Poverty in America

Poverty in America

A Handbook

John Iceland

UNIVERSITY OF CALIFORNIA PRESS
Berkeley · Los Angeles · London

University of California Press
Berkeley and Los Angeles, California

University of California Press, Ltd.
London, England

© 2003 by the Regents of the University of California

Library of Congress Cataloging-in-Publication Data

Iceland, John, 1970–.
 Poverty in America : a Handbook / John Iceland.
    p.   cm.
 Includes bibliographical references and index.
  ISBN 0-520-23868-0 (cloth : alk. paper).—
ISBN 0-520-23959-8 (paper : alk. paper)
   1. Poor—United States—History.   2. Poverty—
United States—History.   3. Economic assistance,
Domestic—United States—History.   I. Title.

HC110.P6 I25   2003
339.4'6'0973—dc21   2002041368

Manufactured in the United States of America
10 09 08 07 06 05 04 03
10 9 8 7 6 5 4 3 2 1

For Jeannie and Jakob

Contents

Figures

Tables

Acknowledgments

My thinking on poverty issues has over the years been significantly influenced by the work of Sheldon Danziger, whose clear and provocative writing sparked my interest in problems of poverty when I was a student and afterward. I would also like to thank a number of people who provided helpful comments on drafts of chapters and the organization of the book, including Gordon Fisher, Patricia Ruggles, Daniel T. Lichter, Andrew Beveridge, Josh Kim, and Susan Ferber. Other colleagues deserving recognition for their general support and insight include Daniel H. Weinberg, Charles T. Nelson, Kathleen Short, and Larry Long.

Over the years, I have received significant encouragement and advice from Michael J. White and Hilary Silver, to whom I owe much gratitude. I would like to thank Sidney Goldstein, who encouraged me to study sociology many years ago, as well as Calvin Goldscheider, David Meyer, and David Lindstrom. Naomi Schneider and Sierra Filucci at the University of California Press provided crucial direction for the project during the publication process.

Most of all, I would like to thank my friends and family for support and encouragement, including my wife, Jean, who inspired me to write this book. I would also like to thank my son, Jakob, for giving perspective on life; my parents, Harry and Joan; my brother, Charles; my grandmother Libby; and Matt, John, Edna, Debbie, and Mathew.

The views expressed in this book are those of the author alone and should not be construed as representing the official position or policy of any institution or agency.

CHAPTER I

Introduction

In 1971, Robert Lampman, who had been a key economic adviser to President Lyndon Johnson on anti-poverty initiatives, predicted that poverty would be eradicated by 1980.[1] James Tobin, another policy adviser, had been equally hopeful when he declared his views in a 1967 *New Republic* article entitled "It Can Be Done! Conquering Poverty in the U.S. by 1976."[2]

Today these predictions seem decidedly naive. In fact, by the mid-1970s, with the country in the midst of a recession and an oil crisis, it had already become clear that these optimistic forecasts would prove inaccurate. Poverty rates fluctuated in response to economic booms and busts in the last decades of the twentieth century but saw no further overall decline; they are still particularly high among minority groups, children, and female-headed families. It now seems as unlikely as ever that we will witness drastic falls in poverty in the near future. This leads one to ask: Were Lampman and Tobin fabulously misguided, or did they in fact offer reasonable predictions given the trends at the time? Why does poverty remain so pervasive? Is poverty unavoidable? Are people from particular racial and ethnic backgrounds or family types inevitably more likely to be poor? What can we expect over the next few years? What are the limits of policy?

In addition to providing an in-depth examination of trends and patterns of poverty in the United States, I advance several arguments through the course of this book. First, views of poverty vary over time and place. What it meant to be poor in the early twentieth century is not the same today. Nor is the standard of what constitutes poverty in the United States the same as that in the developing world. Second, the persistence of poverty in the United States reflects more than just an aggregation of individual failings. Structural factors, such as the way we understand and define poverty, the inherent features of our economic system that produce income inequality, social inequities, and our policy responses to these problems shape current trends. Third, contrary to conventional wisdom, shifts in family structure have not been the most important factor explaining trends in American poverty rates in recent decades, though they were related to increasing child poverty rates in the 1970s and 1980s. Economic changes—such as economic growth and income inequality—have had the strongest association with trends in overall rates, regardless of how we measure poverty. Fourth, anti-poverty policies constitute a relatively small part of the federal budget and have only a moderate impact on poverty. The effect of policy on poverty is limited by the role of government in society the public supports. Public sentiment is in turn affected by trust in government, the development of communal institutions, and a belief in a common good. Racial conflict, confusion about the causes of poverty, and parochial concerns all stand in the way of efforts to reduce poverty and inequality.

These analyses are based on a synthesis of a wide range of studies and a firsthand examination of information collected in a variety of social surveys, such as the decennial census and the Current Population Survey. Thus, large portions of this study are based on statistical information about poverty rather than anecdotes or case studies. The strength of these data is that they provide us with a comprehensive overview of poverty across the United States. By combining this information with the historical record and social scientific theory, I am able to present a more complete understanding of the general nature and causes of poverty in America.

WHY LOOK AT POVERTY?

There are several reasons why poverty continues to be a critical issue in the United States. First, the hardship that often accompanies poverty plainly has adverse effects on individuals' physical and psychological well-being. A number of studies have shown that children raised in poor families are less healthy and worse off in terms of their cognitive development, school achievement, and emotional well-being.[3] Poor adolescents, for example, are more likely to have low self-esteem, act out antisocial behaviors, and become delinquent. Poor individuals are also more likely to have health problems and die at younger ages. Some of the harmful effects of poverty are due to low income, while some result from other family conditions that often accompany poverty, such as family instability and low levels of education. Poverty often begets more poverty, as those who grow up in poor families are more likely to be poor themselves as adults. Many if not most people would probably agree that the continued suffering of some Americans in the midst of plenty is morally troubling.

Second, poverty has broader economic consequences. Economies thrive in societies with a vibrant middle class. Much of the strong economic growth in the United States in the twentieth century was fueled by the expansion of consumer markets. As the demand for new products soared, do did technological innovation, productivity, and wages and benefits. Declining levels of poverty contribute to a healthy economy by increasing the number of people who can purchase goods and services; that increase, in turn, stimulates economic growth and raises average standards of living.[4]

Third, high levels of poverty have serious social and political consequences. Poor people often feel alienated from mainstream society. Poverty also provokes social disorder and crime, and it reduces public confidence in democratic institutions if people do not feel their needs are being addressed by the prevailing system. The ghetto riots of the 1960s, for example, reflected the economic, social, and political marginalization of African Americans in U.S. cities. The unequal distribution of resources has contributed to the fragmentation of society we experience today, both nationally and globally.

MYTHS ABOUT POVERTY

Myths about poverty abound. For example, a common misperception is that a majority of the poor are African American residents of inner cities. Even though blacks are overrepresented among the poor, they make up only about one-quarter of the poverty population.[5] Another common misperception is that the poor do not work; in fact, nearly half of the poor of working age work at least part-time. William O'Hare describes this and a number of other common myths, including the widespread misperceptions that poor families are trapped in a cycle of poverty that few escape and that welfare programs are a major part of the federal budget.[6]

Throughout this book I discuss three other general misperceptions. First is the common assumption that poverty represents a fixed measure of economic deprivation. Yet the historical record reveals that people's views of what it means to be poor have varied considerably over both time and place. Not only are poverty standards lower in developing countries than in the United States, but American standards of poverty were much lower in the early part of the twentieth century than they were just decades later.

A second common misperception is the belief that the growth in the number of female-headed families was largely responsible for stagnant poverty rates in the last few decades of the twentieth century. However, I present evidence indicating that trends in poverty were most strongly related to economic changes over this period. While changes in family structure had a strong association with child poverty rates, particularly in the 1970s and 1980s, this relationship disappeared by the 1990s, mainly because of a slowing of shifts in family structure during that decade.

A final misperception is that recent debates about welfare reform reflect distinctly modern social issues. Quite the contrary, debates about the effect of government transfers on markets, individual conduct, and poverty go back to the nation's earliest days. From the beginning, Americans have argued about the relative importance of alleviating hardship, on the one hand, and discouraging and limiting socially undesirable behaviors, on the other. The problem with these debates is that they have often been based on only a partial understanding of the causes of poverty and people also have different goals and priorities when seeking to address them.

PLAN OF THE BOOK

In chapter 2, I discuss views of poverty in America from colonial times to the present. Familiarity with the historical context helps inform current poverty and inequality issues. For example, one way in which recent debates on welfare reform echo past debates lies in how we decide who is worthy of support. There has long been a distinction between the "deserving" poor, such as the elderly, and the "undeserving" poor, such as able-bodied men and unmarried mothers. Until relatively recently, these distinctions could neither be refuted nor supported because of the lack of data and uniform measurement techniques.

Even as some of the central issues of poverty have remained the same, views of what it means to be poor have changed over time. As standards of living have risen, so have assessments of how much money it takes to support a family. Dollar estimates early in the twentieth century were about 50 percent of the estimates made a little over half a century later. Many believe that the current official poverty line, devised in the 1960s and updated annually to account for inflation, is now too low. In 2000 the average poverty line for a family of four was $17,603.

In chapter 3, I review alternative methods of measuring poverty. As the number of antipoverty initiatives grew in the wake of Lyndon Johnson's War on Poverty, it became clear that a standard poverty measure was needed to assess the effectiveness of these programs. The official poverty measure defines poverty lines for families of different sizes and composition and compares a family's reported income to that line to determine if that family is poor. These poverty lines are updated annually for inflation. This poverty measure remains in use to this day, though not everyone agrees that it represents the best way to estimate economic deprivation.

The two basic types of poverty measures are absolute measures and relative measures. Each of these has several possible variants. Absolute measures, such as the current U.S. official measure, typically attempt to define a truly basic needs standard and have thresholds that remain constant over time. Relative measures define poverty in terms of comparative disadvantage, which changes as living standards change. Each of these measures has its own strengths and weaknesses, and both are informative about the changing nature of economic well-being in society.

In my view, the best general measure of poverty has both absolute and relative components. The absolute core of poverty is not being able to meet basic needs; people who cannot meet them should be considered poor, regardless of general living standards. Yet poverty is relative in that people's beliefs about the amount of money needed to live within society rises as overall standards of living rise. One way to keep an absolute poverty measure meaningful is to simply revamp it by adjusting poverty thresholds every generation or so (or as needed). An alternative is a quasi-relative measure recommended by the National Academy of Sciences (NAS) Panel on Poverty and Family Assistance.[7] Its basic strength is a poverty line that increases with inflation-adjusted

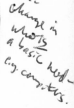

spending on basic goods. Because of this and other advantages, this measure represents a strong, viable challenger to the current official U.S. poverty measure.

Chapter 4 describes the poverty population in detail. In 2000, for example, 11.3 percent of the U.S. population, or 31.1 million people, were poor, according to the official measure. Poverty rates are a little higher when using the NAS measure and significantly higher if using a common relative measure. As is well-known, poverty is more pervasive among some demographic subgroups—such as minorities, children, people with less education, and female-headed families—regardless of the poverty measure used. Poor people are also, unsurprisingly, considerably more likely to report material hardships, such as sometimes not having enough food to eat or missing utility payments. However, both rich and poor Americans alike report having basic consumer items such as TVs and refrigerators.

Evidence from studies looking at the dynamics of poverty indicates that a majority of people who fall into poverty remain in poverty for only a short time. Nevertheless, many families frequently move into and out of poverty, and a significant proportion of the poor also suffer long-term poverty spells. Studies show that the large majority of children who grow up poor do not remain so as adults. Nevertheless, as adults, they are considerably more likely to be poor than those who did not grow up poor.

Poverty varies widely across states and has become more concentrated within cities over the last few decades, though some rural pockets of poverty persist. Some argue that people living in high-poverty neighborhoods (and in remote rural areas) are not only spatially isolated from mainstream society but often socially isolated as well. Many urban problems, such as crime, welfare dependency, drug use, and substandard educational outcomes, are more common in high-poverty areas. Increasing poverty concentration has a variety of sources, including the decline in the number of economic opportunities for many inner-city residents and continued high urban levels of racial, ethnic, and class segregation.

When comparing poverty in the United States with poverty in countries around the world, two findings stand out. First, poverty in developing countries qualitatively differs from that in the United States and other developed countries. In impoverished countries, particularly in South Asia and Africa, a high proportion of the population fails to earn even $1 or $2 a day. Second, while the United States has virtually the highest gross national product (GNP) per capita in the world, it has higher levels of both absolute and relative poverty than other rich countries in Northern and Western Europe. It also has higher levels of relative poverty than just about all European countries.

In discussing the causes of poverty in chapter 5, I consider not only conventional theories about the effect of individual characteristics, such as educational attainment, but also theories that focus on the impact of structural factors. Understanding the workings of economic systems and social inequality is essential for explaining why poverty exists and why members of some groups are more likely to be poor than others. For example, factors that account for the racial-ethnic gap in poverty over the last few decades include not only differences in educational attainment and the prevalence of female-headed families but also residential segregation, economic inequality, and discrimination.

Some of the rapid decline in poverty among minorities over the last half century reflects the fall of legal barriers and the decline of discrimination. Today, past poverty, economic dislocation, wealth differentials, and family instability are barriers at least as important as racism and discrimination in explaining poverty levels among minority groups. Nevertheless, despite this progress, racial and ethnic disparities remain a critical problem in America.

While discrimination against women in the labor market has also declined, gender differences in earnings and poverty have not disappeared. Single-parent families headed by women are considerably more likely to be poor than other family types because they face the challenge of supporting a family on one income and often paying for child care while they work. Lower levels of education among women who head such families also contribute to their lower earnings, as does the fact that many such families do not receive sufficient child support from the absent father. Despite these obstacles, poverty rates among single-parent families, while still significantly higher than poverty rates among other subgroups, have declined over much of the 1990s, largely because of greater employment and earnings among single parents.

In chapter 6, I assess the relative association between trends in poverty and income growth, economic inequality, and changes in family structure over the last half of the twentieth century by analyzing decennial census and Current Population Survey data over that time. I find that income growth had the strongest correlation with trends in absolute poverty, and economic inequality had a larger association with trends in relative poverty rates. The negative association between both poverty measures and family structure changes—mainly the growth in female-headed families—increased from 1949 through 1990 and was greatest among African Americans and children. The relationship disappeared, however, for all groups during the 1990s, mainly as shifts in family structure slowed over the decade.

The analysis in chapter 6 also illustrates how our view and measurement of poverty affect our understanding of the processes that affect it. For example, if we view poverty in terms of absolute material deprivation, then it is clear that economic growth can play an important role in diminishing it. But if we view poverty as a relative phenomenon, then growth does less to reduce it, and wage inequality or policies that redistribute income may play a larger role. Technical issues, such as the way we measure income, also have consequences for our estimates of both poverty and the impact of growth and inequality.

Chapter 7 examines policy issues. The history of American welfare policy has been characterized by a perennial tension between the goal of giving aid in a humane manner to those in need and the attempt to ensure that such efforts do not promote dependence or provide work disincentives. Colonial programs tended to provide sufficient benefits to needy community members, though they were unkind to outsiders, able-bodied men, and pariahs. The poorhouses of the nineteenth century attempted to supply very basic care while discouraging residents from becoming dependent on handouts. These institutions ended up doing little to address the roots of poverty. Scientific charities at the turn of the twentieth century sought to professionalize welfare assistance; their efforts to reform the poor morally often failed miserably.

In the 1930s, the Great Depression showed that local efforts alone were insufficient to combat poverty in times of national economic crisis. It became clear that poverty, even among able-bodied individuals, can result from broader structural forces. In the post–World War II period, even as living standards grew, so did concern that not everyone was benefiting. The War on Poverty and the civil rights movement sought to bring prosperity to those who had previously been ignored by policy or had only marginally benefited from it, such as racial and ethnic minorities. These movements brought a lot of change, though many believed that welfare policies were too expansive and did not do enough to prevent dependency.

Some of the frustration with welfare policy in the late twentieth and early twenty-first century has stemmed from misperceptions about the size of various government programs. Controversial programs such as cash welfare assistance consume only a relatively small part of the federal budget, and indeed, government transfers are often not high enough to lift recipients' income over the poverty line. The relatively popular social insurance programs, such as Medicare and Social Security, make up the largest proportion of income-assistance spending. The cost of medical benefits has risen by more than the cost of other programs since the 1970s. These social insurance programs lift the greatest number of people out of poverty, especially among the elderly. The Earned Income Tax Credit is more effective for helping working families with low wages.

Today's welfare system once again attempts to strike a delicate balance: providing at least some sort of safety net while also promoting work. Given this system's long-term, broad-based social support in the United States, most people seem to accept the extent of inequality built in the economy. The general consensus is that the welfare reform of the late 1990s has worked so far, though many vocal dissenters argue that it does not do enough to check material hardship. Welfare reform legislation mainly addressed one facet of the broader problem of poverty—dependency. The efforts to reduce dependency worked in part because of the prevailing social and economic situation: steady economic growth and declining poverty. Yet history has also taught us that what works in a period of strong economic growth may not suffice in a depression. We therefore need to be attentive to continuing material hardship in society and flexible in our attempts to address it.

CHAPTER 2

Early Views of Poverty in America

What does it mean to be poor? While most people would be hard-pressed to give a precise answer, many of us feel we can recognize poverty when we see it. For example, a news story accompanied with images of malnourished children in a troubled region can vividly display extreme poverty. As one moves away from this kind of obvious example, however, it becomes more difficult to distinguish just what people mean when they refer to "the poor," as opposed to lower-income people more generally.

In 1993 the General Social Survey fielded the following question about poverty: "People who have income below a certain level can be considered poor. That level is called the 'poverty line.' What amount of weekly income would you use as a poverty line for a family of four (husband, wife, and two children) in this community?" Answers ranged from as low as $25 to as high as $1,500 per week. The average response was $341 (about $424 in 2002 after adjusting for inflation).[1] Most families would find it difficult to live on $25 a week. At the other extreme, $1,500 per week (about $1,866 in 2002 dollars) seems excessive as a minimum standard. At what point does luxury become a necessity? More to the point, why did this question elicit such a wide variety of responses?

While poverty—or economic deprivation—is a concrete phenomenon for those who live it, the answer to these questions is that what people judge to be poor varies across both time and place. A working-class laborer in a developing country would likely be considered poor in Western Europe. In fact, the World Bank uses a poverty standard of $1 to $2 per person per day, or $1,095 to $2,190 per year, for a family of three in developing countries in Africa or Latin America.[2] In contrast, the average official poverty threshold for a family of three in the United States was $17,738 in 2000.

As far back as 1776, Adam Smith noted the importance of *social perceptions* in determining what constitutes economic hardship. In the *Wealth of Nations,* he defined the lack of "necessaries" as the experience of being unable to consume "not only the commodities which are indispensably necessary for the support of life, but whatever the custom of the country renders it indecent for creditable people, even of the lowest order, to be without."[3] More recently, Peter Townsend observed that people are social beings who assume many roles in a community—worker, citizen, parent, friend, and so on. He maintained that poverty should be defined as the lack of sufficient income for people to "play the roles, participate in the relationships, and follow the customary behavior which is expected of them by virtue of their membership of society."[4]

In order to understand who we, as a society, consider poor, we must therefore begin by examining how our views have evolved. This chapter begins by tracing views of poverty in America before 1900. I place these views in their economic, social, and political context, noting how these forces subsequently affected twentieth-century efforts to measure and understand poverty. I end by describing the emergence of the current official poverty measure in the 1960s.

VIEWS OF POVERTY BEFORE 1900

Views of poverty reflect social conditions. In the United States, a common assumption in the colonial period, extending through the nineteenth century, was that the roots of poverty lay primarily not in structural economic causes but in individual misbehavior.[5] The poor were often thought of as either "deserving" or "undeserving" of public support. Voluntary idleness was regarded as a vice, and unemployed men were often either bound out as indentured servants, whipped and forced out of town, or put in jail. The Virginia assembly as early as 1619 ordered that idle able-bodied persons should be bound over to compulsory labor. Likewise, in 1633 the General Court of Massachusetts decreed harsh punishment on those who spent their time "idly or unprofitably."[6] Yet hardship among the elderly and children was usually viewed sympathetically, as many colonists recognized that poverty was widespread and sometimes unavoidable. Communities therefore often accepted responsibility for the well-being of the elderly in need.[7]

By the early nineteenth century, many craftsmen and farmers displaced by the mechanization of agriculture and goods production struggled to earn a living, as did unskilled laborers.[8] These groups constituted an economically insecure "floating proletariat," some of whom traveled extensively to find jobs. Some also became "tramps"—jobless men and, to a lesser extent, women who moved continuously from place to place in search of employment.[9]

The perceived distinction between the deserving and undeserving poor persisted in the nineteenth century. For example, in 1834 the Reverend Charles Burroughs spoke about the differences between poverty and pauperism: "The former is an unavoidable evil, to which many are brought from necessity, and in the wise and gracious Providence of God. It is the result, not of our faults, but of our misfortunes. . . . Pauperism is the consequence of willful error, of shameful indolence, of vicious habit."[10]

The word *pauper* generally refers to someone receiving relief or assistance—usually from local or county governments. As illustrated in the quote above, it also has a connotation that paupers are among the "undeserving" poor, as the public tended to have a dim view of people who sought assistance. The poor were also sometimes stigmatized with other labels such as "dependent, defective, and delinquent."[11]

The nineteenth century saw the growth of poorhouses, also known as "indoor relief," as a method of dealing with the poor. Starting in the 1830s, state governments began to write laws mandating that counties have a poor farm or poorhouse. Many of those who needed short-term aid nevertheless still received "outdoor relief," which did not require those seeking help to enter institutions, from local agencies or private charities.[12] The poorhouses were harsh; their purpose was to deter all but the most desperate from applying for help. Poorhouse inmates were expected to work as a form of punishment, moral training, education, and reform.[13] It was not until the beginning of the twentieth century that poorhouses fell out of favor, as public officials and social professionals realized that such institutions did little to reduce poverty and sometimes even exacerbated family instability when family members were interned in these institutions.[14]

Current concerns about the concentration of poverty and the under-class echo fears voiced by many nineteenth- and early-twentieth-century commentators. Indeed, in the middle decades of the 1800s, some middle-class and wealthy city residents began to build new homes in outlying areas in a few cities such as New York and Boston.[15] Michael Katz recounts how in an 1854 annual report, as head of New York City's Children's Aid Society, Charles Loring Brace argued that the "greatest danger" to America's future was the "existence of an ignorant, debased, and permanently poor class in the great cities. . . . The members of it come at length to form a separate population. They embody the lowest passions and the most thriftless habits of the community. They corrupt the lowest class of working-poor who are around them. The expenses of police, prisons, of charities and means of relief, arise mainly from them."[16]

S. Humphreys Gurteen, a writer and preacher, also decried the problems of both poverty and pauperism in his 1882 description of poor city districts: "large families huddled together in tenements and shanties which barely afford protection from wind and storm; dwellings where the laws of health are defied, where the most ordinary sanitary arrangements are unknown, and where 'boards of health' fail to penetrate; . . . human forms, even those of children, shivering in rags; hunger written upon care-worn faces; and despair everywhere triumphant." He blamed these problems on the abandonment of the poor by the well-to-do, on immorality, and on the ineffectiveness of charity, which he believed often fostered dependence.[17]

Nevertheless, aside from some of these small, highly visible "slum" districts, cities were not nearly as highly segregated by class as later in the twentieth century. Urban working-class neighborhoods were in constant flux, with steadily employed workers sharing the same buildings, streets, and residential districts as the those with less steady employment.[18] This is a natural consequence of the fact that poverty was endemic in cities and rural areas across the country.

Katz ventures that perhaps half the population of typical nineteenth-century cities were poor, though this judgment is based more on contemporary notions of poverty than actual standards of the time.[19] He does note, however, that the "working-class experience was a continuum; no clear line separated the respectable poor from paupers."[20] According to another estimate, roughly 10 to 20 percent of late-nineteenth-century Americans lived in a family with a member who had "tramped" at some point—moved from place to place in search of work.[21] The receipt of government aid was far less common. According to an analysis of 1860 census data, 7.9 people in 1,000 received public relief.[22] Robert Hunter, in his 1904 book, *Poverty,* estimated that at least 10 million people were poor, which represents about 13 percent of the American population in 1900. Hunter also asserted that a vast majority of the poor were such because of social and economic conditions, not their own vice.[23]

African Americans in particular continued to face a severely constrained labor market throughout the nineteenth century. Largely concentrated in southern and rural areas, black sharecroppers struggled to earn a living. Blacks were barred by law or custom from almost all full-time jobs, leaving agricultural wage labor as the most common occupation.[24] As the new system of Jim Crow, disfranchisement, and racial violence escalated during the late nineteenth century, southern blacks began to migrate to northern cities in growing numbers. This migration north would swell in the following century. Most blacks who lived in cities were employed as common laborers or as domestic and personal servants. Opportunities for promotion and advancement were uncommon, if not impossible, for blacks in these and other occupations.[25]

Because of their precarious economic position, African Americans were more likely to be very poor and receive public assistance in some cities.[26] W. E. B. DuBois, in his well-known study *The Philadelphia Negro* estimated that about 9 percent of black families were very poor and another 10 percent were simply poor, earning less than $5 per week.[27] As there was no official poverty measure at the time, DuBois's estimates of poverty are based on his own assessment. And as will be discussed in more detail shortly, Dubois's standard of poverty was meager as compared with other appraisals. While African Americans made up about 4 percent of Philadelphia's population in the 1890s, they constituted about 8 percent of those either residing in the city's almshouses or receiving assistance from the county poor board or aid for orphans.[28] DuBois believed that high levels of poverty among African Americans had a number of causes, including slavery's legacy, white racial beliefs and practices, low levels of skill and education, and moral deficiencies of new black migrants from the South.[29]

The United States continued its rapid industrialization and urbanization in the early decades of the twentieth century. Between 1860 and 1920 the nation's urban population rose from 6.2 million to 54.0 million, an increase from about 20 percent of the total U.S. population to over 50 percent. Immigrants from Europe poured into eastern and Mid-western cities in growing numbers. And beginning in about 1915 and continuing for the next thirty years or so, the migration of blacks in search of better economic opportunities in northern cities accelerated. Corporations with their large factories in industries such as steel and automobiles found a large pool of cheap and willing labor in the immi-grant and black communities.[30]

While standards of living rose over this period and many workers found employment in steady jobs, a large part of the workforce, espe-cially those in peripheral industries, remained vulnerable to the periodic and often severe downturns characteristic of the economy. Sugrue describes the plight of these workers: "Trapped in insecure jobs with small companies increasingly marginal to a market dominated by large corporations, they shared with their nineteenth-century predecessors susceptibility to bouts of poverty."[31] It was in this social and economic context that an interest in studying and documenting poverty and hard-ship arose.

THE BEGINNING OF POVERTY MEASUREMENT

The issues described above—economic dislocation, racial/ethnic inequal-ity, immigration, and uncertainty concerning how to address poverty—provide the substantive backdrop for the rise of efforts to measure poverty. Many of these very same issues remain important today.

It was not until the late nineteenth and early twentieth centuries that techniques to measure and examine poverty began to be developed, in part because many social science disciplines and statistical methods themselves are relatively recent phenomena. For example, sociology arose in the nineteenth century through the writings of such people as Auguste Comte, Herbert Spencer, and Karl Marx.[32] While economics has a longer history, the discipline's sophisticated quantitative methods are more recent in origin. In short, while there has long been an interest in poverty issues, the "science" of examining poverty began only in the last century and a half.

Concerned over working-class unrest that fed the revolutions of 1848, European statisticians began about 1850 to study the incomes and expenses of working-class families. This lead to the development of "standard budgets," which basically refer to the cost of goods and serv-ices that families need to achieve a certain standard of living. Influenced by these studies, early efforts in the United States to develop standard budgets began in the 1870–1895 period. Sometimes different budgets were constructed for people of different social classes or occupational groups. While most were constructed to represent a minimum subsistence level, others were meant to represent minimum comfort levels.[33]

Charles Booth came up with the term *line of poverty* in his well-known, multivolume study of poverty and society in London.[34] He defined his concept of poverty in the following way: "The 'poor' are those whose means . . . are barely sufficient for decent independent life; the 'very poor' those whose means are insufficient for this according to the usual standard of life in this country."[35]

In fact, it was around the end of the nineteenth century when the word *poverty* became less associated with receiving public relief or private charity (i.e., "pauperism") and more with having insufficient income to live appropriately. This concept of poverty became widely accepted among the social workers, sociologists, and others in the first two decades of the twentieth century who studied these issues more systematically. It was also around this time that people began to accept the view that poverty was also due to economic and other social factors rather than just individual weakness.[36]

In a careful review of early poverty measurement efforts, Gordon Fisher suggests that these attempts to define poverty (or income inadequacy) inform us not only about economic deprivation but also about the social structure of the time and the social processes by which poverty lines are drawn. Illustrating how the tendency of successive poverty lines to rise in real terms as the real income of the general population rises, early budgets and other measures of income inadequacy were quite low by recent standards. For example, Fisher notes that the 1890–1891 report of the Iowa Bureau of Labor Statistics included a standard budget showing the "minimum cost" of "the necessary living expenses of laboring men with families" at $549.84 for a family of five. In constant, inflation-adjusted dollars, this would be roughly equal to 52 percent of today's official poverty threshold for a family of five.[37]

DuBois's 1896–1897 poverty line (which was meant to be a standard budget rather than a bare-necessities demarcation line) of $5 a week, or $260 a year, represents only about 26 percent of the official poverty line (after adjusting for inflation) for a family of five. This poverty line was markedly lower than every other contemporary American standard budget. Other minimum subsistence budgets and poverty lines developed before World War I tended to represent from 43 to 54 percent of the current official poverty line.[38]

Some Progressive Era advocates of the poor recognized that the standard budget methodology could be misused in ways that were unfair to working-class families. In 1918 William Ogburn, a University of Washington professor who had gone to work for the National War Labor Board, noted in a discussion of standard budgets: "We can not go on the assumption that the housewife can purchase food value with the skill of a domestic-science expert, or that she has the will power of a Puritan, or that no allowance would be made to the man for drinks and tobacco."[39] Indeed, Fisher notes:

> Lower-income homemakers were consistently being expected to show a skill in food buying that would have actually been greater than that of most middle-class homemakers—and were being stigmatized as "ignorant" and having "poor buying habits" when they failed to exhibit such impossible talents. Scott Nearing's [a researcher who had written about family expenditures early in the twentieth century] trenchant analysis was correct: any "superwoman" who could live up to the expectations of such budgets would not have to be subjected to them in the first place, as she would already be earning almost twice the poverty level in private industry.[40]

Into the 1940s there was still no consensus in the literature regarding "poverty" or "poverty lines." Federal government employees, labor union personnel, advocates for income redistribution and greater economic growth, and a handful of academics tried to develop or revise poverty lines during the 1946–1965 period, but many were unaware of the work being done by others in different organizations.[41]

Between 1949 and 1958 a common low-income line that was often cited, originally proposed by the congressional Subcommittee on Low-Income Families (SLIF), was $2,000 a year (in 1948 dollars), a figure higher in real terms than most pre–World War II poverty lines and subsistence budgets; the $2,000 figure (which was for families of all sizes) was equal in constant dollars to 81 percent of today's official poverty threshold for a family of four. The poverty lines offered after 1958 and before the official poverty line was introduced in 1965 tended to be even higher, again reflecting growing standards of living of the time.[42]

THE DEVELOPMENT OF THE OFFICIAL POVERTY MEASURE

The late 1950s and early 1960s saw the publication of several books and reports that drew the attention of policy makers and the public to the problem of poverty. One was John Kenneth Galbraith's *The Affluent Society*. Galbraith argued that, while rising standards of living reduced hardship, the materialism of American consumer culture contributed to inequality and that some pockets of poverty were resistant to the effects of economic growth. He also discussed the relative nature of poverty:

> In part [poverty] is a physical matter. . . . But . . . it is wrong to rest everything on absolutes. People are poverty-stricken when their income, even if adequate for survival, falls markedly behind that of the community. Then they cannot have what the larger community regards as the minimum necessary for decency; and they cannot wholly escape, therefore, the judgment of the larger community that they are indecent.[43]

In 1962 Michael Harrington's *The Other America: Poverty in the United States* was published; reviews of this book and other contemporary reports caught the eye of the Kennedy administration and influenced its views and policies on poverty issues. Harrington's basic aim in the book was to draw attention to the poverty that persisted despite the plenty that many Americans enjoyed. He argued that the poor, black and white alike, were subjected to a chronic suppression of their living standards. This led to a culture of poverty that was perpetuated by an endless cycle of neglect and injustice.[44]

Within the Kennedy administration, the economist Walter Heller, chairman of the Council of Economic Advisors (CEA), wanted to "launch a Kennedy offensive against poverty."[45] The CEA favored doing so within the framework of the broader economic agenda they had been pursuing since 1961, which aimed at faster economic growth and full employment by means of tax cuts. Robert Lampman, a CEA economist at the time, also sought to devise a politically acceptable definition of poverty that would focus less on income inequality and more on the amount needed to achieve a minimum living standard. A narrower income definition would lend itself to the growth-centered economic policy (as opposed to income or wealth redistribution policies) the CEA was advocating.[46]

Following up on the Kennedy administration's decision to commit more funds to anti-poverty programs, President Lyndon Johnson announced his War on Poverty in his January 1964 State of the Union address. In 1965 Mollie Orshansky independently published an article in the *Social Security Bulletin* in which she presented two sets of thresholds—"economy level" and "low-cost level." These were a refined and extended version of thresholds that she had described in a July 1963 *Social Security Bulletin* article.[47]

At that time, poverty measurement had been a major item on the Office of Economic Opportunity's (OEO's) research agenda. Influenced by CEA views on the political feasibility and desirability of defining poverty as a lack of income, the OEO adopted the lower of Mollie Orshansky's two sets of poverty thresholds—the set based on the economy food plan—as a working definition of poverty for statistical, planning, and budget purposes. In 1969 the U.S. Bureau of the Budget (now the Office of Management and Budget) designated the thresholds as the federal government's official statistical definition of poverty. The weighted-average nonfarm poverty threshold for a family of four was $3,128 for the base year, 1963. In the following chapter, I discuss this measure, along with other types of poverty measures, in more detail.

CHAPTER 3

Methods of Measuring Poverty

A 2000 *Baltimore Sun* story declared that "for more than 30 years, the U.S. government has defined who is needy by using a measure known as the 'poverty line.' . . . But experts of virtually every stripe agree that the nation's official measure of poverty—never designed to be permanent—is outdated. And despite years of studies by economists and poverty experts, there is no agreement on how to repair it."[1] This aptly summarizes the current state of poverty measurement: agreement that the existing measure has lost some meaning over time, but little consensus on what type of measure would be better.

The story also notes that poverty could rise with a new measure: "Although the numbers are adjusted for inflation, the method of determining the poverty threshold—published annually by the Census Bureau —hasn't changed. But living and spending patterns have changed. Housing and transportation costs each now require a larger share of the family budget than food, according to consumer surveys. . . . Child care has become another significant expense."

Contrast this with the following stark assertion about the meaning of poverty, written in 1904: "Whether it be directly through starvation, or indirectly through sickness brought on by insufficient nourishment, poverty must necessarily lead to the extinction of the physical life."[2]

These quotes raise key poverty measurement issues touched upon in the previous chapter: should poverty refer to a severe state of material deprivation? Or should poverty lines rise over time with standards of living? What items should be included in a poverty measure? In this chapter I review the basic types of poverty measures, discuss their advantages and disadvantages, and describe a measure recommended by a National Academy of Sciences panel that is a strong contender to replace the current official one.

WHAT IS POVERTY?

Poverty, as defined and applied in this book, essentially refers to economic, or income, deprivation. Two basic types of poverty measures are *absolute* measures and *relative* measures. Absolute measures, such as the current U.S. official measure, typically attempt to define a truly basic—absolute—needs standard and therefore remain constant over time. Relative measures, which are more commonly used by researchers and policy makers in Europe and less so in the United States, explicitly define poverty as a condition of comparative disadvantage, to be assessed against some relative, shifting, or evolving standard of living. The key distinction between the measures is not in the specific monetary value of the respective poverty thresholds but rather how these thresholds are updated over time. Absolute poverty lines remain constant, while relative ones rise as standards of living rise.[3]

In the 1990s, a U.S. National Academy of Sciences research panel devised a *quasi-relative* measure, which combines elements of absolute and relative measures.[4] The quasi-relative measure has certain qualities that, in my view, make it conceptually and practically the most viable and useful type of general poverty measure in the United States, even though every type of measure can be informative when trying to understand different social and economic phenomena.

ABSOLUTE MEASURES

Absolute poverty measures have thresholds, or poverty lines, that remain constant over time. These measures are descended from the work on standard budgets and poverty lines described in the previous chapter. The assumption underlying most absolute measures is that there is a measurable subsistence level of income or consumption below which people should be deemed economically disadvantaged or deprived. Early advocates of the poor who developed standard budgets typically attempted to come up with a dollar figure representing the amount of income below which a family or person risked being without adequate shelter, clothes, or food. While absolute thresholds do not necessarily have to represent a severe measure of deprivation, it is nevertheless implicit that they are developed by "experts" with reference to basic physiological needs.[5]

The official U.S. poverty measure is an excellent example of an absolute measure that achieved a wide degree of support and consensus. More specifically, the current official poverty measure has two components—poverty thresholds and the definition of family income that is compared to these thresholds. Mollie Orshansky of the Social Security Administration constructed poverty thresholds by using the "Economy Food Plan" (the lowest-cost food plan) prepared and priced by the U.S. Department of Agriculture. Orshansky actually described her poverty thresholds as a "relatively absolute" measure of poverty, inasmuch as they were developed from calculations that made the use of the consumption patterns (at a particular point in time) of the U.S. population as a whole. Nevertheless, the measure is considered an absolute one because it does not change as standards of living change. The plan was designed for "temporary or emergency use when funds are low." It allowed for no eating at restaurants, called for careful management of food storage and preparation, and was designed to provide a nutritious but monotonous diet.[6]

To get from the food plan cost to an overall poverty threshold figure, Orshansky used information from the 1955 Household Food Consumption Survey, which indicated that families of three or more people spent about one-third of their after-tax income on food in that year. She therefore multiplied the costs of the food plan for different family sizes by three to come up with thresholds for those family sizes. The food plan—and thus the thresholds developed from it—reflected the differing food needs of children and adults.[7] Thresholds have been updated yearly for inflation using the Consumer Price Index (CPI). The definition of family resources used to compare to the thresholds is the Census Bureau's definition of income—gross annual cash income from all sources, such as earnings, pensions, interest income, rental income, asset income, and cash welfare. A family and its members are considered poor if their income falls below the poverty threshold for a family of that size and composition.[8]

The main advantage of absolute poverty measures is that they are conceptually easy to understand and intuitively appealing. There is, after all, an "absolutist core" in the idea of poverty.[9] For example, if

there is starvation and hunger, then there is clearly poverty—regardless
of how high or low the overall standard of living. Furthermore, the history of research on standard budgets exemplifies the widely held belief
that there is some amount of money we need to survive, and that people making less than that amount face substantial economic hardship.

The main disadvantage of absolute poverty measures is that, as standards of living change, generally so do people's perceptions of what
poverty means. Fisher describes how poverty lines and minimum subsistence budgets before World War I were, in constant dollars, generally
between 43 and 54 percent of Mollie Orshansky's poverty threshold for
1963. A U.S. Works Progress Administration "emergency" budget for
1935 was equal to 65 percent of Orshansky's poverty threshold, and
Robert Lampman's low-income line for 1957 was 88 percent of that
threshold.[10]

Economists describe this phenomenon as the income elasticity of the
poverty line—the tendency of successive poverty lines to rise in real
terms as the real income of the general population rises. Reviewing
a number of studies on the issue, Fisher estimates that the amount
of money people think it takes to "get along" rises between 0.6 and
1.0 percent for every 1.0 percent increase in the income of the general
population.[11] He finds similar general patterns in Britain, Canada, and
Australia. Thus, it could be argued that poverty measures are useful
only to the extent that they tell us something meaningful about the conditions in a particular society. Poverty is by its nature at least somewhat
relative; people are poor when others think of them as poor.[12]

The official U.S. poverty measure has some advantages and disadvantages unrelated to the fact that it is an absolute poverty measure.
On the positive side, it has achieved a level of consensus that no other
poverty measure in the United States can claim. As an analytic tool, it
has provided much useful information about trends in economic well-
being, especially now that we have developed a consistent time series of
data since its adoption in the mid-1960s.

Yet the official U.S. poverty measure suffers from notable technical
problems.[13] For one, the definition of money income used is flawed—
gross cash income inadequately captures the amount of money people
have at their disposal to meet economic needs. Second, the thresholds
are not very refined and have become outdated. There are also other,
less central, technical criticisms, such as the unit of analysis (the family)
and the source of data used for official poverty statistics. These short-
comings are now discussed in turn.

① should count in-kind support

Regarding the definition of income, a family is considered poor if its gross cash income falls below the family's designated poverty threshold. Cash income includes earnings and other items mentioned earlier.[14] Yet many argue that in-kind or near-money government benefits that can be used to meet basic needs should also be counted as resources—such as food stamps, housing subsidies, and the Earned Income Tax Credit (EITC). The omission of these items from the official definition of resources has become increasingly serious in recent years because government policies designed to aid low-income families have progressively been concentrated in these noncash programs.[15]

② variation in expenses

Furthermore, some argue that the current income definition does not take into account variation in expenses that are necessary to hold a job and to earn income—expenses that reduce disposable income. These expenses include taxes, transportation costs for getting to work, and the cost of child care for working parents with children. These expenses are taken into account in the resources definition of an experimental poverty measure described in more detail below, but they are not in the current official income definition.[16]

③ crude— not just mult of food

Official poverty thresholds also have problems. For one, they are constructed rather crudely, and as such, they have become outdated. While the thresholds were originally constructed based on the cost of a food budget and then multiplied by three, more recent data indicate that food comprises closer to one-sixth of families' expenses (not one-third). A more refined threshold could price out the cost not only of food but also of other necessities, like shelter and clothing. Some argue that thresholds should also be adjusted for geographic differences in costs of living.[17] The logic behind this is that families in, say, New York City have greater income needs than families in rural Mississippi. The official measure does not take these differences into account.

④ unit of analysis

Fifth, there are a number of other technical elements of the official measure that could be further refined but that I only briefly mention here. For example, the "unit of analysis" used to measure poverty continues to receive scrutiny. The debate revolves around what is the most appropriate unit—the family, the household, or some other grouping. The official poverty measure uses the family as a basic unit. That is, a person is poor if his or her family income falls below the poverty threshold for a family of that size and composition.[18] A problem with this definition is that cohabiting couples are treated as separate units—as if they did not pool resources at all. The rapid growth in the number of cohabiting couples and people living in nontraditional housing arrangements has magnified the effect of this issue.[19]

Other issues range from the best data set to use (the Current Population Survey is the current source of official statistics, though the Survey of Income and Program Participation collects more detailed data), to the proper way for adjusting thresholds for families of different sizes and composition, to the most appropriate method of updating thresholds for price changes. A more detailed discussion of the official measure, its problems, and potential alternatives is contained in the volume authored by the National Academy of Sciences Panel on Poverty and Family Assistance, *Measuring Poverty: A New Approach.*[20]

RELATIVE MEASURES

Relative poverty can be defined as comparative economic deprivation. It is based on the notion that poverty is relative to a society's existing level of economic, social, and cultural development. Implicit is the assumption that people are social beings who operate within relationships. Those whose resources are significantly below the resources of others, even if they are physically able to survive, may not be able to participate adequately in social organizations and relationships, and are thus incapable of fully participating in society.[21] Adam Smith argued that to be poor was to lack what was needed to be a "creditable" member of society. He noted that in his day (the eighteenth century) a man needed a linen shirt if he was to appear in public "without shame."[22]

Relative measures can take different forms. The most common method is setting a threshold at a percentage of the median of household income. Analysts comparing poverty across countries in the European Community and the United Kingdom have often specified a poverty threshold at half the median income.[23] Other relative methods are also possible, such as 60 percent or 40 percent of median income, or using different percentages of mean income, or using household expenditure survey data instead.

Relative measures have advantages and disadvantages. On the positive side, advocates argue that the relative notion underlying these measures fits with both the historical record and changing views of poverty as described above. Second, sometimes real needs do indeed rise in richer countries. For example, while a car may be a luxury in some countries, in a society in which most families own cars and where public transportation services are also poor, a car may often be needed to find a job and commute to work. In her book *Nickel and Dimed: On (Not) Getting By in America*, Barbara Ehrenreich describes how the lack of affordable housing drives up the housing prices for the poor. For example, she reports that a trailer park in Key West convenient to hotel jobs was charging $625 a month for a half-size trailer, forcing lower-wage workers to search for housing farther away in less fashionable areas. She argues, "Insofar as the poor have to work near the dwellings of the rich—as in the case of so many service and retail jobs—they are stuck with lengthy commutes or dauntingly expensive housing."[24]

It is no surprise, then, that relative measures tend to be popular in wealthy industrialized countries. The Organization for Economic Cooperation and Development (OECD) notes that, since very extreme hardship such as starvation is very uncommon in advanced industrialized societies, absolute subsistence poverty lines have little meaning.[25] Some researchers argue that poverty should be thought in terms of exclusion from standards of living generally available to others in the same society. Social exclusion has therefore become a common theme in discussions about poverty in Europe. At a 2000 meeting of European Union countries, for example, the leaders declared that "the number of people living below the poverty line and in social exclusion in the Union is unacceptable."[26]

Detractors point out a few disadvantages of relative poverty measures. Some find these measures conceptually unappealing, believing that poverty is indeed an objective, scientific phenomenon. Scientific reasoning—not value judgments—should drive changing notions of who is poor.[27] Second, relative measures can behave in deceptive ways over time, particularly during periods of economic growth and recession. In particular, relative thresholds often decline in bad times as median incomes fall. This could result in a decline in measured poverty rates, even though low-income people are faring worse rather than better.[28] Some empirical work in the United States suggests, however, that this is often not the case—relative poverty rates do tend to rise during recessions.[29]

Yet there are notable examples of relative poverty reacting counter to the business cycle. For example, in the late 1990s, when the Irish economy grew at an annual rate of 7 or 8 percent, unemployment fell, and wages rose, the relative poverty rate, as measured by the numbers living below 50 or 60 percent of average income, rose. This produced skepticism among politicians and the public about the meaningfulness of reported relative poverty rates there. Similarly, the Czech Republic, Hungary, and Poland all went through serious recessions in the 1990s, but relative child poverty rates, which used a poverty line based on a fixed percentage of average income, did not.[30] The United Nations Children's Fund (UNICEF) Innocenti Research Centre has noted that relative poverty is really about inequality, with a focus on the bottom end of the income distribution; its premise is that what constitutes an acceptable quality of life changes over time and that falling behind the average by more than a certain amount means effective exclusion from the normal life of society.[31]

Another set of arguments occasionally levied against relative poverty lines is that they are often too much of a moving target for policy because they change over time or that relative poverty cannot be eliminated.[32] However, relative poverty, using the measures described above, can theoretically be eliminated if there is very little economic inequality. It is therefore more accurate to say that absolute and relative poverty measures provide different yardsticks for measuring the success of social programs. Absolute poverty tends to be more responsive to economic growth—which raises average living standards. Meanwhile, relative poverty is more responsive to income inequality, which reflects the distribution of resources in society. Which measure one deems of greater importance from a policy standpoint could influence one's choice.

An additional challenge, though not necessarily a drawback, of relative measures is that consideration has to be given to the reference group. That is, should relative poverty be measured in relation to the average standards of living for the country or for the subnational, perhaps community, level? Most relative measures use the nation as the reference point, but it is true that standards of living often vary across states, provinces, and communities in most nations.[33]

Before turning to other types of poverty measures, I will discuss one additional relative type. *Subjective* measures have been used in a number of countries,[34] though their use by researchers is comparatively limited. Subjective measures are based on public opinion—as reported in surveys—of what minimum income is needed for a person or family not to be poor. A common question asks respondents about the minimum level of income or consumption needed to "get along" or to "make ends meet." This overtly subjective component gives the measure its name, even though other measures inevitably also involve some subjective judgments.[35]

subsective measures

Subjective measures contain a relative component, as subjective thresholds usually change over time in response to social and economic trends. The advantage of these measures is that they are easy to calculate and do not rely on expert judgment. In essence, if one accepts the premise that poverty is intrinsically a relative phenomenon based on social conditions, then one might think that asking people about their opinion on poverty is the best and most appropriate way to measure it.

Yet subjective measures suffer from several pitfalls. For one, question wording can have a substantial impact on the types of responses one gets. Furthermore, as mentioned in the previous chapter, responses vary widely, even with a particular question wording, as not all respondents understand a question in the same way. This is because what it takes to "get along" or "make ends meet" can differ significantly in various communities and also reflects individual opinions as much as actual needs. For example, three different studies that tried to estimate an annual subjective threshold for a four-person family reported mean responses ranging from $12,160 to $32,530, in 1992 dollars.[36] Finally, surveys based on small samples can result in imprecise and unrepresentative estimates of what people think poverty means.

OTHER POVERTY MEASURES

Researchers have devised numerous other measures, some of which are variations of either absolute or relative measures, depending on how they are implemented. The goal here is not to provide an exhaustive list but merely to mention that many other measures of poverty are possible and can be informative.

Consumption measures compare not a family's income but rather its consumption of goods to a poverty threshold. If the family spends little, this is an indication of actual material deprivation—insufficient consumption of basic items such as food and shelter. Conceptually, this represents a very powerful and appealing measure. Consumption measures can be either absolute or relative, depending on how the threshold is designed and implemented. That is, one can use an unchanging (absolute) threshold or one that changes with standards of living. The main problem with consumption measures is that few large-scale surveys ask the relevant questions on family consumption patterns needed to construct a consumption poverty measure. In addition, it could be argued that some people consume little by choice. So it is possible to classify relatively wealthy or high-income individuals as poor if they simply choose to spend little.

While consumption measures emphasize actual consumption, self-reliance measures take a different tack, emphasizing earnings capacity. The assumption is that, since tastes and preferences affect both actual consumption and income, a better indicator of poverty is one that reflects the *capability* of families to meet, by their own efforts, some minimum level of living.[37] This measure could potentially be useful for policy makers interested in gauging the effectiveness of social programs in promoting self-reliance.

Self-reliance measures are implemented by using a set of poverty thresholds (either relative or absolute), which are then compared to a family's potential income. Herein lies the difficulty and chief weakness. How does one measure a family's income potential? Statisticians can model and describe the typical earnings of people of different demographic groups (for example, people in different age, educational, and racial groups). But these models inevitably have limited predictive power, and there is always considerable variation in actual family outcomes.

Other poverty-related measures include *hardship measures, social exclusion*, and other multidimensional indexes. Hardship measures are based on respondents reporting a lack of food, heat, access to health care, or adequate housing, to name a few possible dimensions.[38] Hardship measures tend to be close to absolute measures in spirit, though they can also be defined in terms of hardships relative to a particular society's norms. The problem with hardship measures is that there is no consensus yet, at least in the United States, on what exactly they should measure. Some define them in terms of inadequate consumption of basic goods,[39] while others in terms of poor physical living conditions.[40] There is a wide variety of indicators possible, including those relating to housing, nutrition, medical well-being, and neighborhood quality. Within all these categories there are several possible measures. To combine them into an index is a challenging endeavor. Hardship measures may also reflect preferences and tastes, not always involuntary deprivation.[41]

Social exclusion can be defined in a variety of ways and, like hardship, is challenging to measure. The United Kingdom government has defined social exclusion as "a short-hand term for what can happen when people or areas suffer from a combination of linked problems such as unemployment, poor skills, low income, poor housing, high crime environment, bad health and family breakdown."[42] Such people are

alienated from, and living on the fringes of, mainstream society. In the
United States, the term *underclass* has been used to describe a segment
of the population, mainly African Americans in highly segregated inner
cities, that suffers social exclusion. A. B. Atkinson has identified three
elements of social exclusion: (1) relativity—individuals are excluded from
a particular reference community or society; (2) agency—people are
excluded by an act of people or institutions, such as employers, schools,
or government service agencies; and (3) dynamics—exclusion is a function not just of current circumstances but also of future prospects.[43]

Poverty as defined in this book is not the same as, nor does it strive
to be synonymous with, material hardship or social exclusion, though
the concepts are certainly related. The focus of this book is on *income
poverty* rather than on these other measures, in part because the latter are difficult both to define concisely and measure.[44] In chapter 4
I discuss some statistics on various measures of material hardship and
concentrated poverty (the latter of which is associated with social exclusion). Measures of hardship and social exclusion are best viewed as
complementary to income poverty measures, as they all illuminate different aspects of people's well-being.

In addition to hardship and social exclusion measures are multidimensional *income* poverty indexes. Amartya Sen, in a much cited
paper, and others have argued that simple poverty rates—also known as
"head-count ratios"—are flawed because an ideal poverty index should
not only indicate the proportion of people who are poor but also estimate the average shortfall of the poor below the poverty threshold,
often referred to as the *depth* of poverty, and additionally the distribution of income among the poor.[45] Indexes sometimes also incorporate
various elements of material hardship in their estimation. It should be
noted that the depth of poverty can actually be examined using variations of the official (or other) poverty measures. For example, U.S. Census Bureau poverty reports provide figures on "poverty gaps," which are
average income shortfalls vis-à-vis poverty thresholds, and the number
of people falling below specified fractions of the poverty thresholds.[46]
These types of statistics will be discussed in more detail in chapter 4.

A QUASI-RELATIVE POVERTY MEASURE

In response to the increasingly apparent weaknesses of the official poverty measure described earlier, the U.S. Congress appropriated funds

for an independent scientific study of this measure. The job fell to the National Research Council of the National Academy of Sciences (NAS), which established the Panel on Poverty and Family Assistance. This panel reviewed several alternative approaches to measuring poverty, noting that the decision to accept or reject any particular one must involve subjective judgment as well as scientific evidence. It did, however, recommend specific changes, some within a range, to the official poverty measure in its 1995 report, *Measuring Poverty: A New Approach*.[47] In subsequent research undertaken by the Census Bureau, a few experimental poverty measures based on small variations of the panel's recommendations were implemented and published.[48]

Specifically, the NAS panel recommended that a new poverty threshold be calculated by determining, for a reference family of two adults and two children, a dollar amount for food, clothing, shelter, and utilities and then increasing that dollar amount by a modest percentage to allow for other needs (such as household supplies, personal care, and non-work-related transportation). The dollar amount would be scaled down from the median spending for those four basic items, using data gathered in the Consumer Expenditure Survey.

The NAS panel's recommended poverty measure is essentially relative in nature because the thresholds would be updated based on changes in real expenditures for certain consumption categories—which typically rise as the general standard of living rises. The recommended measure is quasi-relative because the proposed update would be based on consumption expenditures for only basic categories of goods and services—food, clothing, housing, utilities—that would be expected to rise less rapidly than total consumption expenditures (or median income).

The details of this measure are as follows: rather than recommending a specific dollar figure for the total threshold, the panel recommended a range of possible values based on its own judgment, informed by a consideration of expert budgets, relative poverty thresholds, and "subjective" poverty thresholds. A subsequent Census Bureau report used the midpoint of the panel's recommended range; this figure, for the four basic categories plus other needs, turned out to be roughly equal to the median actual expenditure for the four basic categories alone in 1997.[49] According to the panel's recommendations, the reference family threshold is then adjusted, using an equivalence scale, to reflect the needs of different family sizes and types.[50] Unlike the official U.S.

poverty measure, these thresholds are further adjusted for geographic variations in housing costs in different regions and metropolitan area population sizes.

Family resources in the NAS panel measure are defined as the value of cash income from all sources, plus the value of near-money benefits that are available to buy goods and services covered by the new thresholds, minus "nondiscretionary" expenses. Cash income sources include wages and salaries, interest income, and cash welfare assistance. This element of the NAS panel's resource definition is the same as the current official Census Bureau definition of income. The panel's resource definition then also includes near-money benefits such as food stamps, housing subsidies, school breakfast and lunch subsidies, home energy assistance, assistance received under the Women, Infants, and Children (WIC) nutritional supplement program, capital gains/losses, and the Earned Income Tax Credit. Nondiscretionary expenses subtracted include taxes, child care and other work-related expenses, medical out-of-pocket costs, and child support payments to another household. Taxes represent a nondiscretionary expense in that people cannot spend this money that is withheld from their paychecks. Child care and other work-related expenses (such as commuting expenses) are also subtracted because, the panel argued, these costs are often incurred if parents are to work and earn labor market income.[51]

The NAS measure addresses some of the weaknesses of both purely absolute and purely relative measures, though certainly not all of them. One remaining weakness is that, as currently implemented, many elements require complex statistical procedures that could still use further refinement. U.S. Census reports on the issue have presented several alternative experimental poverty measures that generally produce similar poverty rates.[52]

Nevertheless, the NAS measure is clearly a more refined measure than the current official poverty measure in both the construction of the thresholds and the definition of income used. It also has the advantage of increasing, in real terms, as spending on basic items increase, so that it reflects changes in real standards of living. Yet it is not responsive to changes in consumption patterns of other, more discretionary items—such as luxury goods—that may occur. It is also designed to gauge the impact of government programs on poverty, as both cash and noncash government benefits are taken into account in the measure of family income.

COMPARISON OF SELECTED MEASURES

Figure 3.1 compares four-person (two adults, two children) poverty thresholds of four common measures for the years 1947–2000: the threshold of the official U.S. poverty measure, the midpoint of the threshold ranges recommended by the NAS Panel on Poverty and Family Assistance, a relative threshold based on half the median after-tax family income,[53] and subjective thresholds garnered from the question, "People who have income below a certain level can be considered poor. That level is called the 'poverty line.' What amount of weekly income would you use as a poverty line for a family of four (husband, wife, and two children) in this community?"[54]

Since the official threshold is updated solely on the basis of inflation, the threshold dollar amount has remained unchanged. In contrast, subjective and relative thresholds fairly closely track each other over the period. They are below the official threshold until the late 1950s and early 1960s, after which they surpass the official threshold. By 1993, with the official threshold at $17,463 (in 2000 dollars), the subjective threshold was at $21,145, and the relative threshold was at $21,415. The relative poverty threshold rose rapidly in the strong economy of the late 1990s, reaching $25,283 in 2000.

Note that the subjective and relative thresholds cross the official threshold in the period just before the official threshold was originally devised. Thus, at the time, there would have been little difference between poverty rates estimated using any of these three methods. However, since that time, there has been an increasing disjuncture between these poverty rates.

The Census Bureau's experimental threshold time series using the NAS panel's recommendations begins only in 1989. Before trying to compare the experimental thresholds with the current official thresholds, one should note that the NAS thresholds were developed to be used with a specific resource (income) definition that differs significantly from the current official Census Bureau income definition used with the current thresholds. If one looks only at the dollar figures themselves, then the experimental thresholds appear to be approximately equal to the current official ones. However, once one takes into account the significantly different income definitions involved—mainly the subtraction of nondiscretionary expenses in the NAS measure—the experimental thresholds are found to be effectively higher than the official

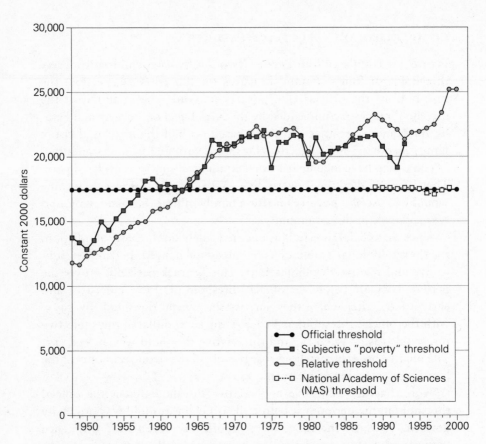

SOURCE: Official thresholds from Joseph Dalaker, "Poverty in the United States: 2000," U.S. Census Bureau, Current Population Report, series P60-214 (Washington, DC: U.S. Government Printing Office, 2001); NAS thresholds from Kathleen Short, "Experimental Poverty Measures: 1999," U.S. Census Bureau, Current Population Report, Consumer Income, series P60-216 (Washington, DC: U.S. Government Printing Office, 2001); relative thresholds, 1947–1992, from National Research Council, *Measuring Poverty: A New Approach,* ed. Constance F. Citro and Robert T. Michael (Washington, DC: National Academy Press, 1995), pp. 132–33; relative thresholds, 1993–2000, from author's tabulations of 1994–2001 Current Population Survey data; subjective thresholds from National Research Council, *Measuring Poverty,* pp. 138–39. Many of the National Research Council thresholds are taken from Denton R. Vaughan, "Exploring the Use of the Public's Views to Set Income Poverty Thresholds and Adjust Them over Time," *Social Security Bulletin* 56, 2 (summer 1993): 22–46.

NOTE: The thresholds are for two-adult, two-children families. Relative thresholds represent one-half the median after-tax income of this family type. The subjective "poverty" thresholds for 1947–1989 are from Vaughan, "Exploring the Use of the Public's Views," table 1. See also National Research Council, *Measuring Poverty,* for more details. Values for the years 1955–1956, 1965, 1968, 1972, 1987–1988, and 1990–1991 are calculated using linear interpolation based on information from adjacent years.

Figure 3.1. Poverty Thresholds for Four-Person Families, 1947–2000

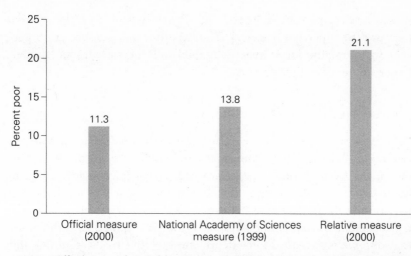

SOURCE: Official measure from Dalaker, "Poverty in the United States: 2000"; National Academy of Sciences measure from U.S. Census Bureau, "Standardized and Unstandardized Experimental Poverty Rates: 1990 to 1999," Poverty 1999 table release package, Internet data release (www.census.gov/hhes/poverty/povmeas/exppov/suexppov.html), October 23, 2000; relative measure from tabulations of 2001 Current Population Survey Annual Demographic Supplement data. The relative threshold equals half the median household income in 2000.

Figure 3.2. Poverty Rates, by Measure

ones. In its 1995 report, the NAS panel pointed out that, after adjusting for the differences between its income concept and the current official census definition, the range proposed for the new threshold would be between 14 and 33 percent higher than the official poverty threshold for 1992.[55] The midpoint of that range (the level used in the Census Bureau reports[56]) would then be equivalent to about 23.5 percent higher than the current official threshold for 1992. The fact that the experimental thresholds are effectively higher than the official ones is borne out when one notes that the experimental measure yields higher poverty rates than the current official measure.

Figure 3.2 shows just that contrast by depicting poverty rates estimated using the official measure, the NAS measure, and a typical relative measure. Note that there are actually many ways a relative poverty measure can be constructed, even after deciding on the particular threshold. The relative measure used here employs a threshold equal to one-half the after-tax median family income. Like the official poverty measure, the income definition used in this relative measure refers to total family income.[57] Unlike the NAS measure, it does not subtract taxes, nor does it include near-cash benefits. Unsurprisingly, results show that poverty rates are lowest when using the official poverty measure (11.3 percent in 2000) and highest when using the relative measure (21.1 percent in 2000). The experimental measure (13.8 percent in 1999, the latest year available) falls between them, though closer to the official measure.

THEORETICAL ISSUES REVISITED

Poverty measurement research efforts in the United States are near a crossroads. There is some movement, at least in the research community, away from absolute methods of measuring poverty toward more relative measures. In the end, the method adopted will likely depend in part on the theoretical considerations. Does *poverty* refer to a *subsistence* standard—that is, the amount of money required to survive—or to *economic marginalization*—deprivation relative to social norms and standards? In addition, can there be such a thing as a legitimate absolute poverty measure that remains constant over time? As I indicated above, a contingent of researchers would contend that defining an absolute standard has serious drawbacks, mainly that poverty is grounded in time and place.

The quasi-relative measure provides a compromise between the extreme absolute and relative ways of thinking and measuring poverty. Most of all, it addresses the unrealistic assumptions behind purely absolute measures—that there can be a single, unchanging absolute standard. For, as has been shown, even the current official measure, while nominally absolute, is still partially relative in that it reflects the standards of the time it was constructed. The quasi-relative measure also addresses the conceptually unappealing nature of purely relative measures—the denial that there is such a thing as purely basic needs. For example, if most people in a society have two luxury cars, should we really consider someone with only one to be poor? The quasi-relative measure explicitly accepts the fact that some relativity is inherent in measuring poverty, but it strives to measure deprivation in relation to the acquisition of an absolutely basic set of goods.

SUMMARY

Poverty refers to economic deprivation. But while poverty represents the struggle to meet basic needs, views about what more precisely constitutes poverty and who the poor are still vary across both time and place. Poverty measurement efforts over the years have shown that, as overall standards of living rise, so do the thresholds deemed necessary to sustain a minimum level of living.

The two basic types of poverty measures are *absolute* measures and *relative* measures. Absolute measures, such as the current U.S. official measure, typically attempt to define a truly basic needs standard. Relative measures define poverty in terms of comparative disadvantage, which is assessed against changing standards of living. Each of these measures has different strengths and weaknesses. Yet if used appropriately, they can also complement each other—as there are various legitimate ways to think about economic deprivation.

In my view, the best general measure of poverty has both absolute and relative components. The absolute core of poverty lies in the feeling that, if people cannot meet basic needs, they are poor—regardless of overall standards of living. Poverty is relative in that people's beliefs about the money needed rises as overall standards of living rise. One way to keep an absolute poverty measure meaningful is to simply revamp it by adjusting poverty thresholds every generation or so, or as needed. An alternative is the quasi-relative measure recommended by the National Academy of Sciences Panel on Poverty and Family Assistance.[58] Because of its strengths, this measure is a strong viable candidate to supplant the current official U.S. poverty measure.

CHAPTER 4

Characteristics of the Poverty Population

Misperceptions about the poverty population are common. For example, in the early 1990s one survey asked, "What percent of all the poor people in this country would you say are black?" The median response was 50 percent. Another 1994 survey asked, "Of all the people who are poor in this country, are more of them black or more of them white?" Fifty-five percent of the respondents thought more blacks than whites were poor, 24 percent thought more whites were poor, and the remaining 31 percent thought there were about equal numbers.[1] According to figures from the U.S. Census Bureau, while blacks have higher poverty rates than whites, they still constituted only 27 percent of the poverty population, and non-Hispanic whites constituted about 48 percent in 1994.[2]

Martin Gilens, who reported the 1994 survey findings, argues that media coverage of poverty and race issues is also frequently skewed. One study of magazine stories on poverty in *Time, Newsweek,* and *U.S. News and World Report* in the late 1980s and early 1990s found that 62 percent of the poor people in photos accompanying these stories were African American—far above their representation in the poverty population. In the same study, while only 15 percent of the working-age poor people pictured in the magazine stories held a paying job, 51 percent of the actual working-age poor are employed at least part-time.[3] In interpreting all of these results, Gilens argues that the public's views reflect negative racial stereotypes, including the assumption that

African Americans are poor and lazy, and negative stereotypes about the poor, such as the view that many are of working age yet jobless. He holds that slanted media coverage contributes to these stereotypes. Finally, he observes that such views may have political consequences, such as by increasing Americans' opposition to welfare.[4]

In this chapter I aim to go beyond conventional wisdom and look at exactly *who* are the poor, focusing on information collected from social and economic surveys. Themes explored in this chapter include patterns of poverty across demographic groups, poverty and material hardship, the dynamics of poverty, poverty's geography, and U.S. poverty in the international context. Having this baseline information is essential to both understanding the causes of poverty and formulating policy responses that make the most sense.

POVERTY IN THE UNITED STATES OVER TIME AND ACROSS GROUPS

Figure 4.1 shows poverty rates over time and for different age groups. After a steady decline in the American poverty rate between 1959 (the first year for which government statistics on poverty are available) and 1973, progress stalled. Whereas 22.4 percent of Americans were poor in 1959 and only 11.1 percent were in 1973, by 2000 the official poverty rate was still 11.3 percent, indicating that 31.1 million Americans lived in poverty—even after years of a strong economy and declining poverty in the 1990s.[5]

The elderly experienced the greater declines in poverty over the 1959 to 2000 period than other age groups. The poverty rate among the elderly was 35.2 percent in 1959, considerably higher than both the child (27.3 percent) and eighteen-to-sixty-four-year-old (17.0 percent) poverty rates. But by the late 1990s, the elderly poverty rate was as low as among people eighteen to sixty-four, whose poverty rates remained stagnant after 1973. A great deal of the reduction in the elderly poverty rate is due to the impact of Social Security and other such programs.[6] Meanwhile, child poverty rates declined from 1959 to 1973, only to rise until the economic boom of the mid-1990s.

Poverty rates vary by the measures we use. Table 4.1 shows poverty rates across different demographic groups using the current official measure of poverty, a relative poverty measure, and a measure recommended by the National Academy of Sciences (NAS) Panel on Poverty and Family Assistance.[7]

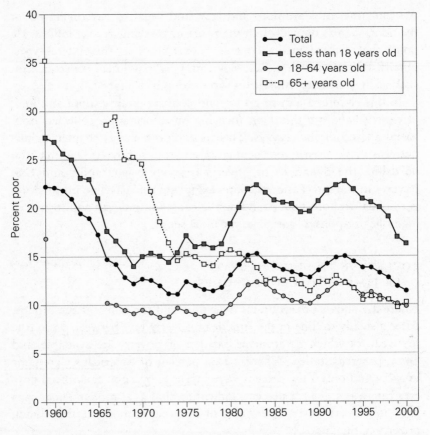

SOURCE: Dalaker, "Poverty in the United States: 2000."

Figure 4.1. Official Poverty Rates by Age, 1959–2000

Survival

vs. Marg.

As described in chapter 3, the current official poverty measure is an absolute one, where the thresholds are meant to represent a truly basic needs standard, and remain constant over time. The relative measure has thresholds that change over time as standards of living change; the thinking behind this measure is that those whose resources are significantly below the resources of others, even if they are physically able to survive, are marginalized from mainstream society. The relative threshold used here is equal to one-half the median family income in the United States in 2000 (the median was $50,565). As in the official poverty measure, the income amount used in this relative measure represents total gross family income.

The NAS measure is a *quasi-relative* one combining absolute and relative elements. It is relative because the thresholds are updated based on changes in real expenditures for certain consumption categories but is less than fully relative because only basic categories of goods and services—food, clothing, housing, utilities—are considered. The amount spent on these items tends to rise less rapidly than median family income. The NAS measure also aims to correct some of the technical deficiencies of the official measure and the relative one used here. In particular, it aims to more accurately measure a family's disposable (net) income by including noncash benefits, such as food stamps, and by subtracting nondiscretionary expenses, such as work-related expenses and medical out-of-pocket costs. Under this measure, thresholds also vary across geographic areas with different costs of living.

As of 2000, 11.3 percent of the population was poor, according to the official measure. Poverty rates are higher when using either the NAS (13.8 percent) or relative measure (21.1 percent). While 7.5 percent of the non-Hispanic white population was poor, according to the official measure, a little over a fifth of both African Americans and Hispanics were poor. According to all measures, the poverty rate among African Americans and Hispanics was between two and three times the non-Hispanic white poverty rate. According to the official measure, about 1 in 10 Asian Americans were poor. The poverty rate among Native Americans was 25.9 percent over the 1998 to 2000 period.[8] Less educated people were far more likely to be impoverished than those with more education, regardless of the measure used.

Among people in families with children, those in married-couple ones were considerably less likely to be poor (6.9 percent, according to the official measure) than single-parent male-headed (17.5 percent) or female-headed (35.3 percent) families in 2000. Unrelated individuals—that is, people living alone or with housemates—had a poverty rate of 18.9 percent. Citizenship status also matters; native-born people and naturalized citizens have fairly similar poverty rates, while noncitizens have considerably higher poverty rates.

While the overall patterns of poverty under the NAS and official poverty measures were similar, official poverty rates were a little lower than NAS rates for most groups. Poverty rates also tended to be modestly higher when using the NAS measure vis-à-vis the official measure among groups that receive fewer noncash government transfers (such as food stamps) and have higher work-related or medical expenses than

TABLE 4.1. POVERTY RATES FOR INDIVIDUALS BY DEMOGRAPHIC CHARACTERISTICS

	Official poverty measure (2000)	National Academy of Sciences (NAS) poverty measure (1999)	Relative poverty measure (2000)*
All Persons	**11.3**	**13.8**	**21.1**
Age			
Children	16.1	17.6	26.4
Non-elderly adults	9.4	11.8	17.6
Elderly	10.2	15.8	27.7
Race/Ethnicity			
White, non-Hispanic	7.5	9.7	15.7
Black, non-Hispanic	21.9	23.4	35.5
Hispanic	21.2	26.9	37.0
Asian/Pacific Islander, non-Hispanic	10.6	15.5	18.9
Native American**	25.9	—	—
Sex			
Male	9.9	12.5	19.1
Female	12.5	15.0	23.1
Family Type			
Married couple	5.6	8.3	12.7
Married couple with children	6.9	9.0	14.2
Male headed	12.6	16.8	23.9
Male headed with children	17.5	20.7	29.8
Female headed	28.2	31.4	44.6
Female headed with children	35.3	35.9	52.6
Unrelated individuals	18.9	19.6	34.1
Education (of those age 25+)			
Less than high school	22.2	26.9	42.6
High school	9.2	11.9	19.8
Some college	5.9	7.9	13.4
College graduate +	3.2	4.2	6.4
Citizenship Status			
Native	10.7	12.7	20.2
Naturalized citizen	9.7	13.8	19.7
Not a citizen	19.4	28.6	34.4

SOURCES: Official and relative measures from tabulations of the 2001 Current Population Survey Annual Demographic Supplement data. NAS measure from tabulations of the 1999 Experimental Poverty Measures Research Data file. American Indian poverty rate from Joseph Dalaker, "Poverty in the United States: 2000," U.S. Census Bureau, Current Population Reports, series P60-214 (Washington DC: U.S. Government Printing Office, 2001).

*The relative threshold equals one-half the median household income in 1999. See text for details on all three measures.

**Given the small sample size, the poverty rate for Native Americans refers to the 1998–2000 three-year average.

[handwritten: 17,463 / 6,820 / 12,643]

others, as these are among the elements taken into account in the NAS measure but not in the official poverty measure.[9]

Relative poverty rates are higher than both the official and NAS poverty rates, though the patterns across groups tend to be similar, with a couple of exceptions. For example, while nonelderly adults and the elderly have fairly similar poverty rates when using the official poverty measure, the elderly have considerably higher poverty rates than other adults when using the relative measure, mainly because more of the elderly have incomes above the official poverty lines but below the relative ones. Perhaps one way to interpret the overall difference between the relative poverty rates and the official (and to a lesser extent, the NAS) poverty rates is that, as we would expect, the proportion of people who did not meet a socially acceptable standard of living in 2000 was higher than that of those who struggled to meet the most basic of physical needs.

Most of the rest of this chapter focuses on research that uses the official poverty measure, as this is the most common measure used in the United States and is therefore the one about which the most is known.

THE DEPTH OF POVERTY AND MATERIAL HARDSHIP

The poverty figures discussed above tell us something about the extent, or breadth, of poverty across demographic groups and over time. Amartya Sen has argued that it is important to know not only the number of poor people (known as a "head-count ratio") but also the average shortfall of the poor below the poverty threshold and the distribution of income among the poor.[10] Figure 4.2 therefore shows levels of "extreme" poverty, or the proportion of people with family incomes less than half the official poverty threshold, and "near" poverty—the proportion with family incomes less than 1.25 of the poverty threshold. While the overall official poverty rate was 11.3 percent in 2000, a smaller proportion of people—4.4 percent—were in extreme poverty, while 15.8 percent of all people were near poor and poor.

Rates of extreme poverty are higher among children and African Americans and lower among whites, Asians, and the elderly. Among families in poverty, the amount by which their incomes fell below the official poverty line averaged $6,820 in 2000.[11] This figure has remained fairly stable over time: it declined a little in the 1960s, increased in the late 1970s through the early 1990s,[12] then declined modestly in the late 1990s.

[handwritten margin notes: "depth of pov.", "extreme poverty", "near poverty", "12,643"]

[handwritten at bottom: "Do as a variety of charts"]

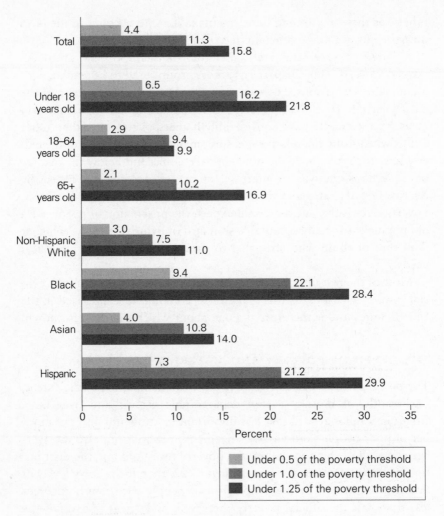

SOURCE: Dalaker, "Poverty in the United States: 2000."

Figure 4.2. Ratio of Family Income to the Poverty Threshold, 2000

Unsurprisingly, poor people are considerably more likely to report suffering a variety of material hardships than the nonpoor. Table 4.2 shows reports of selected measures of hardship by poverty status, using thresholds that are 200 percent of the official poverty thresholds. That is, people are considered poor here if they have a family income less than twice the official poverty line. Heather Boushey and her coauthors

TABLE 4.2. PERCENT OF PEOPLE EXPERIENCING
VARIOUS HARDSHIPS BY POVERTY STATUS,
1995–1996

	Below 200% poverty	Above 200% poverty
Critical Hardships		
Food Insecurity		
Not enough food to eat*	12.6%	1.6%
Missed meals	17.5	3.4
Insufficient Health Care		
Did not receive or postponed necessary medical care	12.7	8.0
Housing Problems		
Evicted*	1.1	0.1
Utilities disconnected*	4.1	0.6
Doubling up with friends or family	2.4	0.3
Serious Hardships		
Food Insecurity		
Dissatisfaction with kind of food*	28.8	8.4
Worried about having enough food	41.1	11.0
Insufficient Health Care		
Emergency room is main source of care	7.3	2.3
No health insurance coverage	35.9	9.9
Housing Problems		
Unable to make housing or utility payments	25.0	7.8
Telephone disconnected	10.4	3.0
Inadequate Child Care		
Child cares for self	5.1	6.8
Child not in after-school or enrichment activities	21.2	8.5
Inadequate adult-to-child ratio in childcare facility	6.0	8.5

SOURCE: Heather Boushey et al., *Hardships in America: The Real Story of Working Families* (Washington, D.C.: Economic Policy Institute, 2001), table 8.
*Data for these variables come from the 1993 Survey of Income and Program Participation (for calendar year 1995); data for all others come from the 1997 National Survey of American Families (for calendar year 1996).

divided hardships into two types: critical and serious.[13] They define critical hardships as those that threaten basic needs for survival, and serious hardships as those in which families "lack the goods, services, and financial ability to maintain employment and a stable, healthy home environment." They further break down hardships into four categories: food insecurity, insufficient health care, housing problems, and inadequate child care. Data for their findings come from the 1993 Survey of Income and Program Participation (SIPP) and the 1997 National Survey of American Families (NSAF).[14]

With regard to specific hardships reported in Table 4.2, about 1 in 8 people of the population under 200 percent of the poverty threshold reported not having enough food to eat sometimes or often, and 18 percent missed meals sometimes or often. About 1 in 8 also reported that in the last twelve months a member of their family did not get, or postponed, necessary medical care. About 1 percent were evicted, and 4 percent had their utilities disconnected. People with family incomes over 200 percent of the poverty line were considerably less likely to report all of these problems.

As would be expected, serious hardships were more common than critical hardships. Of those with family income below 200 percent of the poverty line, over a quarter of the families reported lacking the kinds of food they liked to eat, and 2 in 5 worried that food would run out before they could buy more. Over a third of the poor lacked health insurance; a quarter reported that there had been a time in the past twelve months when their household was not able to pay the mortgage, rent, or utility bill; and about a fifth did not have a child in after-school or enrichment activities. Among people in families with children, about 5 percent lived in one in which a child had cared for him- or herself in the past month or stayed alone with a sibling under thirteen years old. Nonpoor families reported these problems at considerably lower rates, except for two of the child care items.

Boushey and her collaborators state that, overall, 29 percent of families below the official poverty threshold and 25 percent of families between 100 percent and 200 percent of poverty experienced critical hardships, while about 11 percent over the 200 percent poverty level experienced such hardships. About 63 percent of those under the official poverty line, 74 percent between 100 and 200 percent of the poverty line, and 30 percent of the population with incomes over 200 percent of the poverty line reported experiencing one or more serious hardships.

A moderate number of poor American households own common consumer items. Figure 4.3 indicates, for example, that 41 percent of poor households (using the official poverty definition) owned their own home (as compared to 65 percent of all households) in 1995, and about 70 percent owned a car or truck (compared to 90 percent of all households).[15] The fact that many poor households owned a number of

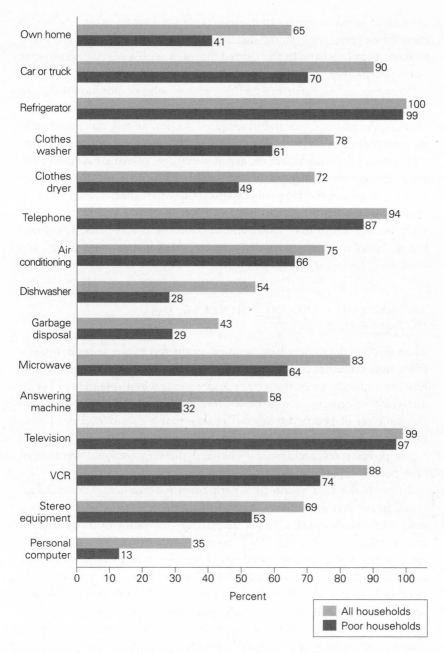

SOURCE: Robert Rector, Kirk A. Johnson, and Sarah E. Youssef, "The Extent of Material Hardship and Poverty in the United States," *Review of Social Economy* 57, 3 (September 1999): table 3, p. 359.

Figure 4.3. Percent of Households with Various Consumer Goods, 1995

consumer goods suggests that poverty in the United States differs in nature from poverty in many developing countries, as will be discussed in more detail shortly. In the United States, a wide variety of consumer items is available at a range of prices and quality levels.

However, in the American context, people who do not have access to a car may have trouble holding a job, given the decentralized character of many American cities and inadequate accompanying municipal public transportation systems. The poor may also often pay more for goods and services than the nonpoor, as supermarkets offering low prices are often less common in poor urban neighborhoods or rural places.[16] It could also be argued that American families that do not own some of these basic consumer goods may both feel marginal and be treated as such and therefore may lack sufficient income to, as Peter Townsend put it, "play the roles, participate in the relationships, and follow the customary behavior" of their society.[17]

THE DYNAMICS AND INTERGENERATIONAL TRANSFER OF POVERTY

Most poverty data come from studies conducted at one point in time or from annual studies conducted on a different set of people every year. It has been mainly since the 1970s and 1980s, when researchers began analyzing information from newer longitudinal studies—which follow the same set of people for several years—that a dynamic view of poverty has emerged. The findings from these longitudinal studies surprised many poverty researchers and changed the conventional wisdom of how people experience poverty over time.

Many had had a vision of a permanently dependent "underclass," mired in poverty and utterly dependent on the government or others.[18] And while traditional, cross-sectional (or one-point-in-time) surveys indicate that poverty is a fairly constant feature of society—the poverty rate, for example, has fluctuated only from about 11 to 15 percent since the mid-1960s—the newer longitudinal data show that a majority of poor individuals actually remain poor for only short periods of time and a relatively high proportion of people have experienced poverty at one point or another.[19] One study found that 1 in 3 Americans experienced at least one year in poverty between 1979 and 1991.[20]

Among documented spells of poverty in which the beginning is observed in a survey, about 45 percent end within one year and 70 percent are over within three years.[21] Only 12 percent of poverty spells last ten years or more.[22] If we calculate poverty using a monthly rather than an annual time frame, we see even more turnover in the poverty population. For example, while the proportion of people who were poor for at least two consecutive months in 1994 was 21 percent, the percent who were poor every month of both 1993 and 1994 was 5 percent.[23] Of course, many of those who are poor for just a couple of months are people who may have higher annual incomes but who may work seasonally.

Despite the shortness of many poverty spells, it is quite common for people who leave poverty to fall back into it a short time later. In fact, when measuring poverty on an annual basis (the most common way), about half of those who end poverty spells return to poverty within four years. Accounting for multiple spells shows that approximately 50 percent of blacks and 30 percent of whites who fall into poverty in some year will be poor in five or more of the next ten years.[24]

recurrence

Moreover, despite the high level of movement in and out of poverty, more than 50 percent of those who are poor at any given time are in the midst of a spell of poverty which will last ten years or more. This apparent contradiction—that most people who enter poverty are poor for only a relatively short time but most of the people currently in poverty are in the midst of a long-term spell—can perhaps be best explained by an analogy: in most hospitals, while the chronically ill are only a small part of those admitted on a daily basis, they still represent a large portion of the patients in the hospital at any given time.[25]

others are moving in & out

A number of factors affect the length of time people are poor. As might be expected, people are less likely to escape poverty in recession years than in other years.[26] In addition, the longer one is in poverty, the less likely one is to escape it. For example, while the probability of escaping poverty after being poor for one year is 0.53, the probability after four years drops to 0.23.[27] Families headed by white men tend to leave poverty more quickly than those headed by others, such as black women.[28] While fewer than 1 in 50 whites was poor for ten or more years from 1979 to 1991, 1 in 6 African Americans was.[29] In a study of children's poverty spells over a fifteen-year period beginning in 1968, Greg Duncan found that nearly 30 percent of African American children were poor in ten or more years and that they constituted almost 90 percent of long term–poor children.[30]

factors in length

Another issue is the extent that poverty is passed from one generation to the next. Before relatively recent research, conventional wisdom had it that the debilitating effects of poverty are indeed passed on to successive generations. The fact that people were trapped in long-term

generational?

poverty was one of the motivations for President Johnson's War on
Poverty.[31] If poverty is indeed routinely "transmitted" across generations and unequally distributed across demographic groups, U.S. norms
of fairness and meritocracy can very justifiably be called into question.

Research has shown that there is about a 0.40 correlation between
fathers' and sons' income.[32] With regard to poverty, about 1 in 4 who
were consistently poor before age seventeen were still poor at ages
twenty-five to twenty-seven. But poor African American children are
less likely to escape poverty than others—1 in 3 were still poor at ages
twenty-five to twenty-seven, as compared to 1 in 12 white children.[33]

Researchers debate which factors do most to explain the moderate
correlation of poverty across generations. Four common theories are
the "economic resources" model, the "noneconomic resources" model,
the "welfare trap" model, and the "structural/environmental" model.[34]
According to the economic resources model, parents' lack of money
and time hinders the ability to invest in children's education, which in
turn hurts the children's ability to find well-paying jobs. Poor parents
may also be less able to afford housing in safe neighborhoods and high-
quality schools and may be less connected to job networks than nonpoor parents.

According to the noneconomic resources model, poor parents lack
other resources that often contribute to children's economic success.
For example, poor parents with less education may be less able to
encourage and help their children to obtain a good education. The
material hardship associated with poverty may also increase psychological stress on both parents and their children. Poor single parents may
face the added difficulties of providing appropriate parental supervision
or serving as successful role modes for marriage or work, which in turn
affect the probability that their children will be poor.

According to the welfare trap model, intergenerational poverty is
fueled not by a lack of resources but by the government welfare system.
Lawrence Mead has argued that, when individuals rely heavily on welfare, the stigma associated with welfare disappears and welfare recipients develop self-defeating attitudes and poor work ethics that are then
transmitted to their children.[35] Finally, structural/environmental models
assert that labor market conditions, migration patterns, racial discrimination, and racial and class segregation all play a role in perpetuating
poverty across generations. William Julius Wilson, perhaps the best-
known proponent of this view, argued that the loss of well-paid blue-

collar manufacturing jobs from the inner city and the out-migration of middle-class African Americans from poor urban areas increased the intergenerational transfer of poverty among inner-city residents.[36]

There is no consensus on which of these models is the best, though some research has provided the strongest support for the economic resources model, where parents' lack of money and time hinders their ability to invest in their children. Growing up poor is consistently associated with higher chances of being poor, even when we take into account other factors such as family structure and neighborhood poverty rates. Structural economic conditions, such as high unemployment rates in the local labor market, have small but significant effects on the intergenerational transmission of poverty. There is only modest support for the welfare trap and noneconomic resources models.[37]

THE GEOGRAPHY OF POVERTY

Where one lives affects the opportunities one has and the type of living one earns. The economic, social, cultural, and political features of places vary tremendously. Many cities in the Northeast and Midwest, for example, long had economies based on manufacturing. Deindustrialization in the post–World War II period had a profound effect on people living in these cities. Many who had worked in manufacturing plants lost their jobs as plants closed and moved their operations to the South, overseas, or elsewhere. These people were forced to find other types of employment, and some became poor.

This type of local change helps produce considerable differences in the extent of poverty across states, regions, and metropolitan areas. Concentrated poverty—sometimes referred to as "ghetto" poverty— is also a topic that received considerable attention, particularly in the 1980s and 1990s. These topics are discussed below.

Poverty by Region, State, and Metropolitan Status

Poverty rates vary enormously across states. Data from decennial censuses—the most reliable sources of information on poverty across geographic entities—show that poverty rates in 1999 in the fifty states and the District of Columbia ranged from 6.5 percent in New Hampshire to 20.2 in the District of Columbia. Mississippi, at 19.9 percent, was the state with the highest poverty rate. Ten years earlier, the gap between the highest and lowest state was even wider, when Missis-sippi's poverty rate was 25.2 percent and New Hampshire's was 6.4 percent (see Table 4.3).

The national poverty rate, according to the decennial censuses, declined in the 1990s from 13.1 percent to 12.4 percent. However, poverty rates across American states converged over time, as the states with the highest poverty rates in 1989—such as Mississippi, Louisiana, and New Mexico—experienced larger declines than the U.S. average. In contrast, states with very low poverty rates in 1989—such as New Hampshire, Connecticut, and New Jersey—experienced little change or small increases in poverty.

The Northeast and Midwest continued to have lower poverty rates in 1999 than the South and West. The South and Midwest saw larger than average declines in poverty over the period. Metropolitan areas also continued to have lower poverty rates than nonmetro areas, though there was convergence over the 1990s. Within metropolitan areas, central cities continued to have considerably higher poverty rates than suburbs.

Some researchers have noted that there are some persistently poor and economically depressed rural areas, such as in the Mississippi Delta, Appalachia, and the lower Rio Grande Valley.[38] These are areas where educational levels are low and job opportunities scarce. Unemployment rates have been persistently higher in rural than in urban areas since the mid-1990s. A higher proportion of rural workers also earn low wages than urban workers.[39] Rural areas are often characterized by spatial isolation; inadequate physical infrastructure, such as public transportation and schools; and limited social support services.[40]

Daniel Lichter and Martha Crowley assert that rural poverty is distinctive because it is often extreme and has persisted over decades, especially in the South. While the poor in Appalachia are predominantly white, the poor in other rural pockets tend to be minorities, such as African Americans in the South, Mexican-origin inhabitants in the South and West, and American Indians on reservations. They note that "many Americans assume that disadvantaged minorities are concentrated exclusively in urban ghettos, but some of the most impoverished American minorities live in isolated, economically depressed rural areas.[41]

Concentrated Poverty

What is so important about concentrated poverty? Its significance stems from the fact that many urban problems such as crime, welfare

	1990 census	2000 census	2000–1990 change
U.S. Total	**13.1**	**12.4**	–0.7
Region			
Northeast	10.6	11.4	0.8
Midwest	12.0	10.2	–1.8
South	15.7	13.9	–1.8
West	12.6	13.0	0.4
Metropolitan Area Status			
Metropolitan areas	12.1	11.8	–0.3
Central city	18.0	17.6	–0.4
Suburbs	8.1	8.4	0.3
Nonmetropolitan areas	16.8	14.6 *Rural pov*	–2.2
State			
Alabama	18.3	16.1✓	–2.2
Alaska	9.0	9.4	0.4
Arizona	15.7	13.9	–1.8
Arkansas	19.1	15.8✓	–3.3
California	12.5	14.2	1.7
Colorado	11.7	9.3	–2.4
Connecticut	6.8	7.9	1.1
Delaware	8.7	9.2	0.5
District of Columbia	16.9	20.2	3.3
Florida	12.7	12.5	–0.2
Georgia	14.7	13.0	–1.7
Hawaii	8.3	10.7	2.4
Idaho	13.3	11.8	–1.5
Illinois	11.9	10.7	–1.2
Indiana	10.7	9.5	–1.2
Iowa	11.5	9.1	–2.4
Kansas	11.5	9.9	–1.6
Kentucky	19.0	15.8	–3.2
Louisiana	23.6	19.6	–4.0
Maine	10.8	10.9	0.1
Maryland	8.3	8.5	0.2
Massachusetts	8.9	9.3	0.4
Michigan	13.1	10.5	–2.6
Minnesota	10.2	7.9	–2.3
Mississippi	25.2	19.9	–5.3
Missouri	13.3	11.7	–1.6
Montana	16.1	14.6	–1.5
Nebraska	11.1	9.7	–1.4
Nevada	10.2	10.5	0.3
New Hampshire	6.4	6.5	0.1

TABLE 4.3. *(continued)*

	1990 census	2000 census	2000–1990 change
New Jersey	7.6	8.5	0.9
New Mexico	20.6	18.4	–2.2
New York	13.0	14.6	1.6
North Carolina	13.0	12.3	–0.7
North Dakota	14.4	11.9	–2.5
Ohio	12.5	10.6	–1.9
Oklahoma	16.7	14.7	–2.0
Oregon	12.4	11.6	–0.8
Pennsylvania	11.1	11.0	–0.1
Rhode Island	9.6	11.9	2.3
South Carolina	15.4	14.1	–1.3
South Dakota	15.9	13.2	–2.7
Tennessee	15.7	13.5	–2.2
Texas	18.1	15.4	–2.7
Utah	11.4	9.4	–2.0
Vermont	9.9	9.4	–0.5
Virginia	10.2	9.6	–0.6
Washington	10.9	10.6	–0.3
West Virginia	19.7	17.9	–1.8
Wisconsin	10.7	8.7	–2.0
Wyoming	11.9	11.4	–0.5

SOURCES: 1990 figures from U.S. Census Bureau, "Persons by Poverty Status in 1969, 1979, and 1989, by State," Census Historical Poverty Tables, Table CPHL-162 (Internet data released December 13, 2000, at www.census.gov/hhes/poverty/census/cphl162.html), except metropolitan area figures, which are from U.S. Census Bureau, "Summary of Occupation, Income, and Poverty Characteristics: 1990," 1990 Census of Population: Social and Economic Characteristics, series CP 2-1 (1993), U.S. Summary, table 3. 2000 figures from U.S. Census Bureau, Census 2000, "DP-1. Profile of General Demographic Characteristics: 2000," summary file 1 (SF 1), 100-Percent Data Quick Table (2000, American Fact Finder tabulation available at: factfinder.census.gov).

dependency, drug use, substandard educational outcomes, and out-of-wedlock births are most prevalent in high-poverty areas. Poor people living in these neighborhoods are often both spatially and socially isolated from mainstream society. Their families must therefore often cope not only with their own poverty but also with the poverty and its accompanying problems of hundreds of other families near them. In essence, the premise is that people are affected by their neighbors and that the economic and social environment of high-poverty areas negatively affects those who live there.[42]

The spatial concentration of poverty in American cities is a relatively recent phenomenon. Social historians who have reconstructed urban

neighborhoods hold that in the nineteenth century the poor were generally, with some exceptions in large cities, clustered into pockets and
alleyways near the homes of the affluent.[43] Class and racial segregation
began increasing by 1920 with improvements in transportation and the
rise of the automobile industry, which made the suburban lifestyle more
accessible. After World War II, suburbanization surged dramatically;
early suburban migrants were overwhelming white and middle class.

It was not until the 1960s and 1970s that people began to talk about
sharp increases in "ghetto" or "barrio" poverty, the rise of the "underclass," and increases in "concentrated" poverty. The term *ghetto* or
barrio poverty connotes both economic and racial and ethnic population concentrations. The term *underclass* typically refers to "nonnor-
mative" behaviors present in many high-poverty neighborhoods, such
as dropping out of school, having children out of wedlock, receiving
welfare, having low attachment to the labor force, and abusing drugs
and alcohol. Concentrated poverty refers more strictly to neighborhoods with high poverty rates.

High-poverty neighborhoods are typically defined as those where
over 40 percent of the population is poor, though 20 and 30 percent
thresholds have sometimes been used. Qualitative research suggests that
neighborhoods where 40 percent or more of the residents are poor are
ones that tended to have a "threatening appearance, marked by dilapi-
dated housing, vacant units with broken or boarded-up windows, aban-
doned or burned-out cars, and men 'hanging out' on street corners."[44]

While overall metropolitan area poverty rates were relatively stable
between 1970 and 1990, the number of people in high-poverty neighborhoods increased from a little over 4 million to 8 million people
over the same period. This 92 percent increase far surpasses the overall
28 percent increase in metropolitan area populations as a whole (see
Table 4.4). Nearly half of the people living in these poverty areas are
themselves poor, though only 15 percent of the total poverty population live in such neighborhoods.[45] Almost half (49 percent) of the poor
live in neighborhoods with poverty rates above 20 percent.[46] Results on
this topic from the 2000 Census, unavailable at the time of this writing,
will shed light on whether poverty has become more or less concentrated
in the 1990s.

Whites, African Americans, and Hispanics all had increases in
their numbers living in high-poverty areas over the 1970 to 1990
period. For whites, the biggest increases occurred in the 1980s. For

TABLE 4.4. POPULATION IN HIGH-POVERTY AREAS,
BY RACE AND ETHNICITY, 1970–1990

	Number of people (000s)			1970–1990 % change
	1970	1980	1990	
All Metropolitan Areas	139,328	157,405	177,913	28
White	114,712	124,848	135,098	18
Black	17,000	20,351	23,927	41
Hispanic	7,616	12,206	18,888	148
High-Poverty Areas	4,149	5,174	7,973	92
White	972	1,030	1,843	90
Black	2,447	3,097	4,152	70
Hispanic	729	1,048	1,978	171

SOURCE: Paul Jargowsky, *Poverty and Place: Ghettos, Barrios, and the American City* (New York: Russell Sage Foundation, 1997), table 2.2, p. 38.

blacks, it was fairly evenly spread over the 1970s and 1980s. Among Hispanics, who experienced the largest increases (in part because the Hispanic metropolitan-area population also grew the fastest), the largest increases occurred in the 1980s. In 1990 about half those in high-poverty areas were African American, and nearly a quarter were white and Hispanic each.[47]

People in high-poverty areas fare worse along a number of social and economic indicators. While 71 percent of all men aged sixteen and over are employed across all metropolitan areas, the figure is 46 percent in high-poverty neighborhoods. While female-headed families comprise under a fifth of all metropolitan families, well over half of families in high-poverty neighborhoods are female headed. Over half of people aged twenty-five and over in high-poverty areas never finished high school in 1990, versus 23 percent in metropolitan areas as a whole.[48]

While many residents in high-poverty areas face multiple disadvantages, Paul Jargowsky also emphasizes that these neighborhoods are not homogeneous. Many of those living in high-poverty areas are not public-assistance recipients and do participate in the labor market, albeit in lower-skill occupations and for fewer hours and lower wages than in other areas. He adds that "the extreme poverty of ghetto neighborhoods notwithstanding, the popular and politically exploitable image of ghettos as places where everyone drops out of school, where no one works, and where everyone receives welfare is a gross distor-

tion of reality . . . the data do not suggest the residents of ghettos constitute a separate 'underclass,' hopelessly at odds with the mainstream
culture."[49]

Concentrated poverty results from several factors, including past
government policies, racial and ethnic discrimination, residential segregation, economic changes and employment dislocations, the movement
of prosperous residents to the suburbs, and finally other, less definable
social and cultural forces. In terms of the negative effect of policy, some
federal housing policies, such as the building of low-income projects in
already poor inner-city neighborhoods in the post–World War II period,
contributed to poverty concentration. Federal assistance to highway
construction and mass transit also accelerated the suburbanization of
the middle and upper classes. Infrastructure and tax policies, such
as investment tax credits favoring construction of new plants and facilities—often built in the suburbs—over rehabilitation, also facilitated
suburbanization.[50]

Discrimination has also played a role. Douglas S. Massey and Nancy
Denton described how real estate brokers, speculators, developers, and
banks, acting on the racial animosity within the population, preserved
racial divisions in housing markets. The official policy of the real estate
agents in the Detroit area, for example, was expressed in the "Code
of Ethics" of the National Association of Real Estate Boards, which
explicitly banned racial mixing in neighborhoods through the 1940s
and later more tacitly.[51] Massey and Denton also argue that the resulting residential segregation, interacting with economic change and social alienation, played a key role in the perpetuation of concentrated
poverty:

> Deleterious neighborhood conditions are built into the structure of the
> black community. They occur because segregation concentrates poverty to
> build a set of mutually reinforcing and self-feeding spirals of decline into
> black neighborhoods. When economic dislocations deprive a segregated
> group of employment and increase its rate of poverty, socioeconomic dep-
> rivation inevitably becomes more concentrated in neighborhoods where
> that group lives.[52]

Other theories emphasize the impact of economic changes on
poverty concentration. Two of these are referred to as the "spatial mismatch" hypothesis and the "skills mismatch" hypothesis. According to
spatial mismatch theory, originally proposed by John Kain, increases in
the concentration of the inner-city poor are directly linked to the elimi-

nation of low-skill manufacturing jobs and the deconcentration of employment from central cities to the surrounding suburbs.[53] A related economic process, the emergence of the service economy, has resulted in the lack of well-paying job opportunities that match the skills of inner-city residents—a skills mismatch.[54] Many of the new jobs in the cities are high-paying service jobs that require high levels of education, or low-skill and low-wage service jobs that are unattractive as lifetime employment opportunities. The result is increasing poverty in the inner cities and growing affluence in the suburbs.

William Julius Wilson, in *The Truly Disadvantaged,* builds on the mismatch hypothesis. He argues that, because of economic restructuring and the accompanying flight of blue-collar jobs from the city, many middle-class blacks with sufficient money to leave their old inner-city neighborhoods did just that. As a consequence, the neighborhoods they left became even poorer when their economic vitality was drained. The result was neighborhoods whose people are increasingly socially isolated and face a shrinking job market; hence, an increase in concentrated poverty.

Others have argued that welfare policy and changes in norms have contributed to concentrated poverty.[55] The argument is that welfare makes people less self-reliant and provides positive incentives for out-of-wedlock births and female-headed households. Crime also rose in cities, and elsewhere, because the criminal justice system decreased sanctions against aberrant behavior. Government policies that discouraged personal responsibility, combined with social isolation and an ingrown expectation of failure among the poor, led to increasing dependency in poor areas.[56] A culture of poverty based on aberrant norms and behaviors emerged in the ghetto, where the poor do not take advantage of new opportunities that may arise.[57]

That welfare policy has played a role in exacerbating concentrated poverty has been contradicted by a number of arguments. On a theoretical level, it is argued that cultural values do not ultimately determine behavior or success. Existing opportunity structures are more important. William Julius Wilson has argued:

> Cultural values emerge from specific social circumstances and life chances and reflect one's class and racial position. Thus, if underclass blacks have limited aspirations or fail to plan for the future, it is not ultimately the product of different cultural norms but the consequence of restricted opportunities, a bleak future, and feelings of resignation resulting from bitter personal experiences.[58]

There is also empirical evidence against the welfare argument. Mainly, welfare payments have decreased in real dollars since 1972, while concentrated poverty continued to rise in the years after.[59] Finally, the general de-emphasis of the economic opportunity structure's impact on poverty is a general weakness of these types of explanations.

Which factors, then, are the most salient for understanding rates of concentrated poverty and changes in concentrated poverty? The jury is still out on the matter, and it is likely that all play at least some role. Jargowsky concluded, in his book *Poverty and Place,* that economic opportunities at the metropolitan level were the most important factor determining patterns of ghetto and barrio poverty, while neighborhood sorting processes, such as residential segregation and the growing economic segregation among African Americans, also played important roles.[60]

U.S. POVERTY IN THE INTERNATIONAL CONTEXT

Comparing poverty across countries provides greater insight into the nature and severity of poverty in the United States. Two distinct patterns emerge from this type of comparison. First, in absolute terms, poverty in the United States qualitatively differs from that in the developing world, where poverty is measured in terms of having sufficient resources to stay alive. Second, despite high general standards of living, the United States suffers from considerably more poverty and inequality than most other developed countries with similar standards of living. These two themes are now explored in turn.

Poverty in the Developing World

Globalization has had a dramatic impact on countries around the world. The market system has now become the organizational model for a majority of rich and poor economies alike. On the positive side, it has generated an enormous amount of material progress around the world. In the decades following World War II, absolute poverty declined worldwide, and there was improvement along other social indicators, such as broad-based declines in infant mortality, a reduction of child malnourishment, and an increase in school enrollment.[61] Yet globalization has also contributed to growing inequality across countries and to social and economic exclusion and marginalization.[62] The poorest 20 percent of the global population has not benefited much

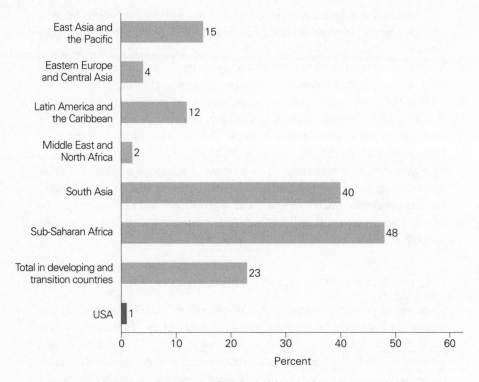

SOURCE: World Bank, "Income Poverty: The Latest Global Numbers," Data on Poverty (www.
worldbank.org/poverty/data/trends/income.htm), 2001; USA estimate from 1999 Current Population
Survey March supplement tabulations.

Figure 4.4. Percent of People Living on Less Than $1 a Day, by World Region,
1998

from general improvements.[63] Of the world's population living in developing and transition economies, 2.8 billion, or almost half, live on less
than $2 a day, and about 1.2 billion, or 23 percent, live on less than
$1 a day, with 44 percent of these people living in South Asia.[64]

Figure 4.4 shows the percent of people living on less than $1 a day in
1998, by global region.[65] This extreme measure of poverty indicates
considerable material deprivation across several regions. Poverty is especially severe in South Asia and Africa, where 40 and 48 percent of the
population is poor, respectively. Acute poverty is somewhat lower in
East Asia and the Pacific, where the percent earning under $1 a day fell
from 27 percent in 1987 to 15 percent in 1998. In terms of absolute
numbers, the count of those earning under $1 fell from 420 million to

280 million from 1987 to 1998. Yet in Latin America, South Asia, sub-Saharan Africa, and Eastern Europe and Central Asia the total number of poor has been rising.[66]

The average income in the richest twenty countries is thirty-seven times the average in the poorest twenty—a gap that doubled in the past forty years.[67] These patterns are associated with other key measures of well-being. While in the thirty member nations of the Organization of Economic Cooperation and Development (OECD, which consists of many Western European countries plus other industrialized countries, such as Japan and Australia) 6 out of every 1,000 children die before the age of one; in the sub-Saharan region 92 out of 1,000 die before that age (see Figure 4.5).[68] In the United States, the infant mortality rate is about 7 per 1,000, though it is almost 15 per 1,000 among children born to African American mothers.[69] Nevertheless, in the poorest countries as many as 1 in 5 children dies before the age of five. Similarly, while fewer than 5 percent of all children in rich countries are malnourished, in poor counties as many as 50 percent are.[70]

Poverty in Wealthier Countries

While poverty in the Unites States is qualitatively different from poverty in most of the developing world, it is still more common than in other countries with similar levels of development. This is true whether we use an absolute or relative poverty measure. Figure 4.6 compares poverty rates of eleven wealthy countries using an absolute, or constant, poverty line that does not vary across place (or time). Timothy Smeeding and his colleagues applied the 1994 or 1995 U.S. poverty line, depending on the year of the data in the country in question, using "purchasing power parity" (PPP) exchange rates, which convert the dollar-denominated poverty line into different currencies.[71] Because of complexities in determining the exchange rate, the exact poverty rates shown should be viewed with caution and are discussed for general comparative purposes rather than used as precise measures of material deprivation.[72]

According to Figure 4.6, the United States does not compare particularly favorably to other rich countries in terms of absolute poverty levels, where a similar poverty line is used. The U.S. poverty rate of 13.6 percent is surpassed only by Australia and the United Kingdom. The other countries of Western and Northern Europe, along with Canada, have lower absolute poverty rates.

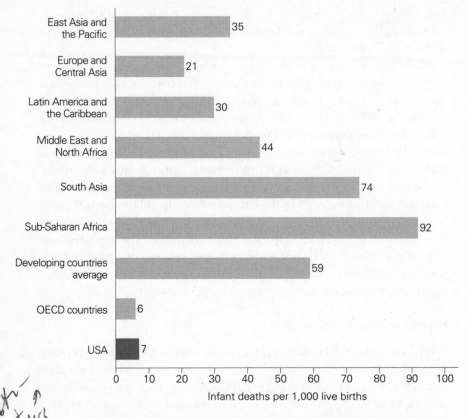

SOURCE: Estimates from World Bank, "Social Indicators—Health: Life Expectancy, Infant and Child Mortality, Malnutrition," Data on Poverty (www.worldbank.org/poverty/data/trends/mort.htm), 2001, except USA estimates, which are from Centers for Disease Control and Prevention, "Infant Mortality Rates, Fetal Mortality Rates, and Perennial Mortality Rates, According to Race: United States, Selected Years, 1950–99," National Center for Health Statistics, Health Data, table 23 (www.cdc.gov/nchs/about/major/dvs/mortdata.htm), 2001.
NOTE: OECD, Organization for Economic Cooperation and Development.

Figure 4.5. Infant Mortality, by Region, 1999

Figure 4.7 compares the United States to these same countries, but this time using a relative poverty measure—where the poverty line represents 40 percent of the median adjusted disposable personal income in each of those countries. The poverty measure is relative because the poverty line varies across countries based on local levels of income.[73] According to this measure, the United States fares even worse when compared to other countries. It has the highest relative poverty rate of all the countries shown—almost double that of the United Kingdom and three times the relative poverty rate of France.

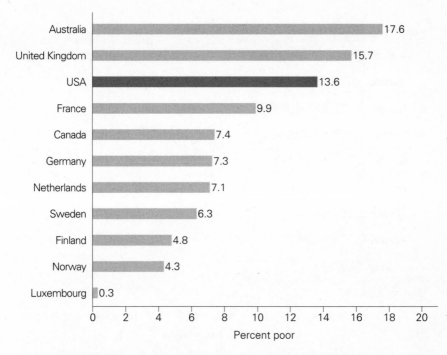

SOURCE: Timothy Smeeding, Lee Rainwater, and Gary Burtless, "United States Poverty in a Cross-National Context," Luxembourg Income Study Working Paper no. 244 (September 2000), table 1.

Figure 4.6. Absolute Poverty Rates for Selected Rich Nations, Using the U.S. Poverty Line, Mid-1990s

In their analysis of both absolute and relative poverty levels, Smeeding and his colleagues assert, "Although the high rate of relative poverty in the United States is no surprise, given the country's well-known tolerance of wide economic disparities, the lofty rate of absolute poverty is much more troubling. After Luxembourg, the United States has the highest average income in the industrialized world. The per capita income of the United States is more than 30 percent higher than it is, on average, in the other ten countries of our survey."[74]

Susan Mayer, in a comparative study of income poverty and material hardship in the United States, Sweden, Germany, and Canada, also finds that there are more poor people in the United States, the U.S. safety net is weaker, and poor Americans are poorer than the poor in the other countries.[75]

When comparing measures of material hardship other than pure income insufficiency, however, Mayer concludes that poor Americans

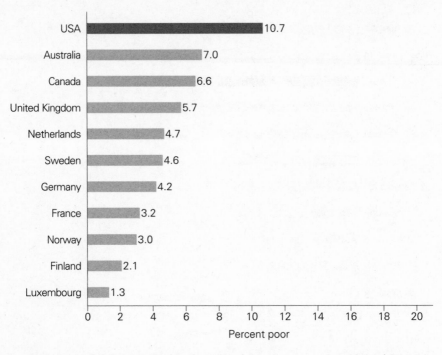

SOURCE: Smeeding, Rainwater, and Burtless, "United States Poverty in a Cross-National Context," table 2.
NOTE: The poverty line is defined as 40 percent of median adjusted disposable personal income in each country.

Figure 4.7. Relative Poverty Rates for Selected Rich Nations, Mid-1990s

do not live with more material deprivation than poor Swedes, Germans, or Canadians. For example, discussing the ownership of consumer durables, she reports that people who are designated poor using a relative measure (below 50 percent of national median income) are more likely to have a motor vehicle in the United States than in Sweden or Canada but not more likely to have a washer or dryer, or telephone. Notably, she adds that American blacks clearly fare worse than other poor people in the United States and in the other countries. Overall, Mayer posits that unmeasured wealth, availability of credit, and a better measure of income in other countries may explain some of these findings or that the findings may reflect differences in tastes among the poor, where the purchase of certain consumer goods may receive higher priority in the United States than other countries.[76]

Regardless of the material deprivation *among* those who are poor, the United States clearly has higher levels of poverty (i.e., a greater proportion of people who are poor) than other wealthy countries. Poverty rates are higher in the United States because many jobs, even full-time ones, pay low wages and because public benefits are more limited. Considering market income alone, relative U.S. poverty rates are higher than in some of the rich countries and lower than in others. However, because of lower government benefits in the United States, the net beneficial effect of universal transfers, such as child allowances, and the effect of targeted social assistance transfers, such as food stamps and guaranteed child support for single parents, is smaller in the United States than in other countries.[77] Indeed, government expenditures on social welfare programs as a percentage of gross national product are considerably higher in Western European countries than in the United States.[78]

Figure 4.8 shows poverty rates once again across countries, but this time the focus is on children. In addition, a greater number of countries are considered, including some lower-income countries in Eastern Europe, where economic transition and turmoil were occurring in the mid-1990s. According to the figure, the child poverty rate in the United States is fairly high—18.5 percent of children are poor. However, illustrating the qualitatively different nature of poverty in poorer countries and the difficulty of comparing material deprivation across vastly different social and economic contexts, we see that some Eastern European countries have extremely high child poverty rates of 85 percent and over. In Russia, for example, virtually all children were poor by this particular measure. This is not shocking, given that the Russian gross national product (GNP) per capita was $4,100 in 1996 (in 1995 U.S. dollars), or about one-seventh the U.S. per-capita GNP of $26,400. Child poverty rates using this absolute poverty measure are also high in countries such Ireland, Spain, Israel, and Italy. Bruce Bradbury and Markus Jantti note that, while there is no doubt that absolute poverty is high in these countries, the precise estimates should be viewed with a grain of salt because of the difficulties in estimating accurate PPPs for countries with widely different income levels. Finally, the figure shows that the Western and Northern European countries—those that are truly comparable to the United States in terms of GNP per capita (though all except Luxembourg have lower GNP per capita than the United States)—have lower absolute poverty rates.[79]

Figure 4.9 shows relative child poverty rates for the same set of countries, setting poverty thresholds at 50 percent of the median income in each country. When using this relative measure, the United

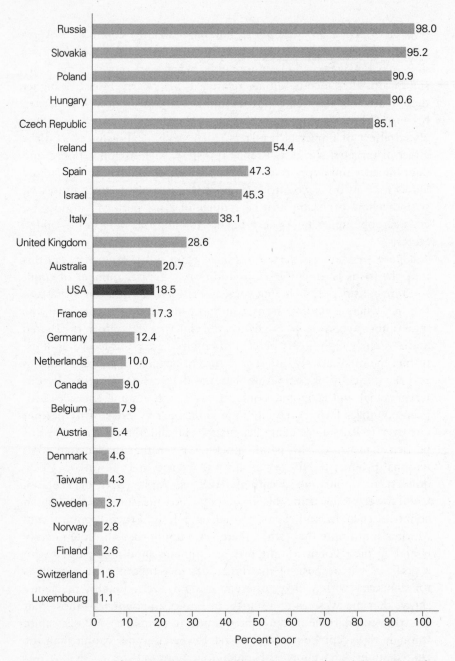

SOURCE: Bruce Bradbury and Markus Jantti, "Child Poverty across Twenty-Five Countries," in *The Dynamics of Child Poverty in Industrialised Countries,* ed. Bruce Bradbury, Stephen P. Jenkins, and John Micklewright (Cambridge, UK: Cambridge University Press, 2001), table 3.2.

Figure 4.8. Absolute Child Poverty Rates for Selected Countries, Using the U.S. Poverty Line

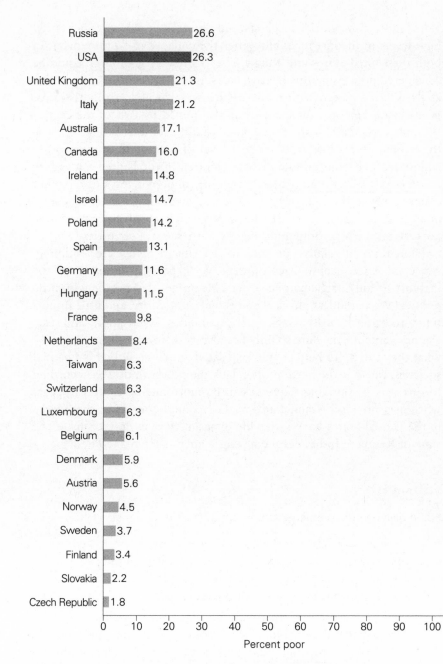

SOURCE: Bradbury and Jantti, "Child Poverty across Twenty-Five Countries," table 3.2.
NOTE: The poverty line is defined as 50 percent of the median income in each country.

Figure 4.9. Relative Child Poverty Rates for Selected Countries

States fares very poorly, surpassed only by Russia, which experienced high levels of income inequality after the collapse of Communism. In both the United States and Russia, over 1 in every 4 children could be considered poor using this relative measure. Every other country in this analysis fared better, with many of the Western and Northern Europeans again amongst the lowest but also joined by two of the central European countries. It should be noted that the flip side is that, because the United States has a higher real level of income than most other countries, high- and middle-income children in the United States fare considerably better than relatively well-off children in most of the other countries. It is the high levels of income inequality that causes low-income American children to have both high absolute and relative poverty rates when compared to many of these same countries.[80]

High rates of relative poverty in the United States are troubling. Amartya Sen conceptualizes poverty as "capability failure," or the inability to fully participate in society. He argues that people with little political voice, modest physical and economic security, and little opportunity to better their lives lack basic capabilities. While goods and services are valuable, they are so only because of their instrumental value—what they can do to help people lead satisfying lives. In highly unequal societies, those at the bottom often lack the power to do so. According to this way of thinking, poverty can be more intense than it appears when measured using family income. For example, Sen notes that blacks in the United States have lower life expectancy than do citizens of the state of Kerala in India, despite having higher absolute incomes.[81]

SUMMARY

Some basic patterns emerge from a number of national surveys:

- Declines in poverty in the United States more or less stalled by the early 1970s. Poverty is also more pervasive among some groups, such as minorities and female-headed families. Patterns vary somewhat by measure of poverty used.

- Poor people are, unsurprisingly, considerably more likely to report material hardships, such as sometimes not having enough food to eat or missing utility payments. Yet both rich and poor Americans alike report having basic consumer items such as TVs and refrigerators.

- While a majority of people who fall into poverty remain poor for only a short time, many families frequently move into and out of poverty, and a significant proportion of the poor suffer long-term poverty spells.

- Poverty varies widely across states and has also become more concentrated within cities over the last few decades, mainly because of economic reorganization and residential segregation. Rural pockets of deep poverty also persist in some places.

- When comparing poverty in the United States with poverty in countries around the world, research indicates that poverty in developing countries—because it is so widespread and severe—differs qualitatively from that in the United States and other developed countries. Nevertheless, despite the fact that the United States has virtually the highest GNP per capita in the world, it has higher levels of both absolute and relative poverty than other rich countries in Northern and Western Europe. It also has higher levels of relative poverty than just about all European countries.

CHAPTER 5

Causes of Poverty

[handwritten margin notes: CST — Both/and analysis — (go from other book — false trade-off —]

It is commonly believed that individual failings or wayward values propel people into poverty. In the 1960s, anthropologist Oscar Lewis wrote:

> By the time slum children are age six or seven they have usually absorbed the basic values and attitudes of their subculture and are not psychologically geared to take full advantage of changing conditions or increased opportunities which may occur in their lifetime.[1]

[handwritten margin note: Poll Split]

A 2001 poll in the United States asked: "In your opinion, which is the bigger cause of poverty today—that people are not doing enough to help themselves out of poverty, or that circumstances beyond their control cause them to be poor?" Responses were nearly evenly split between "people not doing enough" (48 percent) and "circumstances" (45 percent). More affluent people were more likely to believe that poor people themselves were not doing enough, while the poor were more likely to point to circumstances rather than themselves. The same poll also showed that about two-thirds of Americans believe that the poor have the same values as other Americans, and about a fifth thought they had lower moral values.[2]

[handwritten margin note: neoclass. econ]

In the social sciences, *neoclassical economic theory* also emphasizes the role of individual-level traits, such as family background and educational level, in affecting people's economic well-being. For example, many studies have shown that people who invest in their education or skills can expect higher incomes. This view dominates economic research on poverty in the social sciences. Alice O'Connor has argued that "the ubiquity of the neoclassical model as a way of explaining the causes and consequence of poverty—alternately labeled human capital, social capital, or cultural capital—indicates the extent to which that central theoretical framework still prevails. So, too, does the overwhelming emphasis on individual-level attributes as the 'causes' of poverty, an emphasis that avoids recognition of politics, institutions, or structural inequality."[3]

While neoclassical economic studies are informative, as both human capital traits and individual actions do affect outcomes, researchers who conduct these types of inquiries today often overlook, as O'Connor noted, the enormous impact of social, economic, and political systems on poverty. In this chapter I discuss the underlying structural cause of poverty, including why poverty is more prevalent among some groups than others. I begin with a brief discussion of general sociological theories of social stratification. I then examine the role of the economy and low-wage work in explaining patterns of poverty, analyze changing patterns of racial and ethnic stratification, and finally, discuss gender norms, family structure, and culture and their impact on poverty.

SOCIAL STRATIFICATION

The term *social stratification* here refers to a set of social and economic institutions that generate inequality and poverty. Inequalities have played themselves out in various ways in different social systems, past and present. David Grusky posits that modern industrial societies have egalitarian ideologies that run contrary to extreme forms of stratification found in caste, feudal, and slave systems. Nevertheless, inequality continues to be a prominent feature in advanced economies.[4]

Many of the concepts used to understand stratification today come from sociological theorists of the nineteenth and early twentieth centuries. Karl Marx focused on the role of economic systems in producing inequality. Briefly, he argued that stratification in industrial societies is generated by conflict between two opposing classes: the bourgeoisie and proletariat. The former are the owners of the means of production—the capitalists—and the latter are the workers.[5] The bourgeoisie exploit the proletariat by keeping the surplus value—profit—generated by the work.[6]

Max Weber, whose main body of work dates to the early twentieth century, held that the concept of class alone was not enough to understand stratification. He proposed a triumvirate of concepts: class, status groups, and parties. He defined status groups as communities, often distinguished by a specific lifestyle and value system. If the line between groups is rigid, a status group is a closed "caste." Status groups gain power through the monopolization of goods or control of social institutions. The third concept, parties, refers to political power. Weber makes the distinction between the three concepts in the following way: "Whereas the genuine place of 'classes' is within the economic order, the place of 'status groups' is within the social order . . . 'parties' live in a house of 'power.'"[7]

The concepts of class, status, and party continue to have resonance in discussions of the causes of poverty today. Below I discuss the role of the market system (factors relating to "class") in generating both prosperity and poverty, as well as the social forces ("status") that produce unequal outcomes for different groups. Chapter 7 discusses the effect of policy ("party") on poverty.

The Effect of Economic Processes on Poverty

Economic processes affect trends in poverty in two ways. First, economic growth determines absolute increases and declines in average standards of living. Second, economic inequality affects the distribution of income. A common analogy is that economic growth determines the size of the pie, while inequality affects the size of each slice. I now discuss the impact of each of these on poverty.

Economic growth here refers to increases in overall levels of national income. Economic growth is a function of changes in the size of labor supply, human and capital investment, and technological improvements. The U.S. economy experienced all three of these over the last two centuries. The country's population grew from a mere 3.9 million in 1790, to 76.2 million in 1900, to 281.4 million in 2000.[8] Likewise, whereas only 25 percent of people twenty-five years and older had four years of high school in 1940 (the first year in which the Census Bureau collected these figures), 83 percent had achieved this level by 1999.[9] Technological shifts, in the form of the industrial revolution and, more recently, the Information Age, propelled by computer technology, have also contributed to advances in productivity and growth.[10]

Figure 5.1 shows the trend in both poverty rates, using an absolute poverty standard, and the gross domestic product (GDP)—the output of goods and services produced by labor and property located in the United States—over the 1947–2000 period.[11] As expected, the figure shows a negative correlation between GDP growth and poverty, particularly in the 1947–1973 period. In 1947, by one estimate, the poverty rate was well over 30 percent. By 1973 it had declined to 11.1 percent. Over that period, the GDP rose from 1.5 trillion to 4.1 trillion, in constant 1996 dollars. Note that, when we observe slight dips in the GDP, as during the recessions of 1973–1974, 1981–1982, and 1991–1992, we see corresponding spikes in the poverty rate. Evidence from developing countries around the world also indicates that there is a very strong relationship between economic growth and absolute poverty rates.[12]

The figure also suggests that the relationship between income growth and poverty slowed beginning in the 1970s. This weakening relationship has been noted by a number of studies. Some believe that growing inequality may have also played a role in persisting high rates of poverty after 1970.[13]

Moreover, the rate of GDP growth slowed after 1973. While the economy grew at an average annual clip of 3.9 percent in the 1950s and 4.4 percent in the 1960s, it grew at only 3.2, 2.7, and 2.5 percent rates in the 1970s, 1980s, and 1990s (through 1998), respectively.[14] It has been estimated that a 1 percentage point fall in unemployment reduces the poverty rate by 0.4 points, and a 1 percent change in median earnings reduces absolute poverty by 0.16 percentage points.[15] Hence, the slowing of economic growth had negative consequences for further poverty reduction.[16]

But, as will be discussed in more detail in the following chapter, one caveat to these findings is that the relationship between economic growth and poverty, using a relative or subjective poverty standard, is less straightforward than when we use the absolute poverty standard discussed here. When using relative poverty measures, we find that, as general living standards rise, so do the poverty thresholds, resulting in a much weaker association between income growth and poverty. Inequality therefore tends to have a larger association with trends in relative poverty rates.

Income inequality results from economic systems that foster the accumulation of money and assets in one segment of society, often at the expense of another, or from broad-based economic shifts that

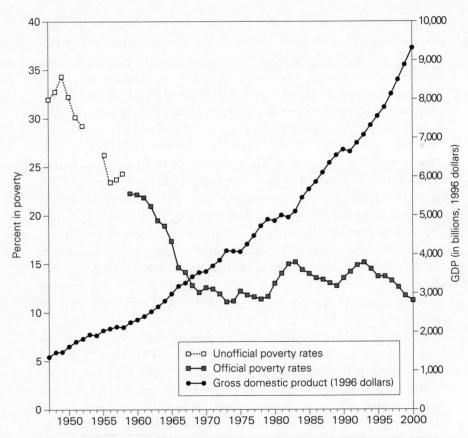

SOURCE: GDP data from Bureau of Economic Analysis, "Gross Domestic Product, in Current Dollars and in Chained (1996) Dollars," Times Series Estimates of Gross Domestic Product (www.bea.doc .gov/bea/dn1.htm), 2002; poverty rates for 1947–1958 from Gordon Fisher, "Estimates of the Poverty Population under the Current Official Definition for Years before 1959" (mimeo, Office of the Assistant Secretary for Planning and Evaluation: U.S. Department of Health and Human Services, 1986), as reprinted in Robert Plotnick et al., "The Twentieth Century Record of Inequality and Poverty in the United States" (paper presented at the General Conference of the International Association for Research on Income and Wealth, Cambridge, UK, August 23–29, 1998), appendix D; poverty figures for 1959–2000 from Dalaker, "Poverty in the United States: 2000," appendix, table A-1.

Figure 5.1. Poverty Rates and Gross Domestic Product, 1947–2000

produce instability and disruption in the labor market. Inequality is built into today's market system, as its foundation rests on people's ability to accumulate capital. To paraphrase Marx, business owners favor having inexpensive labor to maximize their profits (to reap surplus value).

However, it should be noted that the market is not necessarily a zero-sum game—economic growth potentially benefits large segments of society. Average standards of living rose in the United States dramatically over the twentieth century (as measured by per-capita income), as have life expectancies. Still, stratification and inequality generated by the market are phenomena that continue to cause concern among many observers in the United States and abroad. In my view, an economic system—any system—needs to be able to moderate inequality to retain its popular support and legitimacy.

Aside from the issue of how capital is distributed, economic disruptions, which are common in the market system, can also help produce economic instability and inequality. For example, in the nineteenth century, the United States was largely rural, and a majority of people were engaged in farm-related activities. Industrialization, accompanied by urbanization, changed this; many workers in the countryside and in small towns, such as farmers, unskilled laborers, and skilled craftsmen, were displaced by the mechanization of agriculture and the mass production of other goods. These workers, left with few relevant skills, became a mobile surplus of labor. One consequence was widespread poverty in many American cities and towns.[17]

At the turn of the twentieth century, economic instability in the United States continued. This was the era of the consolidation of large corporations. While these corporations provided stability for many workers in core industries, such as the automobile industry, workers involved in more marginal industries were particularly susceptible to low wages, unemployment, and poverty.[18] The conflict between capital and labor reached a fever pitch in the United States early in the twentieth century. Workers in many manufacturing industries tried unionizing to bring about higher wages and better working conditions, and they were bitterly opposed by business owners.

Reformers such as Theodore Roosevelt were dismayed by the concentration of wealth and power among prominent industrialists and giant corporations and favored a more equitable distribution of resources among the population. While World War I shifted the focus of politics to other issues, these basic tensions between capital and labor simmered through the first half of the twentieth century. Slowly, however, labor unions gathered wider acceptance, and membership grew.[19] In addition, most segments of the population shared in the economic boom that followed World War II.[20]

By the early 1970s, the situation had changed once again. In addition to the slowing of economic growth, inequality began to increase. Figure 5.2 compares the annual percentage change in family income across the income distribution for the two time periods of 1947 to 1973 and 1973 to 1995. All groups experienced income increases in the earlier, 1947–1973 period, with the poorest fifth experiencing the greatest growth—a 3.0 percent annual rate. In contrast, after 1973, overall GDP growth rates slowed, so that no group did better than in the earlier period. Moreover, while the richest 20 percent saw their incomes rise by an average of 1.3 percent a year in this period, the poorest 20 percent experienced a 0.6 percent annual decline.[21] One estimate has it that for every 1 percent increase in income inequality (measured by the ratio of median income to income in the lowest quintile), poverty increases by 0.26 percentage points.[22]

Why, after decades of decreasing inequality throughout the middle of the twentieth century, did inequality then rise in the last quarter of the century? Changes in the structure of the economy were clearly important.[23] Some believe that the declining demand for workers at the lower end of the economic ladder vis-à-vis the supply contributed to inequality. In other words, there were shifts in the demand for labor among firms to which labor supply (workers) was slow to adjust. This line of thinking has been referred to as the "skills mismatch" hypothesis. The result was that the level of education or other skills needed for employment was rising more quickly than the level of education of the workforce. A much higher proportion of jobs required, or were most suitably filled by, college graduates than before.[24]

Much of the evidence for this hypothesis comes from the growing inequality in wages by level of education.[25] While average weekly wages rose by 9.8 percent among men who held a college degree between 1979 and 1993, the wages for male high school dropouts fell by 22.5 percent.[26] The distribution of earnings also widened among women over the period, though it was mainly because of higher earnings among more highly educated women rather than declines among others. African Americans were perhaps the most affected by skills mismatches. It has been argued that, while the educational attainment of black city residents improved in the 1970s and 1980s, it was not sufficient to keep pace with even faster rises in the educational attainment of those persons being employed by city industries.[27]

What produced these skills mismatches, and declining wages for less educated workers more generally? Four common explanations are deindustrialization, technological change, globalization, and declining unionism. The premise of the deindustrialization hypothesis is that the shift of employment in the economy from manufacturing to services

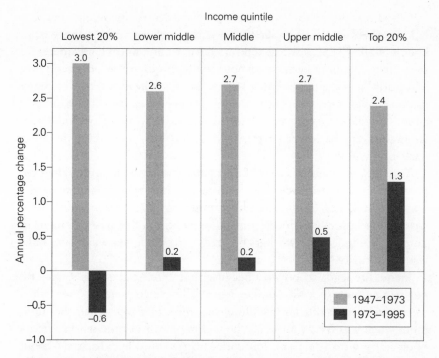

Income quintile

SOURCE: Barry Bluestone and Bennett Harrison, *Growing Prosperity: The Battle for Growth with Equity in the Twenty-First Century* (Boston: Houghton Mifflin, 2000), pp. 183, 185.

Figure 5.2. The Growth of Family Income: 1947–1973 versus 1973–1995

resulted in the destruction of a disproportionate number of higher-wage jobs, especially those whose primary requirement is manual skill. In their place, the service and retail trade sectors of the economy generated millions of new jobs, but these tend to be associated with a polarized earnings distribution and poverty.[28] Yet not all evidence indicates that deindustrialization is solely to blame for persisting high levels of poverty, as wage inequality has also increased *within* industries.[29]

Technological changes in the economy also played a role in increasing inequality by raising the demand for highly skilled workers relative to those with lower skills. For example, computerization increased the demand for engineers and programmers, while it reduced the demand for typists and already lower-paid secretaries. Yet while technological shifts likely explain some of the rising inequality, there is much it also does not explain. For example, real earnings have increased more for some less technically oriented professions, such as among lawyers, brokers, and managers, than among science technicians.[30]

Globalization of the market economy affected inequality because U.S. workers increasingly compete with workers around the world. Highly skilled U.S. workers tend to have a comparative advantage in the global economy because of both the high quality of postsecondary education in the United States and because the headquarters of many multinational corporations, to which profits flow, are located in U.S. cities. Conversely, many less educated American workers are at a disadvantage given the lower costs of living and low wage levels in other parts of the globe.[31]

The decline of unions also likely contributed to inequality. The proportion of the workforce that is unionized has been falling since the 1950s, but it accelerated after the mid-1970s.[32] The proportion of workers in unions declined from 29 percent in 1975 to 14 percent in 1997.[33] Nonunionized workers typically are paid lower wages and have less job security.[34]

Inequality leads to poverty because many low-wage jobs simply do not pay enough to keep families from falling into poverty, even when using the current official (absolute) measure. In 1997, when the minimum wage was $5.15 an hour, the income of a full-time worker (forty hours, fifty weeks) making minimum wage would be $10,300—about $2,500 below the average 1997 poverty line for a three-person family and $6,100 under the average poverty line for a four-person family (though none of these figures takes into account government transfers these low-income families may receive). A family of four in which one person worked full-time and the other half-time at minimum wage would still produce earnings falling $950 below the poverty line for such a family ($16,400).

A majority of the poor do in fact have a family member with some attachment to the labor market. Figure 5.3 shows that, among poor families with children in 1997, 37 percent were in full-time working families, another 35 percent were in part-time working families, and only 28 percent were in nonworking families.[35] When using the National Academy of Sciences (NAS) measure, less than a quarter (24 percent) were in nonworking families. People in full-time working families were particularly more likely to be poor under the NAS measure because their expenses, such as Social Security taxes and other work-related expenses, are higher (these elements are not taken into account in the official poverty measure).[36] Since 1973, both the number and share of the poor who are employed full-time and year-round has risen.[37]

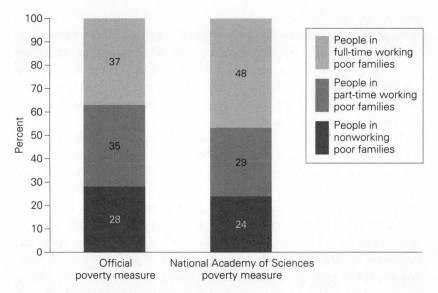

SOURCE: John Iceland and Josh Kim, "Poverty among Working Families: Insights from an Improved Measure," *Social Science Quarterly* 82, 2 (June 2001): 253–67.

Figure 5.3. Distribution of People in Poor Families with Children, by Working Status and Poverty Measure, 1997

Social Stratification—Race, Ethnicity, Gender, and Culture

While the economic forces described above determine overall levels of economic growth and inequality, social stratification across social ("status") groups determine, in a world of finite resources, *who* becomes poor. The main status groups in today's society are defined by the intersection of ethnic, gender, and class affiliations.[38]

Social stratification across status groups occurs when social groups seek to maximize their rewards by restricting others' access to resources and opportunities. Weber noted that usually one social group "takes some externally identifiable characteristic of another group—[such as] race, language, religion, local or social origin, descent, residence, etc.— as a pretext for attempting their exclusion."[39] Caste systems are an extreme form of closed stratification systems; this system prevailed in parts of the United States until the middle of the twentieth century.

Monopolization of social and economic goods and institutions can occur through a number of ways. Discrimination in the form of legal barriers is one mechanism, as described below. Other exclusionary devices include restricting access to people with sufficient wealth or with certain credentials.[40] For example, wealth enables families to obtain high-quality education in private schools and in that way retain their elevated economic and social standing. Obtaining official credentials—such as a degree from a prestigious university, or union membership—is another way access to certain opportunities is controlled and institutionalized.

The process of stratification is usually a cumulative one. A person may begin life at a disadvantage, and disadvantages may be augmented at each stage of the life cycle, such as through the restriction of educational opportunities, then job opportunities, and so on.[41] When stratification is so deeply ingrained in society, ameliorating its effects becomes very difficult. The analysis of trends in poverty that follows indicates that, while social stratification across racial, ethnic, and gender lines inhibits opportunities and serves to increase poverty among some groups, the degree of stratification across these groups clearly diminished over the last half of the twentieth century in the United States.

Racial and Ethnic Stratification

In the U.S. context, several minority groups fare worse than whites according to a number of social and economic indicators. On average, minorities are more likely than whites to have low levels of education, lower levels of employment, lower wages, and have chronic health problems—all characteristics associated with higher poverty rates.[42]

Discrimination against minority group members has historically played a role in producing social inequalities. Discrimination arises out of competition for scarce resources and serves to protect group solidarity.[43] In the educational system, discrimination has contributed to school segregation, classroom segregation, and access to unequal facilities.[44]

Societies characterized by high levels of discrimination also usually have highly segregated labor markets where the price of labor, and therefore wages, for the same work typically differs across groups. In other words, the wages of minority group members are artificially devalued because the labor market is neither fully free nor fully competitive.[45] Disadvantaged group members may be excluded altogether from many better-paying jobs and may thus have to settle for less desirable jobs, whose wages are in turn driven lower by higher levels of competition from others in a similar situation.[46]

A less overt but perhaps more common type of bias in the labor market is "statistical discrimination," which refers to the tendency of employers to use generalizations in their hiring practices. Employers basically lower their search costs for employees by using easily identifiable characteristics, such as sex or race, to predict job performance instead of determining actual individual skill. This reliance on stereotypes is inherently unfair because individuals are judged not by their ability but by their appearance. Shelly Lundberg and Richard Startz note that this can lead to actual differentials in skills and productivity if minority group members invest less in their education or training because they feel this type of investment would not be rewarded.[47]

Racial and ethnic minority groups in the United States, and indeed in multicultural nations around the globe, often struggle to obtain equal access to resources, such as jobs, education, and health services. In the American context, these conflicts have a long history, though their scope and nature have evolved. African Americans, Asian Americans, Hispanics, and Native Americans and even many white ethnic groups, such as the Irish, have all had to cope with limited opportunities, though their experiences have qualitatively differed.

African American Poverty

The official poverty rate among African Americans in 2000 was 22.1 percent. Even though this represented a historic low, it was still almost double the national poverty rate of 11.3 percent (see Figure 5.4). African Americans, who comprised about 13 percent of the U.S. population as of 2000, have long had to contend with acute forms of discrimination and inequality, including a severely constrained labor market throughout the nineteenth century and into the twentieth. After the abolition of slavery during the Civil War, blacks in the South often worked as sharecroppers, mainly because they were barred by law or custom from almost all other full-time jobs. In addition, under the system of Jim Crow, most blacks who lived in cities were employed as common laborers or as domestic and personal servants. Opportunities for promotion and advancement were uncommon, if not impossible, for African Americans in these and other occupations.[48]

William Julius Wilson, among others, has argued that more recently the traditional patterns of interaction between African Americans and whites in the labor market have fundamentally changed, where economic class position is now more important in determining success

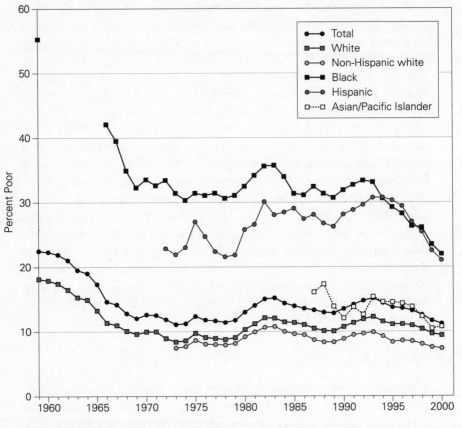

SOURCE: Dalaker, "Poverty in the United States: 2000."

Figure 5.4 Official Poverty Rates by Race and Hispanic Origin, 1959–2000

among African Americans than their daily encounters with whites.[49] From the antebellum period through the first half of the twentieth century, racial oppression was deliberate, overt, and easily observable— ranging from slavery to segregation. By the latter half of the twentieth century, many traditional barriers were dismantled as a result of political, social, and economic changes of the civil rights era. Wilson emphasizes that it is not so much that racial segregation and discrimination have been eliminated as that they have become less rampant, whereas economic conditions play an increasingly important role in determining black disadvantage. He argues that deindustrialization and class segregation in particular have hampered the economic mobility of less skilled blacks in the labor market.[50]

Glenn Loury asserts that, while "discrimination in contract"—the unequal treatment of otherwise like persons based on race in the execution of formal transactions—has declined drastically in the period since 1965, "discrimination in contact" remains more prevalent. *Discrimination in contact* refers to the unequal treatment of persons on the basis of race in the associations and relationships that are formed among individuals in social life. It involves discrimination in the informal, private sphere. Loury argues that economic achievement depends on the nature of social interactions in both spheres because people obtain resources by both formal and informal, by contractual and noncontractual, social relations.[51]

Empirical studies tend to show that the economic penalty of race—of being African American in particular—has declined since the 1960s. Occupational mobility has increased, as has wage parity.[52] Arthur Sakamoto and his coauthors, in their study of declining wage differentials between 1950 and 1990, find that "the net disadvantage of being black was reduced by more than half over this period," even after taking into account changing group educational levels and other factors.[53]

Because the extent of employment discrimination is difficult to measure and quantify, it is difficult to say precisely to what extent discrimination still directly contributes to income disparities and poverty. Studies tend to indicate that discrimination persists in labor markets and other areas. For example, "paired-test studies" in which minority job applicants were paired with white applicants with similar backgrounds and trained to be as similar as possible in behavior, have shown that minorities, particularly African Americans and foreign-sounding Latinos, were less likely to receive job interviews and offers.[54] Racism therefore continues to contribute to a social hierarchy that puts African Americans at an economic disadvantage.

Other factors have also contributed to relatively high levels of African American poverty, some based on social stratification and related to race and others more nonracial in origin. For one, continued high levels of black-white segregation affect individual economic opportunities.[55] Douglas Massey and Nancy Denton, in *American Apartheid,* argued that segregation, interacting with economic forces, reinforces minority poverty by limiting access to the potentially broad range of metropolitan area employment opportunities.[56] The deconcentration of employment from central cities to the surrounding suburbs has also reduced the number of employment opportunities for inner-city blacks.[57]

High levels of residential segregation may contribute to patterns of unequal schooling, perpetuate ethnic stereotypes that give rise to discrimination in employers' hiring patterns, and reproduce segregated job referral networks.[58] In places segregated by both race and class, the poor also often face high rent burdens, lack of access to housing wealth, and housing health risks.[59] These all contribute to feelings of alienation, discouragement, and pessimism, which can in turn reproduce negative economic outcomes.[60]

Deindustrialization and the decline in the strength of unions also appear to contribute to the continued wage and poverty gap between African Americans and whites,[61] as Wilson also argued. Black women have benefited from public sector unionism in particular, and black men benefited from industrial unionism.[62] African Americans have been especially affected by deindustrialization because, as late as the 1968–1970 period, more than 70 percent of all blacks working in metropolitan areas held blue-collar jobs at the same time that more than 50 percent of all metropolitan workers held white-collar jobs.[63]

Another factor that contributes to higher poverty rates among African Americans is human-capital skills differentials. This refers to differences in average levels of education, quality of educational opportunities, and subsequent work experience. The gap in average levels of education has declined over the past few decades. Nevertheless, the quality of schooling received by children varies widely, and African Americans are more likely to attend inferior schools with fewer resources. Lower employment levels among young African Americans subsequently contribute to earnings differentials. Some research has indicated that school achievement, as measured by Armed Forces Qualifications Test (AFQT) scores, and work experience explain a significant portion of the earnings difference between African American and white men under the age of thirty,[64] though these findings are more suggestive than definitive.

Poverty among Other Minority Groups

Some of the processes that have hampered African American economic well-being, such as discrimination, segregation, and human capital differentials, have also affected other minority groups—Latinos, Asian Americans, and Native Americans. Yet the experiences of each group differ considerably because of its regional concentration, population size, and labor market niche and the white population's reaction to its presence in, or immigration to, America.

Hispanics have a long history in the United States, dating at least as far back as the annexation of territory in Florida and, in 1848, huge swaths of land from Mexico extending from Texas westward to California. Asians historically suffered discriminatory treatment in immigration policies limiting their arrival. The 1882 Chinese Exclusion Act barred the immigration of Chinese laborers, and immigration from Japan was completely halted in 1924. By the early decades of the twentieth century, Japanese and Chinese immigrants were denied citizenship and voting rights and were prevented from joining most labor unions. Through intimidation and discrimination, whites limited the economic achievement of Asian Americans.[65]

Latinos and Asian Americans share certain commonalities: they both have historically been discriminated against, have recently experienced increases in their population due to immigration, and are very heterogeneous in terms of their national origins and educational skills. The 1965 Immigration Act, which dropped the bias in favor of immigrants from Europe and set more equitable immigration quotas across global regions, led to immediate, striking, and unexpected shifts in immigration flows. The number of immigrants from Latin America and Asia exploded.[66] In the 1980s, for example, 85 percent of immigrants to the United States were from those two regions.[67]

Despite these similar experiences, poverty rates vary considerably. While the Asian poverty rate in 2000 was 10.8 percent, the Latino poverty rate was about twice as high, at 21.2 percent. While poverty rates among both groups declined significantly in the period of economic expansion in the 1990s, Hispanic rates increased over the 1970s and 1980s (see Figure 5.4).[68] Differences in the characteristics of the immigrants coming to the United States and in the levels of education of immigrants and native-born people of each of the two groups, explain many of these differences.

In general, immigrants often have different labor force outcomes than natives. On one hand, immigrants are often a "select" group of people—they often possess qualities such as ambition and eagerness to learn that are helpful in achieving economic success. On the other hand, limited language proficiency and unfamiliarity with American customs and the labor market considerably hinder immigrant economic mobility, especially in the short run. Overall, immigrant families are at greater risk of poverty than nonimmigrant families. Yet over time and subsequent generations, labor market barriers become less important.[69] Immigrants become more similar to the native-born population in terms of their employment, earnings, English-language fluency, fertility, and poverty the longer they have been in the United States. Some studies show, however, that an increasing number and proportion of immigrants have been arriving with very low levels of skills, contributing to higher overall immigrant poverty rates.[70] In places with many immigrants, the competition for low-wage jobs also appears to drive down wages for these immigrants.[71]

Data from the 1990 Census bear these arguments out (at the time of this writing, results on this topic from the 2000 Census were not yet available). Table 5.1 shows that poverty rates were highest among recent immigrants, particularly among recent immigrants from Mexico. Mexican immigrants had an overall poverty rate of 29.0 percent, higher than the 18.3 percent poverty rate among immigrants from other Latin American countries. The Asian immigrant poverty rate, at 16.5 percent, was lower than the Latino one, though still higher than the poverty rate among immigrants from Europe and Canada. In general, immigrants who have been in the United States longer had the lower poverty rates.[72]

These figures suggest that immigrants from Asia tend to comprise a more "select" group than those from Latin America. Indeed, other evidence indicates that newer immigrants from Korea, India, and the Philippines exhibit higher average levels of education than both Latinos and native-born whites.[73] One factor explaining these differences is that, while many immigrants from Asia become eligible to migrate to the United States because of their work-related skills, a larger proportion of immigrants from Latin America immigrate because they have relatives who are U.S. citizens.[74]

Even among the *native-born,* Asian Americans tend to have high levels of education, which translate into better jobs, higher incomes, and less poverty. Japanese Americans have achieved a level of education similar to that of whites since the early 1940s, as have Chinese Americans since 1960. Asian Americans have also gained greater access to high-tier technical and professional occupations.[75] Latinos are less likely to have a college degree and tend to work in lower-skill, lower-wage jobs.

It is once again difficult to separate the effects of discrimination from those of immigration and human capital in determining why Latinos have higher poverty rates than Asians and why both groups have higher poverty rates than whites. The available evidence tends to suggest that

TABLE 5.1. POVERTY RATES OF THE
FOREIGN-BORN, BY REGION OF BIRTH
AND PERIOD OF IMMIGRATION, 1990

Period of immigration	Europe/ Canada	Mexico	Other Latin America	Asia	Africa	Total
1985–90	22.7	37.3	28.1	27.4	24.6	29.8
1975–84	8.1	28.9	18.3	14.4	13.2	18.7
1965–74	6.4	23.6	12.0	6.6	6.4	12.5
1960–64	5.2	17.3	9.6	5.7	6.9	8.7
1950–59	5.8	17.8	10.9	5.5	9.6	7.9
Before 1950	9.0	20.5	11.2	10.6	3.1	10.6
Total	**9.1**	**29.0**	**18.3**	**16.5**	**15.4**	**18.0**

SOURCE: Barry R. Chiswick and Theresa A. Sullivan, "The New Immigrants," in *State of the Union: America in the 1990's,* vol. 2, ed. Reynolds Farley (New York: Russell Sage Foundation, 1995), table 5.16, p. 265.
NOTE: Native-born poverty rate: 12.4 percent.

native-born Asian Americans' wages, returns to occupational status, and poverty resembles that of otherwise similar whites, though immigrants' economic well-being still lags.[76] The evidence for Latinos suggests the persistence of some racial/ethnic effect on wages and earnings.[77]

The experience of Native Americans differs from all other groups. In addition to being forcibly removed from their land to reservations, Native Americans have had to overcome a dearth of job opportunities in and around reservations and also low levels of educational attainment. The poverty rate among Native Americans in the 1998–2000 period was 25.9 percent, similar to African American and Latino poverty rates. Some evidence indicates a decline (but not elimination) of the net negative effect of being Native American on wages over the last half of the twentieth century.[78] Quantitative research on Native Americans tends to be more limited than that of other groups, in part due to the relatively small Native American population. Additional research on Native Americans, not to mention the other groups, would help shed further light on the complex interrelationship between race and poverty.

Gender, Family Structure, and Poverty

The term *feminization of poverty* was coined by Diana Pearce in a 1978 article in which she argued that poverty was "rapidly becoming a female problem."[79] The term gained further currency in the 1980s and early 1990s. While it originally referred to the process by which the poverty population in the United States became increasingly female, it is currently more often used to refer to the growing number of poor people living in female-headed families (which of course include both male and female children). In 1970, 42 percent of families included an employed father, a homemaker mother, and children; now, only 16 percent of families fit this model, and half of all children will spend some portion of their childhood living with only one parent.[80] Family arrangements today are much more diverse than they were fifty years ago.[81]

Women's poverty rates were 55 percent higher than men's in 1968, then peaked at 72 percent higher in 1978, before declining to 47 percent by the end of the 1980s.[82] In 2000 the female poverty rate (12.5 percent) was 26 percent higher than the male poverty rate (9.9 percent). Women comprise about 57 percent of the poverty population; this figure has changed little since the mid-1970s.[83] Trends differ by age. The gap in poverty rates between working-age women and men has narrowed since 1980, while increasing among young women (those under age twenty-five) and among elderly women (over age sixty-five). Overall, the empirical claims for an accelerating "feminization of poverty" are weak, though female poverty rates do remain disproportionately high.[84]

Women tend to have higher poverty rates than men for two main reasons: (1) they have fewer economic resources than men, and (2) they are more likely to be the heads of single-parent families.[85] Minority women are further overrepresented among the poor because of both their minority status and higher rates of single parenthood.[86] Elderly women are also more likely to be poor than elderly men because of fewer economic resources—such as less Social Security income—but also because of higher female life expectancies, which make elderly women more likely to live alone than men.[87]

Many argue that women's lower economic status reflects the unequal distribution of power in society.[88] It is asserted that men have long maintained control over women's labor power by excluding women from access to some essential productive resources and by limiting women's social roles more generally.[89] Labor market discrimination is a manifestation of unequal power. First, discrimination occurs when men are paid more than women for the same work. Second, discrimination contributes to occupational sex segregation—where men and women are highly concentrated in different types of jobs. The result is that women's work is typically accorded both lower status and lower earnings than occupations with high concentrations of men.[90]

Inequality in the labor market may also occur due to bias or discrimination prior to a person's entrance into the labor market, such as in the education system or in the family.[91] For example, girls are more typically socialized into family-oriented roles, while boys and young men are encouraged to enter careers that emphasize making money and becoming leaders.[92] Women may be more likely to take jobs that are easier to reenter after an interruption in employment, such as for pregnancy and raising young children, and that therefore do not offer as much upward mobility.

Because of the sexual revolution of the 1960s and the high visibility of the women's rights movement, commentators through the 1980s puzzled over why there had been so little accompanying change in the ratio of women's to men's earnings in the labor market. After all, between World War II and 1980, the gap between women's and men's labor force participation rates narrowed steadily, and their college enrollment rates were virtually identical. Between 1970 and 1980, women increased their share of law, medical, and dental school degrees and moved into managerial positions in record numbers. Yet women's earnings hovered around 60 percent of men's throughout the 1955 to 1980 period.[93] Beginning in the 1980s, however, the trend began to change rapidly.

Figure 5.5 shows the change in the female-male ratio of earnings since 1960, using the most commonly used indicator of the gender wage gap—the median earnings of full-time, year-round workers. After 1980, the earnings gap declined rapidly for the next decade or so, before stabilizing. As of 2000, the median annual income of full-time, year-round women workers was 73.3 percent of men's.[94] The mean earnings ratio among young workers (age twenty-five to thirty-four) in 1995, at 78 percent, was considerably greater than the ratio among women thirty-five to forty-four years old (65 percent) and women forty-five to fifty-four (58 percent).[95] Sociologist Suzanne Bianchi has described how much of the movement toward gender inequality has been the result of a gradual process of "cohort replacement," where younger women have been taking on new roles and earning more in the labor market than their mothers. Because of the increase in women's employment and earnings, the relative risk of poverty among working-age women actually declined in the early 1980s.[96]

Nevertheless, despite these improvements, the earnings gap persists. A 1997 study by Francine Blau and Lawrence Kahn of the wage gap in the 1980s found that some of the gap was due to differences in

SOURCE: U.S. Census Bureau, "Women's Earnings as a Percentage of Men's Earnings by Race and Hispanic Origin: 1960 to 2000," Historical Income table P-40 (Internet data released March 21, 2002, at www.census.gov/hhes/income/histinc/p40x1.html).

Figure 5.5. Women's Median Annual Earnings as a Percent of Men's Earnings for Full-Time, Year-Round Workers, 1960–2000

education and amount of work experience. Once they accounted for these, the authors estimated that women earned about 80.5 percent of what men did (rather than about 72 percent). When yet more factors were taken into account, such as the industry, occupation, and union status differences in the jobs men and women occupy, then women were estimated to earn about 88.2 percent of similar men. They therefore concluded that gender discrimination in the labor market still plays a role in depressing women's earnings, though the exact causes of the differential is not yet fully understood.[97] Some of the narrowing of the earnings gap in the 1980s was due not only to gradual increases in women's earnings but also men's losses in employment and wages, particularly among those with less education.[98]

Changes in family structure have also contributed to higher rates of poverty among women. The percent of families headed by single women rose rapidly over the last few decades of the twentieth century, from 10.7 percent of all families in 1970 to 17.6 percent in 1995. The increase among African Americans and Hispanics has been even more rapid (see Figure 5.6). After 1995, however, trends in female headship leveled across all race groups. As of 2000, 17.6 percent of all families were headed by women. For whites the figure was 13.9 percent, and for blacks it was considerably higher at 44.0 percent.

The contribution of single parenthood to higher levels of poverty, particularly among African American families, was discussed by, among others, E. Franklin Frazier in 1932 and 1939, Gunnar Myrdal in 1944, Daniel Patrick Moynihan in 1965, and many others since.[99] Numerous reasons have been offered for changing family formation patterns, including changes in social norms and the declining economic fortunes of men.

The crux of the problem with this trend is that single-parent families headed by women are considerably more likely to be poor. While the poverty rate among people in married-couple families was 5.6 percent in 2000, it was 28.2 percent among female-headed families (see Figure 5.7). Poverty rates also vary by ethnicity, ranging from 5.3 percent among white married-couple families to 38.4 percent among African American female-headed families. Yet it should be noted that the poverty rate for people in female-householder families has declined— from 49.4 percent in 1959 to 38.1 percent in 1970 to 28.2 percent in 2000.[100]

Poverty is high among female-headed families for several reasons. Single mothers (and fathers) often face the challenge of supporting a family on one income, as well as finding and paying for child care while they work and running a household alone when they do not. Children add to living costs but usually do not contribute to family income. Lower levels of education among women who head such families also contributes to their lower earnings.[101]

Furthermore, as discussed above, women tend to earn considerably less than men with comparable qualifications, and mothers tend to accumulate less experience than other workers.[102] Finally, many such families do not receive sufficient (or any) child support from the children's absent fathers.[103] However, research tends to show that, even if

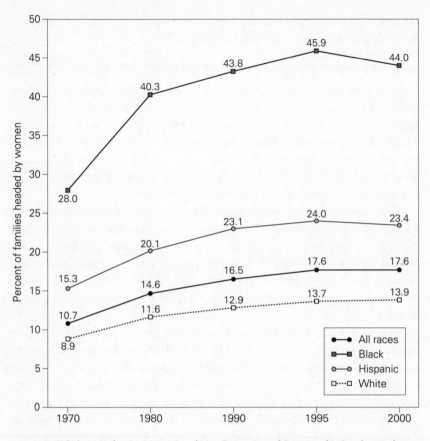

SOURCE: Tabulations of 2001 Current Population Survey Annual Demographic Supplement data.
NOTE: People of Hispanic origin may be of any race.

Figure 5.6. Trends in Female-Headed Families, 1970–2000

all families received the full amount of child support due them, poverty rates would decline only a little. While many fathers deliberately evade their child support obligations, others simply earn too little to pay much.[104]

Poverty is most feminized among African American and some Hispanic (particularly Puerto Rican) families, mainly because these women are more likely to become single-parent householders and to be out of the labor force, live in low-income neighborhoods, have low levels of education, and face labor market discrimination than other women.[105]

Some studies suggest that changes in family structure played a major role in growing child poverty rates from the early 1970s through the

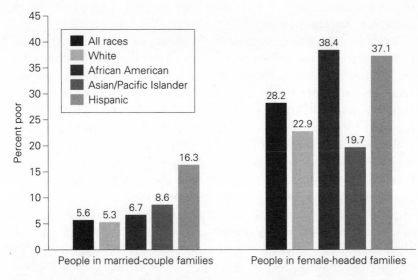

SOURCE: Tabulations of 2001 Current Population Survey Annual Demographic Supplement data.
NOTE: People of Hispanic origin may be of any race.

Figure 5.7. Poverty Rates of People by Family Structure and Race/Ethnicity, 2000

mid-1990s.[106] In 1972, 86 percent of children lived in married-couple families, while in 1999 only 71 percent did. White and Asian children are more likely to be living in married-couple families, and African American children are least likely.[107] It has been estimated that the high proportion of children living in female-headed families accounts for just over half of the difference in child poverty rates between African American and Puerto Rican children on one hand and non-Hispanic white children on the other.[108] Declining real wages among less skilled young adults have also contributed to high child poverty rates and to group differentials.[109]

Yet the poverty rate among female-headed families declined in the 1990s, mainly because of increases in women's employment and wages. The greatest rise in employment among single mothers was concentrated in the mid-1990s. In 1999, employment rates for single mothers of young children were 79, 75, and 59 percent for whites, African Americans, and Hispanics, respectively. Among African American mothers of young children, there was a 22 percentage point increase in employment over the 1990 to 1999 period.[110] The employment rate of never-married mothers, who are the most likely to have little education or job experience and long stays on welfare, rose from 43 percent in 1992 to 65 percent in 1999.[111]

Evidence from other countries also suggests that, while poverty tends to be more common among female-headed families, the poverty rates are not inherently high. Using a relative poverty line equaling 50 percent of the national median income, the poverty rate in 1995 for children in lone-parent families in Sweden (a majority of which are female headed), for example, was 6.7 percent. For children in other family types it was 1.5 percent. In Finland rates were even closer—7.1 percent for children in lone-parent families and 3.9 percent for children in other families. The poverty rates for children in the United States, using that relative measure, were 55.4 in single-parent families and 15.8 percent in other families. Notably, Sweden also has a slightly higher proportion of its children living in lone-parent families than in the United States. High employment rates among women, lower general wage inequality in the labor market, and generous government transfer policies help explain these low poverty rates in single-parent families in Sweden and Finland.[112]

Based on this analysis of child poverty rates across industrialized countries, the UNICEF Innocenti Research Centre argues that reducing poverty in female-headed families would therefore do more to reduce child poverty than reducing the incidence of female headship itself. That is, if the poverty rates of married-couple and female-headed families were more similar, then trends in headship would make little difference.[113] These issues are discussed further in the following two chapters.

Culture and Poverty

Because *culture* has become a politically loaded term in poverty discussions, it is a thorny issue often broached with caution by researchers. Culture is also a complex concept, hard to define and challenging to discern in its effects. Today, the view that cultural behavior contributes to poverty differentials tends to be associated with conservative commentators, though this has not always been the case.

In the 1920s, a number of sociologists from the University of Chicago and their students began to focus more systematically on the effect of social disorganization on the poor. Poverty was thought to result from temporary "cultural breakdown" that occurred in many immigrant and (in the case of African Americans) migrant communities in urban and industrial cities. The breakdown of social controls and customs led to increased crime, sexual promiscuity, family breakup, and economic dependency.[114]

Following the lead of Booker T. Washington (in 1902), sociologists such as Gunnar Myrdal (1944) and E. Franklin Frazier (1932, 1939), in adopting these arguments, were debunking the idea that the poor—and poor African Americans in particular—were genetically inferior.[115] They traced the roots of racial inequality to a wide range of factors, including racism and discrimination, which helped produce a deviant cultural response. Frazier, for example, saw "Negro matriarchy" as an accommodation to slavery and black male joblessness, and therefore a common feature of lower-class culture and poverty.[116] Similarly, other progressives at the beginning of the twentieth century de-emphasized the notion that southern and eastern European immigrants were genetically inferior by arguing that immigrants needed to be Americanized and adapt to mainstream American values and culture.[117]

In the two decades after World War II, however, there was greater discussion of a culture of poverty without reference to other social and economic conditions. These arguments echoed nineteenth-century beliefs about the "undeserving" poor. Oscar Lewis, quoted at the beginning of this chapter, was a strong promoter of the culture of poverty thesis. Lewis believed that the poor contribute to their own impoverishment and identified seventy behavioral traits that distinguish the poor.[118] Similarly, in the late 1950s, Edward Banfield asserted: "The lower-class person lives from moment to moment, he is either unable or unwilling to take into account the future or to control his impulses . . . being improvident and irresponsible, he is likely also to be unskilled, to move frequently from one dead-end job to another, to be a poor husband and father."[119]

Recent observers who have adopted this view—that the poor are essentially different, governed by their own code of values and behavior—tend to emphasize that the poor, or wayward government policies aimed at helping the poor, are often responsible for their degraded position. The argument goes that in the post–Great Society era, high welfare benefit levels provided work disincentives and encouraged dependency. The resulting culture of poverty consists of an eroded work ethic, dependency on government programs, lack of educational aspiration and achievement, increased single parenthood and illegitimacy, criminal activity, and drug and alcohol abuse.[120] Policy did not reward good behavior and did little to penalize harmful behavior. All of these problems in turn have an adverse effect on patterns of income and poverty, producing a vicious cycle of multigenerational dependency, primarily in high poverty areas in many central cities.

While it is likely that "culture" plays some role in reproducing poverty, social and economic structures are probably more important than culture. After all, as described in the previous chapter, many poor people are poor for only a short time, and those living in underclass neighborhoods make up only a small proportion (about 8 percent) of the poor.[121] Even among people who have been poor for a long time and, moreover, live in high poverty areas, differences are likely less rooted in aberrant values and more a result of functional adaptations to a difficult environment.[122] Overall, studies examining cultural differences do not provide overwhelming evidence that most of the poor people adhere to very different value systems than nonpoor people.[123]

CONCLUSION

All too often people assume that personal traits are the sole determinants of economic well-being, and they overlook the impact of environment. This is not surprising given that it is often difficult to recognize how structural forces affect our daily lives. Sociological concepts such as "class," "status" (social group differences), and "party" (policy) are helpful for understanding how stratification systems evolve. This chapter focused on the first two concepts (policy is discussed in chapter 7) by examining how economic and social factors determine levels and patterns of poverty in the United States.

Economic growth tends to drive down absolute poverty rates. As standards of living rise, more and more people earn incomes above the unchanging (absolute) poverty line. However, income inequality, resulting from the ordinary workings of the market system in which the accumulation of assets (profit) is the goal and also from economic shifts and instability, may impede the positive impact of economic growth. If only the rich benefit from growth, then growth will have little impact on poverty. Increasing inequality since the 1970s contributed to stagnant absolute poverty rates in the 1970s and 1980s.

Social stratification by race and gender helps explain why some groups of people are more likely to be poor than others. Notably, however, the effect of social stratification along these group lines on poverty declined significantly over the last half of the twentieth century, likely due in large part to a decline in discrimination—especially in its overt, legal forms. Today, past poverty, economic dislocation, wealth differentials, and family instability are barriers at least as important as racism and discrimination in producing the exclusion of African Americans, Hispanics, American Indians, and some Asian Americans from full and equal participation in American society.[124] Nevertheless, despite this progress, racial and ethnic antipathy and discrimination have not disappeared. Moreover, the simple lifting of many barriers does not mean that equality is immediate or automatic.

Changing patterns of family formation also affected trends in poverty in the United States, though the impact is more pronounced among some racial and ethnic groups. Female-headed families are particularly more likely to be poor because women householders face the challenge of supporting a family on one income and often paying for child care while they work. Lower levels of education among women who head such families also contributes to their lower earnings. Furthermore, women tend to earn considerably less than men with comparable qualifications, and mothers tend to accumulate less experience than other workers. Finally, many such families do not receive sufficient child support from the children's absent fathers. Despite these obstacles, poverty rates among single-parent families, while still significantly higher than poverty rates among others, declined over much of the 1990s, largely because of greater employment and earnings among single parents.

CHAPTER 6

Why Poverty Remains High, Revisited

Consider the following three views concerning current trends in poverty:

View 1

"The major underlying factors producing child poverty in the United States are welfare dependence and single parenthood."[1]

"The lack of progress in child poverty since 1965 can be explained in part by the erosion of marriage and the growth of poverty-prone single parent families."[2]

View 2

"[E]conomywide growth improves the income of poor people."[3]

"[A]lmost all the variation in the poverty rate is tracked by movements in median family income."[4]

View 3

"Economic growth in America no longer guarantees a decline in poverty. A steady decline in wage among less-skilled workers has offset the improved employment opportunities created by economic growth."[5]

"[R]educing poverty by raising the income of the poor and of low-wage workers should be the top policy priority. . . . Poverty remains high today, and inequality has increased, not because of a failure of social policy or of

This chapter is based on a paper presented at the August 2001 American Sociological Association meetings in Anaheim, CA: John Iceland, "Why Poverty Remains High: Reassessing the Effect of Economic Growth, Income Inequality, and Changes in Family Structure on Poverty, 1949–1999."

personal responsibility, but because of a failure of the economy to perform as it did in the past."[6]

While not all elements of these views contradict each other, not all of them can be right either. Poverty debates typically revolve around which factor one considers the most important. There is, at least, broad agreement on a couple of basic points. In the late 1960s and early 1970s, there was growing optimism that poverty was in headlong retreat.[7] At the time, the economy was booming, poverty rates were plunging, and consumer confidence was high. But the hopefulness of the 1960s gave way to more difficult times and higher poverty rates by the late 1970s and 1980s. By the close of the twentieth century, even after nearly a decade of economic growth, nearly 12 percent of the American population remained poor, including nearly a quarter of African Americans.[8]

Whereas in the previous chapter I discussed general causes of poverty and the reasons poverty rates vary across demographic groups, in this chapter I examine a more specific question: what was the relative association between trends in poverty over the last half of the twentieth century and per-capita income growth, economic inequality, and changes in family structure? These are the three factors highlighted in the quotes above.

I also use three measures of poverty here: the current official measure, a relative poverty measure, and for part of the analysis, a technically more refined quasi-relative poverty measure. Examining data from the census and Current Population Survey, I find that income growth is most strongly related with trends in absolute poverty over the half century, while economic inequality plays the most significant role in explaining trends in relative poverty. Rising inequality in the 1970s and 1980s was especially important in explaining increases in Latino poverty. Changes in family structure generally had a smaller effect but did have a significant effect on both African American poverty and child poverty through 1990. Strikingly, however, changes in family structure did little to explain changes in poverty among any group after 1990.

BACKGROUND

Three factors commonly offered to explain trends in poverty in the latter half of the twentieth century are income growth, economic inequality, and changes in family structure. If per-capita incomes increase on average, such as due to increasing employment and wages, then it is natural to think that poverty will decline. However, economic inequality can mitigate the overall positive impact of income growth if unemployed and lower-income workers do not enjoy the fruits of such growth. The third factor, changes in family structure—particularly the increasing number of female-headed families—may be associated with higher poverty rates because such families are economically more vulnerable and are more likely to be poor.

All three undoubtedly affected trends in poverty over the last half of the twentieth century, when two contrasting time periods stand out. In the first, from 1949 to the early 1970s, income growth was rapid, economic inequality declined, the proportion of families headed by a single parent increased but remained at fairly low levels, and poverty declined rapidly.[9] In the second, from the early 1970s to around 1990, economic growth slowed, income inequality increased, the proportion of families headed by a single parent and the number of individuals living alone rose rapidly, and poverty rates stagnated. Less has been written or is understood about trends in the 1990s—a decade when the economy surged, economic inequality slowed, the growth of single-parent families plateaued, and poverty declined.[10]

Disentangling the effect of these three processes on poverty is further complicated if one also takes into account how our views of what constitutes poverty change over time. The current official measure of poverty is an "absolute" one, in that poverty thresholds remain constant (adjusted only for inflation). Some analyses have shown that income growth played the largest role in reducing poverty over the first two time periods when using this absolute measure.[11]

The main disadvantage of absolute poverty measures is that, as standards of living change, generally so do people's perceptions of what poverty means.[12] For example, a common poverty threshold used in 1950 (as defined by the congressional Subcommittee on Low-Income Families) was $2,000 per year, which is about 70 percent of the current official threshold for a family of four when adjusted for inflation.[13] Many people think that the poverty lines from the current official measure, devised in the mid-1960s, are too low.[14] If we were to accept the notion that relative poverty measures are superior to absolute ones, we would likely find that inequality plays a larger role in explaining trends in poverty, because relative poverty measures are designed to capture a dimension of inequality (inequality at the low end of the income spectrum). Conversely, relative poverty is likely less responsive to income growth—which represents changes in average standards of living.

In this chapter I therefore compare the relative association between poverty and income growth, inequality, and changes in family structure, using not only the current official measure of poverty but also a relative measure and the quasi-relative measure recommended by the National Academy of Sciences (NAS) panel described in chapter 3. This permits a more complete measure of the relationship between these factors under differing assumptions of what poverty really means.

DATA, METHODS, AND LIMITATIONS OF THE ANALYSIS

Data used in this analysis come from the 1950 and 1970 decennial censuses, as well as the 1991 and 2000 Annual Demographic (March) Supplements to the Current Population Survey (CPS), all of which collect information about income in the previous calendar year. To gauge the effect of income growth, economic inequality, and changes in family structure on poverty, I use Sheldon Danziger and Peter Gottschalk's method of employing direct standardization and simulations to calculate adjusted rates under different assumptions. Details about the data and methods are described in appendix A.[15]

It is worth noting five limitations of the analysis here. First, it should be said that results below do not represent *causal* relationships, in that we can not definitively say that poverty is caused by changes in income growth, economic inequality, or changes in family structure. Instead, they suggest how strongly phenomena are related. This is a more general limitation of social science statistical models, but it perhaps applies even more to the methodology used here, where simulations and decomposition methods are used to discern general relationships. For example, the analysis below is based on simulations of what the poverty rate would have been in 1999 if per-capita income—everyone's standard of living—had gone up by the same amount over the half century. So rather than directly calculating the effect of economic or income growth on people's poverty status, the analysis examines how much poverty (measured in different ways) would be reduced if everyone's standard of living had risen by the same amount. For ease of exposition, the results below are occasionally described in terms of the effect of one process or another on poverty.

A second limitation, as noted by Danziger and Gottschalk, is that the method ignores any behavioral link between economic and demographic changes.[16] For example, falling wages among men (economic changes) may make them less likely to marry, thus increasing the number of people living in female-headed families. Such an interaction is not directly taken into account by a simple simulation.

Third, the income growth and economic inequality factors in the analysis measure growth and inequality originating from a broad variety of sources, such as greater labor-force participation rates, wages, cash government benefits, and demographic trends not explicitly modeled, such as changes in family size. It does not attempt to sort out the basic sources of income growth and inequality.

A fourth, related limitation of the method used is that economic inequality represents a residual category in the analysis, in that differences in poverty rates in the simulations not accounted for by income growth or changes in family and racial/ethnic composition are attributed to economic inequality. So, for example, if I were to include more detailed family composition or other factors in the model—such as the head's age and education or the number of children in the family—the estimated impact of inequality would likewise be affected (and would probably be reduced). So it is important to keep in mind that the effect of income inequality really represents the effect of factors, detailed in appendix A, not included in the model.

Fifth, the analysis does not focus on the impact of most policies on poverty. The NAS measure discussion highlights the effect of some non-cash policies, but other policies that raise people's total cash income are not directly measured (they are captured in the income growth variable). Chapter 7 contains a detailed analysis of the effect of policy on poverty.

Despite these limitations, the analysis is still informative because it shows the relative association between poverty and broad economic and family structure trends and illustrates how these associations vary by how we think about poverty.

WHAT THE ANALYSES SHOW

Table 6.1 shows basic statistics of the American population, according to the survey data, at four points in time—1949, 1969, 1990, and 1999. The poverty rate using the absolute poverty measure plummeted from 39.5 percent in 1949 to 13.9 percent in 1969. It changed little over the next two decades before falling to 11.8 percent in 1999. Poverty rates fell for all racial/ethnic groups and family types, particularly in the 1949 to 1969 period, but also thereafter. For example, the African

American poverty rate fell from 76.7 percent in 1949 to 35.9 percent in 1969, and then to a historic low of 23.6 percent in 1999. This figure is still three times the 7.7 percent poverty rate among non-Hispanic whites in 1999. Absolute poverty rates among people in female-headed families declined from 62.4 percent in 1949 to 30.8 percent in 1999, a figure still considerably higher than the official poverty rate for people in married-couple families (5.8 percent).

The 1949 absolute poverty rate of 39.5 percent was calculated basically by applying the official poverty methodology, devised in the 1960s, to an earlier time. It should be emphasized that, in 1949, it is unlikely that such a high a proportion of people would have been considered poor by the standards of that day. That is why using a relative poverty measure is perhaps just as, or more, informative. Relative poverty rates do indeed show a somewhat different trend. The relative poverty rate fell from 24.7 percent in 1949 to 20.6 percent in 1969, and thereafter increased to 26.1 percent by 1999.[17] In addition, while the relative poverty rate was considerably lower than the absolute poverty rate in 1949, it was considerably higher than the official poverty rate by the end of the century. So while absolute income deprivation declined considerably over the period, relative deprivation did not.

Relative poverty trends within demographic groups tended to fall across the 1949 to 1999 period (contrary to the overall trend), suggesting that a compositional shift in the population may account for some of the increase in the overall relative poverty rate. The poverty rates among most groups follow a similar trend, with some exceptions, such as Hispanics, who experienced increases in their relative poverty rates over the period. NAS poverty rates, which are available for only the 1990 to 1999 period, tend to follow the official poverty rate trend, though at moderately higher overall levels. The NAS poverty rate in 1999 was 13.8 percent.

Between 1949 and 1999, the data show considerable shifts in the racial/ethnic composition of the population and changes in family structure. The percent of people who were non-Hispanic white declined from 88.2 percent in 1949 to 70.7 percent in 1999. Other groups all experienced increases. Similarly, the percent of people in married-couple families declined from 87.2 percent in 1949 to 65.5 percent in 1999, while those in other family types increased. Note, however, that the percent of people in female-headed families changed little between 1990 (14.1 percent) and 1999 (14.4 percent), a difference that is not

TABLE 6.1. DESCRIPTIVE STATISTICS, BY YEAR, 1949–1999

| | Year | | | |
	1949	1969	1990	1999
Poverty Rate Using Official Methodology	**39.5**	**13.9**	**13.5**	**11.8**
By Race				
Non-Hispanic white	34.8	10.3	8.8	7.7
Non-Hispanic African American	76.7	35.9	31.8	23.6
Hispanic	65.3	25.4	28.1	22.8
Other	69.9	20.2	14.9	14.1
By Family Structure				
Married couple	37.0	8.8	6.9	5.8
Female-headed family	62.4	40.2	38.1	30.8
Male-headed family	43.8	16.1	12.7	12.2
Unrelated individual	53.9	35.9	20.7	19.1
Relative Poverty Rate	**24.7**	**20.6**	**23.4**	**26.1**
By Race				
Non-Hispanic white	20.6	16.3	17.7	19.7
Non-Hispanic African American	58.4	46.6	45.3	42.7
Hispanic	41.6	35.8	42.8	46.2
Other	49.6	27.1	23.8	27.3
By Family Structure				
Married couple	21.7	14.7	14.8	16.9
Female-headed family	51.1	52.0	52.7	54.7
Male-headed family	32.5	24.7	25.9	29.0
Unrelated individual	44.0	45.6	34.8	37.4
National Academy of Science (NAS) Poverty Rate	—	—	**16.8**	**13.8**
By Race				
Non-Hispanic white	—	—	11.8	9.7
Non-Hispanic African American	—	—	33.1	23.4
Hispanic	—	—	37.0	26.8
Other	—	—	18.6	16.8
By Family Structure				
Married couple	—	—	10.7	8.3
Female-headed family	—	—	40.6	31.4
Male-headed family	—	—	19.7	16.8
Unrelated individual	—	—	21.3	19.6

TABLE 6.1. *(continued)*

	Year			
	1949	*1969*	*1990*	*1999*
Distribution of the Population by Race/Ethnicity				
Non-Hispanic white	88.2	83.5	75.7	70.7
Non-Hispanic African American	9.6	10.9	12.2	12.5
Hispanic	1.8	4.5	8.6	11.9
Other	0.4	1.2	3.5	4.8
Distribution of the Population by Family Type				
In married couple family	87.2	81.2	68.1	65.5
In female-headed family	6.6	8.9	14.1	14.4
In male-headed family	2.3	2.3	3.3	4.2
Unrelated individual	4.0	7.6	14.5	15.9
Per Capita Income, $1999*	6,768	12,684	18,296	21,290
Median Income of 2-Adult, 2-Child Families, $1999**	22,750	46,076	51,025	59,488
Sample Size	429,541	1,969,674	158,318	133,380

SOURCES: Tabulations of data from the 1950 and 1970 Integrated Public-Use Microdata Series (IPUMS) and the 1991 and 2000 Current Population Survey (CPS).

*Per capita income calculated from data published in U.S. Census Bureau, "Historical National Population Estimates: July 1, 1900, to July 1, 1999," Population Estimates Program, Population Division (Internet data released, April 11, 2000; revised June 28, 2000 at www.census.gov/population/estimates /nation/popclockest.txt; U.S. Census Bureau, "Standardized and Unstandardized Experimental Poverty Rates: 1990 to 1999," Poverty 1999 table release package (Internet data released October 23, 2000, at www.census.gov/population/estimates/nation/popclockest.txt).

**Median income of 2-adult, 2-child family is the reference family poverty threshold in the relative poverty measure.

statistically significant, given the margin of error associated with each of those estimates in the CPS. Finally, the table shows that per-capita and median family incomes increased over the period. Per-capita income represents the measure of income growth used in this analysis, while median family income is used in the calculation of the poverty threshold in the relative poverty measure, as described in appendix A. It is important to note, however, that, while both increased over the period, the rates of growth for each were not the same in all periods.

For example, per-capita income increased by nearly half between 1969 and 1990, while median income increased only modestly over the period. This has implications for the estimated effect of income growth on relative poverty, as discussed below.

Poverty and Income Growth

Figure 6.1 shows the relationship between income growth and trends in absolute and relative poverty rates over the three time periods, on one hand, and the NAS measure, on the other, over the 1990–1999 time period. Much of the large decline in the official (absolute) poverty rate over the 1949 to 1969 period (–25.6 percentage points) is explained by rapid income growth (–18.6 percentage points).

While absolute poverty rates changed little in the 1969 to 1990 period (–0.3 percentage points), income growth still served to decrease poverty (–5.6 percentage points). The fact that poverty declined by only 0.3 percentage points means that other forces (income inequality and family structure changes) had an association with poverty in the opposing direction, as will soon be shown. From 1990 to 1999 we see yet a third trend emerging. The official poverty rate declined by a modest amount (–1.7 percentage points), and the effect of income growth further slowed (–2.5 percentage points).

Results differ when we look at the relative poverty measure. Although relative poverty rates declined considerably between 1949 and 1969, they rose thereafter. Between 1949 and 1969, income growth was not related to the decline in relative poverty; the simulation shows that it was actually positively associated with it (by 2.3 percentage points). This is explained by the fact that, as was shown in Table 6.1, per-capita income simply did not grow as fast over the period as the median family income of a two-adult, two-child family (the relative poverty threshold). That is, the poverty line rose even more rapidly than per-capita income.

In contrast, in the 1969 to 1990 period, income growth was simulated to have a substantial beneficial impact on relative poverty, as per-capita income grew at a faster pace than the median income. Finally, over the 1990s, income growth had little relation to trends in relative poverty, which increased by 2.7 percentage points.[18]

Data concerning the NAS measure are available only from 1990 to 1999. As discussed earlier, the NAS measure is a quasi-relative measure, for which the thresholds are updated annually for changes in real expenditures on basic goods (food, clothing, shelter, and utilities). Fur-

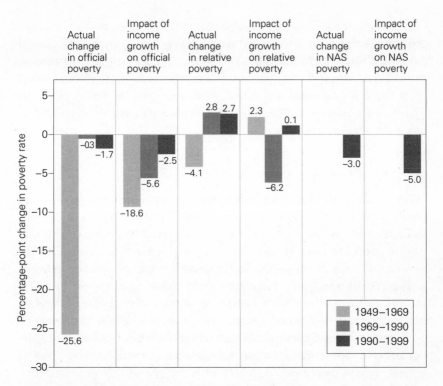

SOURCE: Tabulations of data from the 1950 and 1970 Integrated Public-Use Microdata Series (IPUMS) and the 1991 and 2000 Current Population Surveys (CPS).
NOTE: NAS, National Academy of Sciences.

Figure 6.1. The Effect of Income Growth on Poverty, by Measure and Time Period, 1949–1999

thermore, it is technically more refined than the official poverty measure, in that the family resource measure more fully captures disposable income than the current gross cash income measure, and thresholds are also constructed in a more refined manner.

Overall, the NAS measure fell by 3 percentage points over the period, a greater decline than that according to the official measure. Results indicate that, if everyone's income had increased by the same proportion over the period as the population average, the poverty rate would have declined by 5 percentage points—a larger simulated effect than we see when using the official measure (2.5 percentage points). One of the main reasons for these differences across the two measures is that income growth was more rapid when using the NAS definition of income than when using the official measure.

The inclusion of capital gains income in the NAS measure of income growth, but not the official measure, plays a role. Including capital gains as a form of income tends to produce higher estimates of income growth than when they are omitted. If capital gains were to be omitted from the NAS measure, the effect of income growth would fall from −5.0 to −3.2 percentage points—more similar to patterns found when using the official measure.

Poverty and Economic Inequality

Figure 6.2 shows the relationship between economic inequality and poverty, using the three poverty measures. The decomposition analysis indicates that, while economic inequality served to decrease absolute poverty over the 1949 to 1969 period (−9.3 percentage points), by the 1969–1990 this relationship had reversed (+2.4 percentage points). These results are quite consistent with other findings on growing income and wage inequality beginning in the early 1970s.[19] Danziger and Gottschalk examined sources of increasing inequality between 1973 and 1991 and concluded that changes in labor markets, and particularly the substantial increase in inequality in men's earnings, played a major role in increasing inequality over the period.[20] In the third time period, the 1990s, results in Figure 6.2 show little association between economic inequality and absolute poverty.

The relationship between *relative* poverty and inequality is either about the same as or larger than the relationship between absolute poverty and inequality, depending on the time period. The simulated effect of economic inequality on relative poverty is also larger in two of the three time periods than the effect of income growth. This supports the notions that relative poverty tends to be more sensitive than absolute poverty to trends in economic inequality, and also more sensitive to economic inequality than to income growth.

Inequality was associated with slight increases in the NAS poverty rate over the 1990 to 1999 period, in contrast to the effect when using the official measure. Since dollar amounts of the NAS and official thresholds are fairly similar, the difference in the effect has more to do with the measurement of income used in the two measures. As described earlier, capital gains increase the simulated effect of income growth on NAS poverty; conversely, they also produce higher simulated effects of economic inequality on poverty than when they are omitted. If capital gains were omitted from the NAS measure, the simulated effect of inequality

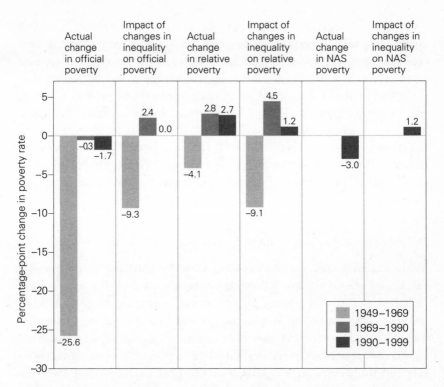

SOURCE: Tabulations of data from the 1950 and 1970 IPUMS and the 1991 and 2000 CPS.

Figure 6.2. The Effect of Changes in Economic Inequality on Poverty, by Measure and Time Period, 1949–1999

would change from +1.2 to –0.5 percentage points—more similar to patterns found when using the official measure. It should be noted that other elements in the NAS measure also have an effect, sometimes in an opposing direction. For example, the inclusion of the Earned Income Tax Credit (EITC) in the NAS but not the official measure of income actually serves to reduce the simulated negative impact of income inequality. This tax credit was designed to raise the incomes of low-wage workers. Excluding the EITC from the NAS definition of income would increase the effect of changes in inequality from +1.2 to +2.2 percentage points.

Poverty and Family Structure

Figure 6.3 decomposes the effect of changes in family structure on poverty. The effect is actually fairly similar across all three poverty measures. Changes in family structure had a small positive (harmful) correlation with poverty from 1949 to 1969 (+1.3 when using the official measure, +1.5 when using the relative one). Between 1969 and 1990, the effect of changes in family structure, while moderate, was nevertheless about double the effect in the 1949–1969 period. Notably, from 1990 to 1999 the relationship between changes in family structure and poverty disappeared (it was statistically insignificant, regardless of the poverty measure used). Over all the time periods, the association between trends in poverty and family structure changes tended to be smaller than those between poverty and income growth and economic inequality.[21]

Poverty across Racial and Ethnic Groups

Table 6.2 provides a more detailed view by showing results across racial and ethnic groups. All groups experienced their biggest declines in both absolute and relative poverty in the 1949 to 1969 period. As in the total population, while income growth had the strongest association with declining official poverty rates for all groups, it was simulated to increase relative poverty in the first time period (given that the poverty thresholds rose at a quicker rate than per-capita income over the period). In the 1969–1990 period, income growth was simulated to have a significant beneficial effect on official poverty rates of all groups, though it was smaller than in the earlier period. It also had a beneficial relationship with relative poverty rates, as per-capita income rose more quickly than median incomes.

In the 1990–1999 period, blacks and Hispanics experienced large declines in official and NAS poverty rates, fueled mainly by income growth. The relationship between income growth and poverty among whites was in the same direction but smaller. As mentioned before, the inclusion of capital gains in the income definition in the NAS measure helps produce a larger simulated effect of income growth than in the official measure.

Declining inequality appeared to have a very substantial role in reducing both absolute and relative poverty rates in the 1949–1969 period for all groups, and the effect was larger among groups that experienced bigger overall declines in poverty (Latinos and African Americans). There was a notable reversal in the 1969–1990 period. Inequality was associated with increases in poverty among all groups, especially relative poverty, with the greatest effect on Hispanics (+14.1 percentage

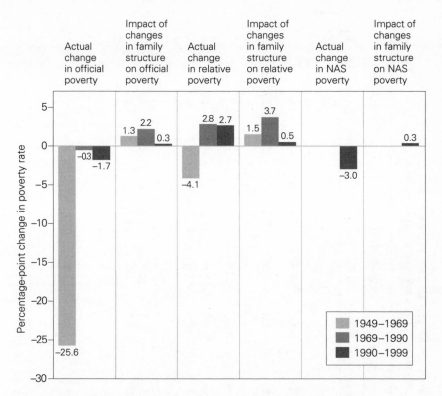

SOURCE: Tabulations of data from the 1950 and 1970 IPUMS and the 1991 and 2000 CPS.

Figure 6.3. The Effect of Changes in Family Structure on Poverty Rates, by Measure and Time Period, 1949–1999

points). The 1970s and 1980s was a time when many low-skilled workers from Mexico and other Latin American countries immigrated to the United States.

In the 1990 to 1999 period, the effect of inequality on official poverty rates was generally small, with the largest effect shown among African Americans (−3.1), who experienced the largest overall declines in poverty over the period. Inequality served to decrease African American relative poverty rates and modestly increase non-Hispanic white and Hispanic relative poverty rates. Inequality had a small harmful effect on NAS poverty among whites, though the association is insignificant among blacks and Hispanics.

The effects of family structure on poverty were generally small in the 1949–1969 period, with the largest effect among African Americans (+2.4 when using the official measure). However, the relationship

TABLE 6.2. DECOMPOSITION OF CHANGES IN THE POVERTY RATE, BY POVERTY MEASURE, RACE/ETHNICITY, AND YEAR, 1949–1999

	1949–1969			1969–1990			1990–1999		
	Whites	Blacks	Hispanics	Whites	Blacks	Hispanics	Whites	Blacks	Hispanics
Actual Change in Poverty Rates									
%-point change in official poverty	-24.5	-40.8	-39.8	-1.4	-4.0	2.6	-1.2	-8.2	-5.3
%-point change in relative poverty	-4.3	-11.8	-5.8	1.4	-1.3	7.0	2.0	-2.6	3.5
%-point change in NAS poverty	—	—	—	—	—	—	-2.1	-9.7	-10.1
Effect of Income Growth									
On official poverty	-17.7	-24.7	-29.3	-4.3	-12.6	-10.9	-1.9	-4.7	-4.6
On relative poverty	2.1	3.8	4.9	-5.3	-11.0	-11.1	0.1	0.2	0.2
On NAS poverty	—	—	—	—	—	—	-3.6	-9.9	-10.3
Effect of Inequality									
On official poverty	-7.8	-18.5	-11.5	1.1	2.8	10.7	0.5	-3.1	-0.6
On relative poverty	-7.6	-17.9	-11.8	3.8	2.4	14.1	1.4	-2.4	3.4
On NAS poverty	—	—	—	—	—	—	1.3	0.5	0.2
Effect of Changes in Family Structure									
On official poverty	1.0	2.4	1.1	1.8	5.8	2.9	0.3	-0.5	-0.1
On relative poverty	1.2	2.3	1.1	2.8	7.2	3.9	0.5	-0.4	-0.1
On NAS poverty	—	—	—	—	—	—	0.2	-0.3	0.0

SOURCE: Tabulations of data from the 1950 and 1970 IPUMS and the 1991 and 2000 CPS.

between poverty and changes in family structure were significantly larger in the 1969 to 1990 period, regardless of the measure, with the largest association again with poverty among African Americans (+5.8 percentage points when using the official poverty measure).

Results again show the waning relationship between poverty and changes in family structure in the 1990–1999 period. Changing family formation patterns had no statistically significant association with poverty rates of any racial/ethnic group, signifying a reversal of a long-term trend, particularly among African Americans. This is explained by the fact that the trend showing a greater number of African Americans living in female-headed families halted by the end of the decade. In 1999, 37 percent of blacks lived in female-headed families, down from 39 percent in 1990. The proportion in married-couple families remained about the same, at 42 percent, while changes in other living arrangements made up the difference.

Child Poverty

Among children we see many of the same patterns that characterized the general population. In the 1949 to 1969 period, we see large declines in the official poverty rate and a more modest, though still substantial, decline in the relative poverty rate (see Table 6.3). As in the total population, income growth served to decrease official poverty of all groups of children but served to increase relative poverty (because thresholds rose more quickly than per-capita income). Between 1969 and 1990, child poverty rates rose for nearly all groups (the change in the official African American poverty rate was not statistically significant), according to both poverty measures. The increase in poverty was greater for children than for the total population. Income growth was simulated to decrease both absolute and relative poverty rates, with larger effects among African American and Latino children. This indicates that the other factors served to increase child poverty rates, as discussed below. In the 1990s, when official and NAS child poverty rates again declined, particularly for African American and Latino children, income growth played a prominent role. The effect is again particularly large when looking at the NAS measure, which includes capital gains. Income growth had little effect on relative poverty.

As in the total population, declining inequality served to reduce poverty among all groups of children in the 1949 to 1969 period. Between 1969 and 1990, when child poverty rates rose, inequality

TABLE 6.3. DECOMPOSITION OF CHANGES IN THE CHILD POVERTY RATE, BY POVERTY MEASURE, RACE/ETHNICITY, AND YEAR, 1949–1999

	1949–1969			1969–1990			1990–1999		
	Whites	Blacks	Hispanics	Whites	Blacks	Hispanics	Whites	Blacks	Hispanics
Actual Change in Poverty Rate									
%-point change in official poverty	−31.3	−43.5	−42.3	2.2	0.7	7.2	−3.0	−11.6	−8.2
%-point change in relative poverty	−6.4	−13.7	−5.1	5.7	3.0	11.3	0.3	−3.4	2.1
%-point change in NAS poverty	—	—	—	—	—	—	−4.5	−13.4	−14.7
Effect of Income Growth									
On official poverty	−22.8	−24.7	−32.1	−4.2	−15.1	−13.6	−2.2	−5.2	−5.3
On relative poverty	2.7	4.3	5.8	−5.7	−12.3	−12.8	0.1	0.3	0.2
On NAS poverty	—	—	—	—	—	—	−4.7	−13.9	−13.2
Effect of Inequality									
On official poverty	−9.5	−21.9	−12.0	4.7	7.6	17.1	−1.2	−5.3	−2.5
On relative poverty	−10.4	−20.9	−13.1	8.8	5.2	18.9	−0.5	−2.8	2.3
On NAS poverty	—	—	—	—	—	—	−0.2	1.3	−1.4
Effect of Changes in Family Structure									
On official poverty	1.1	3.1	1.9	1.7	8.1	3.6	0.4	−1.1	−0.4
On relative poverty	1.3	2.9	2.1	2.6	10.1	5.2	0.7	−0.9	−0.4
On NAS poverty	—	—	—	—	—	—	0.4	−0.7	−0.2

SOURCE: Tabulations of data from the 1950 and 1970 IPUMS and the 1991 and 2000 CPS.

served to increase them substantially, with the greatest association, as in the total population, among Hispanic children. While income growth was simulated to decrease the official Hispanic poverty rate by 13.6 percentage points in the 1969–1990 period, income inequality served to increase it by 17.1 percentage points. The effect on the Hispanic relative poverty rate was even larger, at +18.9 percentage points. By the 1990s, inequality no longer served to increase child poverty for any group, with only a couple of modest exceptions.

As with the total population, the association between child poverty and changes in family structure were modest in the 1949–1969 period. By the 1969–1990 period, however, changes in family structure had a particularly strong association with black and Hispanic child poverty rates, both absolute and relative. These changes played a significant role in increasing child poverty rates over the period. For example, among African American children, while income growth alone would have produced a very substantial 15.1 percentage-point decline in the official poverty rate over the period, increasing income inequality served to increase the poverty rate by 7.6 percentage points, and changes in family structure increased it by another 8.1 percentage points— together completely nullifying the positive relationship between poverty and income growth. Among Hispanic children, changes in family structure served to increase the official poverty rate by 3.6 percentage points (and the relative poverty rate by 5.2 percentage points) from 1969 to 1990, while the effect on white child official poverty rates was much more modest, at +1.7 percentage points.

Despite some methodological differences (and differences in the years examined), the findings concerning the association between poverty and family structure are generally consistent with findings from other studies.[22] One of those studies, by David Eggebeen and Daniel Lichter, concluded that changes in family structure served to increase the official and relative poverty rate among children, particularly in the 1980s, and that the racial divergence in family structure since 1960 exacerbated the persistent black-white difference in children's economic status.

As in the analysis of the total population, the 1990s witnessed a dramatic reversal in the association of changes in family structure with child poverty, particularly black child poverty rates. African American children experienced declines in poverty regardless of the measure. While changes in family structure appear to slightly contribute to this decline, the relationship is not statistically significant. The fact that it did not have a harmful association bucks the decades-long trend. While the proportion of African American children in married-couple families declined precipitously from 65 percent in 1970 to 40 percent in 1990, by 1999 the proportion had changed little more (the 42 percent figure in 1999 is not statistically different from the 1990 estimate).

For whites, the relationship between changes in family structure and poverty rates is statistically insignificant. The trend away from married-couple families continued for white children in the 1990s, albeit at a slower rate. The proportion of white children in married-couple families dropped from 90 percent in 1970 to 82 percent in 1990, and then to 80 percent in 2000. Among Hispanics, changes in family structure had no significant association with poverty in the 1990 to 1999 period. After years of decline in the proportion of Hispanic children in married-couple families in the 1970s and 1980s, the proportion stabilized at about 69 percent in the 1990s.

CONCLUSION

Overall, results from this decomposition analysis suggest that income growth explained most of the trend in absolute poverty over the last half of the twentieth century, particularly in the 1950s and 1960s. So why did poverty remain high thereafter? As economic growth slowed in the 1970s and 1980s, inequality and demographic changes together served to keep it that way. Yet the strong economy, coupled with a waning effect of income inequality and demographic change, once again decreased absolute poverty in the 1990s.

The negative effect of family structure changes—mainly the growth in female-headed families—increased from 1949 through 1990, regardless of the poverty measure used. Remarkably, however, the effect of changes in family structure disappeared during the 1990s. A slowing of shifts in family structure explain this.[23]

Two findings across racial and ethnic groups were notable. First, rising income inequality in the 1970s and 1980s had a particularly large negative association with Latino poverty, regardless of the measure used. This could be due to the concentration of Hispanics in low-skill occupations, whose wages eroded over the period, and perhaps also to rapid increases in low-skill Latino immigration. Second, changes in family structure had a larger negative effect on African Americans than others from 1949 to 1990, and particularly between 1969 and 1990—consistent with trends showing rapid increases in black female-headed families over those decades. But by the 1990s, changing family formation patterns no longer had any association with trends in poverty rates of African Americans or others.

This study also illustrates how our views of poverty affect our understanding of the processes that affect it. In particular, economic inequality played the most prominent role in explaining trends in *relative* poverty rates, while the effect of income growth took a back seat. Even as absolute levels of material deprivation and hardship fell spectacularly over the 1949 to 1999 period, relative deprivation fell only modestly, before slowly climbing over the last three decades of the twentieth century. So while certainly fewer people struggled to meet the most basic of physical needs in 1999 than in 1949, a greater number strained to attain a socially acceptable standard of living by century's end.

By the late 1990s, lower-income working parents often faced the challenge of obtaining what many now consider basic needs—such as affordable care for their children or perhaps a car that allowed them to get to work across town in places far from economical housing.[24] Thus, while we should not reject the positive role of income growth in increasing standards of living and reducing absolute poverty, we ought still recognize persisting inequality and its impact on those who fall behind.

Poverty and Policy

The struggle between providing aid to the poor and not promoting socially "undesirable" behaviors is a central one in ongoing debates concerning the future of welfare reform. In 1998 Sar Levitan and his coauthors attempted to summarize public opinion on poverty policy: "We cannot for our own comfort let people starve and freeze on our streets, but we resent their accepting our largesse while indulging in counterproductive habits that we know would decrease our own productivity and well-being if we so indulged."[1]

These issues are not uniquely modern. Nearly a century earlier, in 1904, Emil Munsterberg posited strikingly similar sentiments, even if in different terms:

> The conduct of society toward poverty continues to oscillate between two evils—the evil of insufficient care for the indigent, with the resulting appearance of an ever-increasing impoverishment . . . and the evil of a reckless poor-relief, with the resulting appearance of far-reaching abuses, the lessening of the spirit of independence. . . . The history of poverty is for the most part a history of these constantly observed evils and of the efforts to remove them, or at least to reduce their dimensions. No age has succeeded in solving this problem.[2]

Historically, the set of policies employed in the United States toward the poor reflect both its market economic orientation and its individualistic social bent.[3] Compared with other developed countries, the emphasis of policies has tended to be on promoting economic growth rather than ensuring income equality, and on promoting individual liberty over collective well-being. Policies have also tended to limit entitlements and promote work for eligibility to receive aid.

This chapter examines the origins of current policy debates in the United States, describes existing policies toward the poor, reviews evidence on the marginal effect on poverty of government transfers, and finally discusses how competing goals and values drive ongoing debates on the size, scope, and direction of the American welfare state.

HISTORICAL ORIGINS OF CURRENT U.S. POLICY DEBATES

Colonial American policies toward the poor drew heavily from English poor laws. The Elizabethan Poor Law of 1601 in England brought together, in a single statute, many years of previous legislation that established a civil system of locally financed and administered relief. According to this system, whose major features were adopted in many colonies, assistance included direct aid to the unemployable, a policy of apprenticeship for the young, and work relief for able-bodied adults. It gave local governments responsibility for helping the poor, who were often thought of as falling into one of three groups: children, able-bodied adults, and incapacitated, helpless, or "worthy" poor.[4]

The law had some features that would be considered unusual, and some harsh, by today's standards. Not only were parents legally liable for children but children were also liable for needy parents and grandparents. Vagrants refusing work could be committed to a house of correction, whipped, branded, put in pillories and stoned, or evicted from the community. Potential recipients also had no measures available to appeal these decisions.[5] The poor in some places could even be auctioned off to the lowest bidder or placed in an asylum, if the town had one.[6]

Residency requirements for the receipt of public assistance were common in American villages and towns. Each town often expelled nonresident vagrants and strangers. There was little social welfare for American Indians or African Americans during the colonial period. Black slaves were the responsibility of their masters, as were sometimes newly freed blacks, while the treatment of other free blacks varied.[7] In some places, such as Pennsylvania, African American paupers were the responsibility of their legal county of residence,[8] while in others they were denied assistance and were forced to rely on their own self-help methods. Overall, colonists tended to accept responsibility for who they viewed as their community members, but not for others.[9]

By the early 1800s, the country was growing rapidly, and the beginnings of industrialization and urbanization were evident in a few areas. Growing social tensions and disarray raised concerns about how to handle poverty. The effectiveness of previous methods of dealing with the poor and the equity of local responsibility were questioned. The rise of laissez-faire philosophy also brought about changes in the way people thought about the poor. Residency rules were thought to interfere with labor mobility, and many believed that poor laws might make the poverty problem worse. It was thought that such laws contributed to overpopulation and lowered wages and living standards and that the money spent to support the poor took money away, in the form of taxes, from industrious workers. Rugged individualism was the ideal, and able-bodied poor people were thought to be lazy and morally degenerate.[10]

There was a growing belief that "outdoor" relief, which did not require recipients to enter institutions, aggravated these problems. Paupers were proof that a modest life could be had without hard labor. By the 1820s, the movement toward "indoor" relief was underway. Indoor relief involved the widespread use of institutions, such as almshouses, workhouses, orphanages, and mental hospitals. They remained a part of the policy landscape until the Great Depression in the 1930s, even though other types of relief supplanted them well before.[11]

These institutions were meant to reform, rehabilitate, and morally educate the poor. Conditions in poorhouses varied widely. Some were places of degradation, disease, and near starvation, while others were not. Most were actually used for temporary shelter during times of personal crisis or economic distress rather than as places for permanent or long-term residence.[12] These institutions were increasingly funded by states rather than localities, even if they were still run at the county level.[13] In part because so many poorhouses were dismal places for residents, poorly managed and underfunded, over time they failed to meet the goals predicted by their sponsors (e.g., efficient places for moral education, reform, and work) and eventually lost general support.[14]

Outdoor relief also continued during the period, some also being supplied by private charities. Even at the height of indoor relief, more people were often served outside poorhouses than within.[15] African American communities in some cities often ran their own mutual aid societies. For example, in Philadelphia the number of black mutual aid societies increased rapidly in the early 1800s, collecting dues from many adult African Americans and distributing benefits to those in need.[16]

During the Civil War and immediately after, the federal government played a role in aiding freed black men and women through the work of the Freemen's Bureau and by implementing policies aiding Union veterans. The Freedmen's Bureau served as an employment agency and was also a significant source of relief for African Americans in the South before it was dissolved in 1872,[17] though it has been argued that it also had the negative effect of tying freed slaves to plantations as sharecroppers.[18]

For the most part, African Americans were treated separately from the white poor and usually in an inferior manner. With the end of Reconstruction (1867–1876), public welfare programs for blacks began petering out, forcing them to turn to self-help, mutual aid, or to private Negro benevolent societies of one kind or another.[19] On the positive side, Civil War benefits were offered to millions of disabled and elderly Union war veterans, including African American veterans. By 1910 more than a quarter of all American elderly men were receiving regular payments from the federal government.[20]

Aside from benefits for veterans, by the 1870s many cities and localities reduced public outdoor relief, and "scientific charities" grew in importance.[21] This represented the trend of coordinating administration and supervision of aid into larger, professionally and privately managed charities. The organized charity movement aimed not only at eliminating fraud and inefficiency in the administration of relief but also at devising a constructive method of treating poverty. It involved having "friendly visitors" look into each case to diagnose the cause of poverty. Investigation was the cornerstone of treatment, followed by personal contact between the rich and the poor, which was aimed at passing on advice and moral training. The philosophy behind the movement rested upon the notion that poverty was an individual and moral problem. In the late 1800s, Josephine Shaw Lowell, founder of the New York Charity Organization Society stated: "Human nature is so constituted that no [working] man can receive as a gift what he should earn by his own labor without a moral deterioration. No human being . . . will work to provide the means of living for himself if he can get a living in any other manner agreeable to himself."[22]

The scientific charity societies were, however, criticized by some as being too uncomprehending of the causes of poverty, too paternalistic, and sometimes cold and cruel. It was assumed that the poor wanted the moral guidance of the friendly visitors, which was rarely the case. The societies also failed to fully recognize the multifaceted causes of poverty, which included not only individual failings but also such factors as accidents, poor health, low wages, and involuntary unemployment. Yet the professional orientation of these societies encouraged good record keeping and the collecting of information about the causes of poverty during the visits. This contributed to the development of a technique of social service and research—casework—and, with it, the growth of social work as a profession.[23]

The early years of the twentieth century were a time of continued rapid industrialization, urbanization, and immigration. Economic insecurity and deprivation were widespread. Some reformers felt that the complex problems associated with these processes required greater monetary support than private charities could provide. Between 1909 and 1920 forty-three states passed legislation that required employers to provide workman's compensation for employees hurt on the job. This was one of the first organized and sustained social insurance programs in the country.[24] A number of programs to help mothers, such as mothers' pensions,[25] and children also arose in this period. In 1912 the U.S. Congress established the Children's Bureau, whose mission was to collect and exchange ideas and information on child welfare. At the bureau's urging, Congress passed the 1921 Sheppard-Towner Act to fund health education programs for mothers with babies.[26]

Other legislation in this period supported extending aid to widows with children, a segment of the "deserving" poor. Thirty-nine states had such statutes in place by 1919, and all but two by 1935. Widow pension laws marked a turning point in the welfare policies of many states because they removed the stigma of charity for a large number of welfare recipients. The early twentieth century also saw the continued professionalization of charity; by the 1920s, charity workers were becoming "social workers," and the number of schools of social work began to grow. The volunteer "friendly visitor" gave way to the paid, trained caseworker.[27]

The stock market crash in the fall of 1929 and the subsequent Depression vastly changed the economic, social, and political landscape. Between 1929 and 1933 the unemployment rate climbed from 3.2 percent to 24.9 percent. The nation's private charity agencies simply lacked the means to meet the growing need across the country. It became quite evident that at least some of the new poverty resulted from social and economic factors that the needy could not control.[28] Herbert Hoover approached the economic crisis timidly, and as conditions failed to improve, he lost the 1932 election to Franklin Delano Roosevelt.

Roosevelt adopted a proactive approach by instituting a large federal relief program to help restore public confidence in the nation's institutions. In the 1930s, a number of measures were taken, including, among others, the creation of the Works Progress Administration, which provided jobs for the unemployed; the National Labor Relations Act, or Wagner Act, which gave unions guarantees of their right to organize; the Farm Security Administration, which aided small farmers and migratory workers; and the Wagner-Steagall Housing Act, which established the U.S. Housing Authority to provide low-interest loans to local officials building public housing. The Federal Emergency Relief Act, signed into law in 1933, opened up the era of federal aid by making available at the outset $500 million of federal funds to be distributed as grants-in-aid to states. African Americans tended to receive less economic assistance than whites due to discrimination and exclusion. Nevertheless, the New Deal programs represented a notable departure from the past in that they officially tried to prohibit discrimination, and they did end up helping a number of African American families.[29]

One of the most momentous pieces of legislation was the Social Security Act, which became law in 1935. It provided both *social insurance,* in the form of pensions for the aged, and *public assistance,* in the form of unemployment insurance for the jobless, Aid to Dependent Children (ADC, later known as Aid to Families with Dependent Children, or AFDC), and assistance to disabled children. Over time, the social insurance portions of the act have tended to be more popular and less controversial than the public assistance portions.[30] Old Age Insurance (OAI) was eventually expanded to cover just about all retired employees, while providing survivors and disability protection as well. The Social Security Act marked the beginning of federal aid to the states on a permanent basis. It introduced the ideas of entitlement into national policy and made the federal government assume responsibility for the welfare of its citizens.[31] In 1932 the federal share of public aid was 2.1 percent; by 1939 it had risen to 62.5 percent.[32]

World War II brought back full employment and rising incomes for most Americans. The GI Bill of 1944 offered a comprehensive set of disability services, employment benefits, educational loans, family allowances, and subsidized loans for homes, businesses, and farms to 16 million World War II veterans.[33]

The late 1940s and 1950s were years of general prosperity, and the general image of the nation was that of an affluent society with the highest standards of living in the world. Despite these advances, poverty remained. Moreover, there were groups of people among whom poverty was widespread and who, for the most part, had been left out of the mainstream of American life: unemployed southern blacks who had migrated to northern cities, some rural whites, Mexican Americans, Native American on their reservations in the West and Southwest, and Puerto Ricans. The civil rights movement brought national attention to the condition of these socially, economically, and politically marginalized groups, many of whom had only modestly benefited from past policy measures. The urban violence and social disarray of the 1960s shattered the image of America as a classless or relatively homogeneous society.[34]

The Kennedy administration advocated a number of new policies aimed at reducing poverty and inequality, such as the 1962 Public Welfare Amendments to the Social Security Act, which increased federal support to the states for providing services to public assistance recipients. Kennedy's successor, Lyndon Johnson, further moved the poor to a prominent place on the public agenda with the launching of the "War on Poverty." Legislation supporting this effort included the Economic Opportunity Act, which among other things, created the Job Corps for school dropouts; Operation Head Start, a project to give preschool training to children; the Legal Services Corporation; and the Community Action Program (CAP), which supported the creation and operation of community action agencies to combat poverty and empower people locally. The last of these, CAP, was designed to address problems in "disorganized" communities with high poverty. CAP programs ultimately failed because they met with significant bureaucratic and political resistance. They lacked political support in part because they were in fact designed to bypass local politicians. Much of the money allocated never made it to those who needed it.[35]

Other legislation during the period that created programs well-known today include the Food Stamp Act (1964), which provided funds for low-income families to purchase food; Medicare (1965), which provided health insurance for the elderly; and Medicaid (1965), which did the same for the poor. Between 1963 and 1966 federal grants to the states for social services more than doubled. In addition, approximately 1 million new public assistance cases were added to the welfare rolls, especially the AFDC program, and another 3.3 million would be added by 1970.[36] In 1974 the Supplemental Security Income program federalized benefits available to the blind, disabled, and the elderly.

Despite some efforts in the 1960s that attempted to give communities greater power (such as CAP), the general trend in the administration of policies for the poor since the 1930s was toward larger bureaucratic structures and increased professionalization. The combination of these two has, at times, made poverty programs less responsive to actual needs and also harder to reform. Over time, this has lead to greater dissatisfaction with these policies and institutions from many parts of the political spectrum.[37]

By the late 1960s, a growing number of people denounced welfare. In addition, antiwar protests, student upheavals, and social change (such as the women's liberation, civil rights, and welfare rights movements) caused resentment among conservatives. Nevertheless, while Richard Nixon, elected in 1968, criticized federal involvement in services to individuals and communities (preferring self-help), he actually ended up supporting a number of proposals that expanded the scope of social programs designed to help "deserving" needy citizens, including the disabled, the elderly, and the working poor. These programs included the Earned Income Tax Credit (EITC), which provided tax rebates for low-income workers, and the Comprehensive Employment and Training Act (CETA), which subsidized public service jobs for the unemployed.[38]

In the mid-1970s, the economy suffered from high unemployment and inflation. By the end of the decade, it was clear that the optimism of the 1960s had given way to pessimism and cynicism; liberals and many social programs came under attack, and Ronald Reagan led the subsequent movement to limit welfare and reduce social spending, believing that widespread freeloading plagued the system. Under Reagan, military budgets were expanded and taxes cut, as were some social programs, such as CETA. Spending on others, such as AFDC, child care, unemployment insurance, food stamps, subsidized housing, public and mental health services, legal aid, was slashed. Reagan also pushed for the transfer of many government functions from the federal level to the states.[39]

Some of these cuts in the early 1980s coincided with perhaps the worst recession since the 1930s. Poverty and unemployment soared to their highest rates in years. By the mid-1980s the economic crisis eased, though unemployment and poverty were slow to decline. The next big piece of welfare legislation was the Family Support Act, signed into law by Reagan in 1988, whose centerpiece was the Job Opportunities and

Basic Skills (JOBS) program, which required single parents on welfare whose children were older than three years to work in order to receive assistance. If they could not get jobs, they had to enroll in education or job training courses, to be paid for by the states and the federal government. Money was also provided for child care, transportation, and other expenses necessary to enable recipients to work or take part in education and/or job training.

The early 1990s witnessed another significant recession and a sharp increase in the number of cash welfare and food stamp recipients. Dissatisfaction with the welfare system remained. Bill Clinton, who had vowed to "end welfare as we know it" in his 1992 campaign, helped do just that, signing a bipartisan bill in 1996, the Personal Responsibility and Work Opportunity Reconciliation Act (PRWORA). This was a dramatic and controversial measure that brought an end to six decades of federal social policy guaranteeing at least a minimum level of aid to those in poverty. The measure abolished AFDC and replaced it with a system of smaller grants to states, which established rules of eligibility but were required to end welfare to recipients after two years, regardless of whether they had found jobs by that time. It also set a lifetime limit on assistance at five years.[40] A number of other social programs to support the poor remained in place, such as housing subsidies, Medicare, assistance for the disabled, and the Earned Income Tax Credit.

CURRENT SOCIAL WELFARE PROGRAMS

There are two basic types of government programs that attempt to alleviate or prevent poverty, as alluded to earlier: social insurance and public assistance. Social insurance policies are broad, "universal" ones that generally do not impose eligibility criteria based on one's income. Social Security and Medicare are perhaps the two most prominent social insurance programs. Public assistance policies specifically target the low-income population. They are "means-tested" or "income-tested," in that a person or family has to earn below a certain amount to qualify. Temporary Aid to Needy Families (TANF) and food stamps are two of the better-known examples of public assistance programs.

Table 7.1 shows the trend in the share of federal spending on various types of income-tested benefit programs. While income-tested benefits comprised 6.4 percent of the federal budget in 1968, by 1978 it had risen to 13.9 percent. There was a dip in the early 1980s before it rose

TABLE 7.1. FEDERAL SPENDING FOR INCOME-TESTED BENEFITS,
BY FORM OF BENEFIT, SELECTED FISCAL YEARS, 1968–1998

	Total	Medical benefits	Cash aid	Food benefits	Housing benefits	Education benefits	Jobs/ training	Other services	Energy aid
1968	6.4	1.5	2.8	0.5	0.4	0.5	0.4	0.0	0.2
1973	10.9	2.7	3.5	1.6	1.4	0.7	0.4	0.0	0.7
1978	13.9	3.2	3.5	1.9	1.6	0.9	2.1	0.1	0.8
1983	11.6	2.9	2.8	2.2	1.5	0.9	0.6	0.3	0.4
1988	11.7	3.6	2.9	1.9	1.4	1.1	0.4	0.2	0.4
1990	12.1	4.0	2.9	1.9	1.4	1.1	0.3	0.1	0.3
1992	15.1	5.7	3.5	2.4	1.6	1.0	0.4	0.1	0.4
1994	16.9	6.4	4.3	2.5	1.7	1.0	0.3	0.1	0.5
1996	16.9	6.7	4.5	2.4	1.6	1.0	0.3	0.1	0.4
1997	16.8	6.7	4.5	2.2	1.7	1.0	0.2	0.1	0.4
1998	16.8	6.9	4.5	2.0	1.6	1.1	0.2	0.1	0.4

SOURCE: U.S. House of Representatives, Committee on Ways and Means, Green Book 2000: Background Material and Data on Programs within the Jurisdiction of the Committee on Ways and Means (Washimgton DC: U.S. Government Printing Office, 2000) Table K-5.

again in the early 1990s. As of the late 1990s, income-tested benefits made up 16.8 percent of the federal budget. While spending on a number of programs has contributed to this overall rise since 1968, the most prominent category is medical benefits, such as Medicaid, whose share of the federal budget rose from 1.5 percent in 1968 to 6.9 percent in 1998. When considering federal, state, and local spending together, in 1998 spending on means-tested medical benefits was greater than spending on all the other forms combined. Cash aid (such as AFDC and later TANF) was the largest component through 1978; in 1998 it comprised 4.5 of the federal budget, only a percentage point higher than its share in 1973.[41]

Figure 7.1 compares federal spending across various types of programs. The biggest single program in 1999 was Social Security, a social insurance program (22 percent), followed by spending on defense (17 percent), interest payments on debt (16 percent), Medicare (12 percent), and then various income-tested programs, such as cash welfare and food stamps, and other domestic programs.[42] In 1996, 24 percent of federal spending on social assistance was on means-tested programs, and 73 percent was on social insurance programs.[43]

These statistics support the notion that social insurance programs (such as Social Security and Medicare) are larger and more costly (and benefit a greater number of people) than means-tested public assistance programs. This perhaps also reflects the greater popularity of these programs among the general population.[44]

Figure 7.2 provides a picture of the proportion of people in the United States who receive benefits from various programs, as reported in the 2001 Current Population Survey (CPS), a household survey. While families tend to underreport government benefits in household surveys, Figure 7.2 still provides a rough approximation of receipt.[45] The non-means-tested programs, Social Security and Medicare, are the most used—a little over a quarter of American households report receiving some income from these programs. As we would expect, other programs are less widely used, ranging from 1.9 percent of households reporting receipt of TANF/General Assistance cash payments to 13.4 percent reporting receiving benefits from Medicaid.[46] An additional program, whose benefits expanded over the 1990s was the Earned Income Tax Credit. In 1996, 18.7 million families received this credit, with an average family credit of $1,341.[47]

Since welfare reform, the percent of people participating in some of the means-tested program, such as cash welfare and food stamps, has

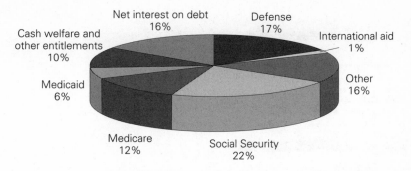

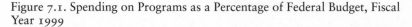

SOURCE: U.S. House of Representatives, Committee on Ways and Means, 2000, *Background Mate-rial and Data on Programs Within the Jurisdiction of the Committee on Ways and Means (Green Book)*. (Washington, DC: U.S. Government Printing Office), table I-3.

Figure 7.1. Spending on Programs as a Percentage of Federal Budget, Fiscal Year 1999

declined. For example, 4.5 percent of the population reported receiving cash welfare (AFDC or non–supplemental security income [SSI] cash assistance) in 1995, as compared to the 1.9 percent figure in 2000. Among the poor, the proportion reporting receiving income from this source dropped dramatically from 22.3 percent in 1995 to 10.2 per-cent just 5 years later. Likewise the proportion of poor householders who reported receiving food stamps dropped from 41.8 percent in 1995 to 29.5 percent in 2000. No such trend was evident in the non-means-tested programs such as Medicare and Social Security, where the proportion of households receiving such income remained fairly steady over those five years.[48]

Given that the means-tested programs are designed to help the low-income population, it is unsurprising that a considerably higher per-centage of households with a poor householder report receiving assis-tance. Nevertheless, about a quarter of the poor did not participate in any major welfare program in 1994, and nearly 60 percent of welfare recipients are not officially designated as poor under the current official poverty definition.[49] While eligibility for welfare programs is based on income, income thresholds are often tied not to the official poverty level but rather often to a multiple of it (for example, families with income 130 percent of the poverty level are eligible for food stamps).

Mean amounts of receipt, among those who report receiving them, were highest for Social Security ($12,276 annually) in 2000 and more moderate for others such as Medicare ($5,316), TANF/General Assis-tance ($3,406), supplemental security income (SSI, $5,247), food

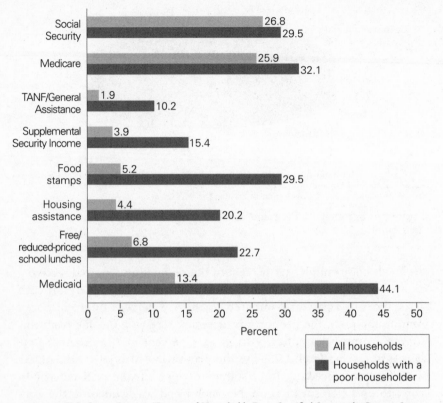

SOURCE: U.S. Census Bureau, "Income of Households From Specified Sources, by Poverty Status: 2000," Experimental Measures of Income and Poverty, Detailed Income Tabulations from the CPS, table 7 (Internet data released September 6, 2001 at ferret.bls.census.gov/macro/032000/rdcall/toc .htm).

Figure 7.2. Percent of Households That Reported Receiving Income from Selected Programs, by Poverty Status, 2000

stamps ($1,565), housing subsidies ($2,182), Medicaid ($2,102), and free/reduced-price school lunches ($664), according to the CPS data.[50] While these amounts are significant, they are often not sufficient to push people's income above the poverty line, even if the noncash bene-fits (such as food stamps, Medicaid, housing subsidies, and school lunches) are included as a source of income (though they are not under the current "official" definition of income).

Figure 7.3 estimates the proportion of the pretransfer poor lifted out of poverty by various safety-net programs in 1996. Social insurance programs—mainly Social Security but also federal pensions and unem-ployment insurance (but not including Medicare)—had the biggest

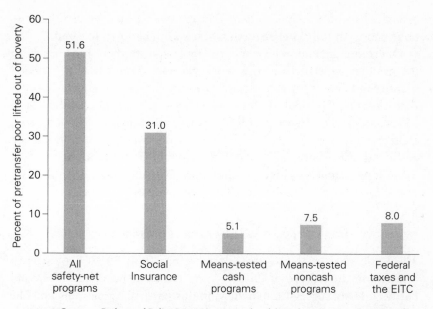

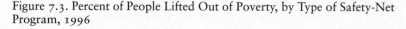

SOURCE: Center on Budget and Policy Priorities, "Strengths of the Safety Net: How the EITC, Social Security, and Other Government Programs Affect Poverty," research report 98-020 (March 1998), table 6; Earned Income Tax Credit (EITC) figures are from table 8.

Figure 7.3. Percent of People Lifted Out of Poverty, by Type of Safety-Net Program, 1996

impact, lifting 31 percent (17.8 million people) of the pretransfer poor out of poverty. Cash assistance programs, such as AFDC and SSI, helped another 5 percent out of poverty. Means-tested noncash programs like food stamps and housing assistance helped 7.5 percent out of poverty, while the Earned Income Tax Credit helped 8 percent out poverty.[51] While the effect of various individual programs has changed over time, the aggregate effect of tax and transfer programs as a whole on the poverty gap was fairly stable over the 1980–2000 period.[52]

As we might expect, programs affect various groups differently. Social Security is the most important safety net program for the elderly. One study in 1996 estimated that 73 percent of the pretransfer elderly poor are lifted out of poverty by Social Security.[53] In large part because of the success of this very popular social insurance program, the elderly poverty rate has, since the 1970s, been close to the overall national poverty rate after years of being considerably above the poverty rate of others. The Earned Income Tax Credit has a particularly large impact on working families and children, and its effect rose significantly over the 1990s as the program was expanded. By one measure, the EITC is estimated to have helped out of poverty over a quarter of otherwise poor people in full-time working families with children in 1998.[54]

One more general achievement of policy since the 1970s has been the gradual construction of a work support system that provides a number of benefits for low-income working families, particularly those with children. This includes housing subsidies, food stamps, the EITC, Medicaid, the Children's Health Insurance Program, the child tax credit, child care subsidies, greater child support enforcement, and school lunch and breakfast programs. Through the combined assistance of many of these, low-income working families with children could, in 1996, convert a $10,000-a-year job into a family income of $16,000.[55]

EVALUATING THE 1996 WELFARE REFORM BILL

The basic goal of the 1996 welfare reform bill, PRWORA, was to "transform the culture of poverty" and reduce dependency.[56] The bill has been fairly successful in achieving this particular goal thus far. The number of people receiving cash assistance dropped dramatically after PRWORA went into effect; some of the decline was due to the bill itself, some to the strong economy, and perhaps some to other unidentified factors. The nation's welfare caseload plummeted from 5 million families in 1994 to 2.2 million in June 2000. While child poverty rates fell, welfare participation fell more quickly. In 1994, 62 percent of poor children received cash welfare; by 1998, the share had fallen to 43 percent.[57] Welfare reform also increased employment rates among single mothers. Employment rates among this group had been slowly increasing for a number of years but then rose from 60 percent in 1994 to 72 percent in 1999, a remarkable jump in such a short time.[58]

A few studies that reviewed a wide array of data found that a majority of welfare leavers were working, though a significant minority were not. Leavers usually had low-wage jobs, so their earnings remained low, and many remained in poverty shortly after leaving welfare. While incomes of single mothers as a whole rose, the income of welfare leavers was often only slightly above what it had been while they were receiving welfare benefits.[59] Working parents who left the welfare roles in the late 1990s reported a median wage of $6.61 an hour and annual earnings of $8,000 to $12,000.[60] There was a significant group of very disadvantaged women with few skills who had difficulty finding work or remaining employed and who suffered from poor physical and mental health.[61]

Many welfare leavers continued to use Medicaid, food stamps, and other government programs, though others did not. Leavers' perceptions of their economic well-being were mixed, though more positive than negative. While most families believed they were better off exiting welfare and were confident they would not need to return to welfare, around a third of families reported problems providing enough food, paying utility bills, and paying rent. A few studies have found significant reliance on family and friends as a means of additional support.[62]

Some of the positive aspects of PRWORA are that it contained a number of features with wide public support—it emphasized work over welfare and in doing so raised employment rates among single mothers, placed the obligation of child support on both parents, supported state-level innovation, emphasized reducing teen pregnancy, and stressed individual responsibility. A negative feature is that it focused more on reducing dependency than on reducing poverty. Work obtained by former (and potential) recipients often does not pay very well. Some hold that the bill also placed too little emphasis on human capital development and support services, that it leaves many very needy families without income support, and that it remains to be seen what happens when there is a deep recession.[63] A serious economic downturn would increase caseloads, strain state budgets, and perhaps force some states to cut benefits.

A number of programs could address some of the negative features above and still be consistent with the goal of reducing dependency. Providing broader services such as affordable child care and health insurance, education or job training, transportation aid, and help with substance abuse, mental health problems, and domestic abuse could reduce hardship and still encourage work.[64] The Earned Income Tax Credit is another program with broad support that essentially increases real wages for workers with low-paying jobs. It has bipartisan support because it assists only those who work, it helps both two-parent as well as single-parent families, and it raises employees' take-home pay without increasing the employer's labor costs.[65] Evidence suggests that the EITC also has a positive effect on the employment of adults from welfare families.[66]

The above studies describe the effect of specific programs and discuss some of the short-term effects of welfare reform. The following section addresses the broader issue of how much policy can achieve and its limitations and identifies the key challenges for policy makers and the public as they consider the most appropriate methods to address poverty.

POLICY IN THE BROADER SOCIAL
AND ECONOMIC CONTEXT

Evaluating policy depends on the criteria by which we judge it. Some
assess policy on the basis of whether it encourages economic growth
and increases average standards of living. Others prefer policy to mini-
mize inequality. Some want policy to promote individual self-sufficiency,
while others are most concerned with reducing material hardship. The
problem with many policy debates—the source of much confusion on
what works and what does not—is that there needs to be greater recognition and discussion of differing underlying aims, priorities, and values.

What should be the basic goals of policy? Hugh Heclo describes
three areas of broad consensus and continuity in policy.[67] First, Americans have generally agreed that there is a public responsibility to help
those lacking the necessities of life. Second, people should strive to be
self-supporting, because full standing as a citizen depends on the inde-
pendence that comes from work and personal earnings. Third, public
spending should attempt to prevent and cure problems of poverty and
welfare dependence. The consensus is more one of mutual obligation,
which combines an obligation on the part of the state to provide services and on the part of recipients to make efforts to achieve independ-
ence through work.[68] A fourth area of broad agreement could probably
be added to this list: policies that promote equity should not unduly
hinder economic productivity and growth—factors that determine
average standards of living.[69]

Problems arise when putting these precepts into practice, and fun-
damental disagreements exist over how to prioritize the objectives.
While PRWORA embodied the general consensus, it clearly put greater
emphasis on ending dependency than on preventing material hardship
and improving the lives of families and children.[70]

Michael Katz, who has written extensively about the history of welfare in America and who places the goal of reducing poverty at the top
of the hierarchy of policy priorities, has argued that markets exist in an
uneasy tension with welfare states. He holds that the increasing use of
market models in the design of policies is an attempt to resolve the contradiction between markets and welfare states by tying benefits more
closely to employment, reducing dependence, and privatizing services.
He maintains that this begs the larger questions: whom do market-
based policies really serve? What are the forms of capital and who controls them? Who participates in the exchange, and who suffers? More

research is needed on where market models work and where they do not, what they can achieve, and where their disadvantages outweigh their benefits.[71]

Those who are most concerned with poverty reduction express concern that government benefits are simply too low to help many people out of poverty. That is, the overwhelming majority of means-tested benefits are designed to sustain people in poverty rather than actually help them move out.[72] Michael Harrington, in an updated introduction to his well-known book on poverty, *The Other America: Poverty in the United States,* argued that this reflects poorly on the country's humanitarian efforts: "The poor are the most sorely tried and dramatic victims of economic and social tendencies which threaten the entire nation. . . . In morality and in justice every citizen should be committed to abolishing the other America, for it is intolerable that the richest nation in human history should allow such needless suffering."[73]

Alternatively, those who prioritize dependency reduction often question the role of government in social and economic affairs. One concern is that welfare programs provide individual disincentives to work. Strident supporters of this view assert that disincentives contribute to a "culture of poverty," consisting of an eroded work ethic, dependency on government programs, lack of educational aspiration and achievement, and increased single parenthood.[74] As described earlier, these general views have a long history in debates about welfare. It should be noted that one need not believe that government programs produce a separate subculture to still accept that benefits may indeed provide some, if small, disincentives to work among individuals.

Among those who place economic growth first, there is the concern about the potential trade-off between economic growth and government spending designed to reduce income inequality. In many European countries, for example, where the welfare state has traditionally played a major role, there have been recent efforts to roll back spending on the welfare state. It has been argued that government spending hampers economic efficiency and growth by limiting flexibility and dampening private investment.[75] Cuts in social transfers are advocated on the grounds that they, or the taxes necessary to finance them, distort the working of the labor market.

What does the evidence on these issues say? The evidence on disincentive effects indicates that various programs do have some, generally small, negative effects on economically "desirable" behaviors. The general decline in welfare rolls after welfare reform supports this notion.

In an extensive review of the pre–welfare reform literature on disincentive effects, Robert Moffitt reports that "econometric studies show that labor supply is reduced by the AFDC and Food Stamp programs, and that the programs affect family structure though usually weakly."[76] Moffitt adds that the labor supply effects are not large enough to explain the high rates of poverty among female heads; most AFDC women would likely be poor even in the absence of the AFDC program. In addition, disincentive effects of welfare on marriage are not large enough to explain long-run declines in marriage rates; broader cultural shifts may also help explain the long-term trend.[77]

Regarding the issue that welfare may inhibit economic growth, evidence suggests that expansive states may have less growth over the longer run, though the evidence is neither definitive nor straightforward. On one hand, more expansive states do, on the whole, have less poverty, particularly relative poverty. Specifically, using relative poverty measures, the U.S. poverty rate is well above the comparable rate in other countries, as described in chapter 4.[78] Even when using the U.S. absolute poverty threshold, the American poverty rate still surpasses those in many European countries, despite the fact that the United States' gross domestic product (GDP) per capita is significantly higher.[79] Although part of the difference may be explained by greater inequality in U.S. market incomes,[80] some of the difference is due to the smaller size of government transfers in the United States.[81]

Poverty rates among single-parent families are also lower in many European countries than in the United States. Such countries often invest heavily in both universal benefits, such as maternity leave, child care, and medical care, and in promoting work among such families.[82] For example, day care is universal in Denmark, Finland, and Sweden. Female labor force participation rates are therefore very high in these countries, averaging over 70 percent in 1997, which in turn serves to decrease child poverty.[83]

The United States, in comparison with other advanced nations, lacks national health insurance, provides less publicly supported housing, and spends less on job training and job creation. In 1990, among eight advanced countries, only Japan, at 11.2 percent of GDP, ranked lower than the United States, at 11.5 percent in public outlays on pensions, health insurance, and other income maintenance.[84]

On the other hand, the long-term unemployed constitute about half of all Western European unemployment, as compared with 10 to 20 percent in the rest of the industrialized world, creating a substantial group of people more or less detached from the labor force in those Western European countries.[85] Welfare disincentive studies in the United States by themselves are evidence that economic productivity is at least slightly affected by certain types of welfare programs. A. B. Atkinson, in a review of evidence from a number of studies linking economic performance to the size of the welfare state, mainly in Europe, asserts that findings across many studies are actually inconclusive: some studies find that high spending on social transfers leads to lower growth; others find the reverse. Effects may depend on the type of spending. Atkinson discusses a number of weaknesses of the various studies, noting that some suffer from theoretical or empirical weaknesses.[86] This does not provide the last word on the issue; the point here is that more research is needed before we can come to firm conclusions on the size of the impact of government transfers on economic growth, and it is worthwhile to look at the impact of different types of programs as well.

Some apprehensions about government programs are motivated less by economic concerns than by suspicion of government's role in social affairs. The devolution of public authority from the federal government to the states reflects the fragmented feelings of nationality and community in the United States and the distrust of centralized authority. People are often cynical of government efforts to provide social insurance programs, sometimes feeling that individuals can do best for and by themselves. Assistance to the poor is often perceived as coming at others' expense.

What are the limits of social obligation—what do we owe one another? Who provides in times of need—families, charities, employers, or the state? Michael Katz notes that these are questions without definitive answers because they are not objective and cannot be resolved by "looking at the data," so to speak.[87] The consensus embodied in welfare reform policy seems to be one of mutual obligation, where the state provides benefits and the able-bodied recipient in one way or another works for these services.[88]

How far should the welfare state go to combat dependency when some resulting material deprivation is inevitable? Even if cuts in social transfers do in fact distort the working of the labor market, we still need to collectively evaluate whether the economic costs are acceptable in terms of social objectives. Markets often enhance risk, while government transfer programs, particularly social insurance ones, are meant to reduce risk.[89]

Reflecting the less expansive welfare state in the United States, social support for welfare programs is lower in the United States than in Europe. For example, a survey conducted in four countries that was published in 1990 found that the percent either "strongly agreeing" or "agreeing" that the "government should provide everyone with a guaranteed basic income" ranged from 20 percent in the United States to 48 percent in the Netherlands, 51 percent in West Germany, and 59 percent in the United Kingdom.[90]

The retreat from expansive welfare states in Europe in the 1990s indicates that there may be at least some convergence in attitudes, partly because of the feeling that the state had become too large and inefficient. The lower unemployment rate and the higher current rate of economic growth and innovation in the U.S. market has spurred other nations to reconsider the extent of their safety nets and give greater reign to the market.

Public pressures to cut back the European safety net have also arisen out of growing social divisions based on race, ethnicity, and nativity. In a discussion of the tensions undercutting social policy issues in Europe, Roger Lawson and William Julius Wilson assert that:

> economic crises in Europe have made it difficult to sustain programs that embody universal and integrative social citizenship rights. . . . Moreover, the increase of racial and ethnic diversity has led some to reexamine the postwar commitment to universal programs and social inclusion, a commitment originally based on conceptions of citizenship that assumed a fair degree of cultural homogeneity. Recent challenges to this commitment often reflect racial bias. As economic conditions have worsened, many in the majority white population view the growth of minorities as part of the problem. Stagnant economies and slack labor markets have placed strains on the welfare state at the very time when the immigrant population, facing mounting problems of joblessness, has become more dependent on public assistance for survival.[91]

The fragmentation of society along racial and ethnic lines has contributed to the lack of a sense of common national community in the United States too. Reflecting policy in colonial times, when American communities provided help for their own while turning their back on outsiders, the lack of a sense of community today contributes to the decline in national civic engagement. Emil Munsterberg, in his 1904 article, noted that "no civilized state is without [policies that address poverty]. . . . Their foundation is laid by a feeling of fellowship."[92] Implicit in this argument is that, in the absence of such a collective feeling of fellowship and citizenship, efforts to alleviate poverty are bound to suffer.

DISTRIBUTIVE JUSTICE AND EQUAL
OPPORTUNITY IN THE MARKET SYSTEM

Do egalitarian and market impulses necessarily collide? What constitutes a "fair" system? Many feel that meritocratic societies have many positive attributes, though "meritocracy" itself is a difficult concept to define, as value judgments determine what actions a society deems to have merit.[93] Should *merit* refer to ability to produce results, which is a function of talent, work, and luck, or should it refer to effort given to produce positive results?

Definitional issues aside, a merit-based society may also be one that generates significant inequality. That is, there is inevitably some trade-off between *equality of opportunity,* which is thought to be an important attribute of meritocracies, and *equality of outcomes.* Roland Benabou argues that equality of opportunity is closely related to social mobility, while equality of outcomes, from an economic point of view, "dulls individuals' incentives to provide the effort required to translate ability into earnings, and this contributes to lower output."[94]

In order to achieve equality of opportunity, some favor enforcing anti-discrimination laws, such as banning discrimination based on race and gender. Others prefer going further by "leveling the playing field" among individuals competing for economic rewards before the competition begins[95]—that is, not only enforcing nondiscrimination but also equalizing opportunity by, say, requiring equal educational expenditures per pupil in public schools.

Along these lines, Samuel Bowles and Herbert Gintis hold that there are such things as economically efficient (productivity-enhancing) egalitarian policies, where states, markets, and communities complement one another. Accepting the market framework as one that raises average standards of living, or the overall "size of the pie," they state that "government policies should seek not to supplant markets and communities but to ensure their accountability and enhance their capacity to support equitable and efficient outcomes. Conversely, markets and communities should be organized to promote the accountability of government to the people."[96]

They offer a few policies that redistribute assets and promote equality of opportunity while still not stifling market incentives. For example, policies that encourage worker ownership of companies, such as profit sharing, tend to stimulate productivity, reduce the cost of monitoring workers, and more equitably distribute wealth than when only a few owners pocket profits. Another policy toward this end involves giving lower-income people greater access to credit, such as encouraging and subsidizing home ownership. Home ownership helps build wealth and encourage investment in communities. Progress was registered in this area over the 1980s and 1990s, as the homeownership rate had never been higher in the United States.[97] Bowles and Gintis also hold that social insurance programs, such as Social Security and employment insurance, provide a much needed safety net and can stimulate productive risk-taking investments in the economy.[98] Whether all of their policy recommendations work effectively is still an open question, but they do provide interesting avenues for exploration.

SUMMARY

Over the course of the history of U.S. welfare policy, there has been a constant tension between the goal of giving aid in a humane manner to those in need and that of not undermining people's incentive to work and be self-supporting. Colonial programs tended to provide sufficient benefits to community members, though they were unkind to outsiders and to able-bodied people. As the social and economic system and the communities embedded in them changed and grew, basic outdoor relief proved insufficient. The poorhouses of the nineteenth century ("indoor" relief) attempted to provide the most basic care while dissuading dependence. These institutions, many of which were poorly managed, were eventually thought to be too inhumane and did little to address the roots of poverty. Scientific charities at the turn of the century sought to professionalize the provision of aid and dissuade dependence, but they were largely not very successful.

In the 1930s, the Great Depression vividly illustrated how local efforts alone are often insufficient in providing a safety net and how poverty, even among able-bodied individuals, is clearly sometimes a result of broader structural forces rather than just individual laziness or other weakness. As general standards of living grew in the post–World War II period, some became concerned that not everyone was benefiting. The War on Poverty and the accompanying civil rights movement attempted to bring prosperity to those who previously had been ignored by, or had marginally benefited from, policy. These movements brought much change, though many thought welfare policies had gone too far in that they did not do enough to prevent dependency.

Some of the frustration from high social welfare costs stems from misperceptions about which government programs consume a large part of the budget. The most controversial programs, such as cash welfare assistance, consume a relatively small part of the budget and have done so for a number of years. Relatively popular social insurance programs, such as Medicare and Social Security, comprise the largest part of income-assistance spending. Medical benefits, such as Medicare and Medicaid, are those whose costs have risen the most quickly over the last three decades.

Government transfers are often not high enough to actually lift people's income over the poverty line. Social insurance programs, such as Social Security, do the most in terms of reducing poverty—especially among the elderly. The EITC does more to help many working families with low wages.

Today's welfare system once again attempts to strike a delicate balance: providing at least some sort of safety net while also promoting work. The general consensus is that the welfare reform of the late 1990s has worked so far, though many vocal dissenters argue that it does not do enough to check material hardship. Welfare reform legislation mainly sought to address only one facet of the much broader problem of poverty—dependency. The efforts to reduce dependency worked in part because of the prevailing social and economic situation: steady economic growth and declining poverty. Yet history also teaches us that what works in a period of strong economic growth will not suffice in a depression. Policy needs to be flexible enough to address the changing economic situation. Economically, we should also look toward policies that promote equality of opportunity without exacerbating inequality.

CHAPTER 8

Conclusion

At the beginning of this book I posed a few questions: why does poverty remain so pervasive? What does it mean to be poor? Are people from particular racial and ethnic backgrounds, age groups, or family types inevitably more likely to continue to be poor? What can we expect over the next few years? What are the limits of policy? I now revisit these questions in turn.

In addition to individual choices people may make, poverty remains pervasive for several reasons: the way we understand and define poverty, the features of our economic system, social stratification across "status" groups (such as racial and ethnic groups), and our policy responses to these issues are the most prominent. People generally think of poverty in terms of comparative disadvantage. While few people die of material deprivation in the United States today, many struggle to attain the basic goods that would allow them to participate in mainstream society. Thus, because the income perceived as sufficient to avoid poverty increases as standards of living rise, achieving inroads against poverty over the long run are difficult.

Poverty is also a common, if not endemic, feature of most economic systems, and the market system—the principle goal of which is the individual accumulation of capital—is not one of the exceptions. On one hand, the system enjoys wide support. As the engine of economic growth and technological change, it contributes to increases in wages and overall standards of living. Economic growth also tends to drive down absolute levels of poverty (where poverty thresholds remain constant over time), particularly when economic growth is accompanied by rising education levels in the population as a whole and driven by a growing middle class.

On the other hand, the market economy often exerts a contrary effect on poverty levels. To maximize profits, businesses usually seek to pay low wages to workers, which increase inequality and poverty. People may also be laid off from work and have trouble finding employment during times of recession or economic transition, such as when deindustrialization hit many northeastern and midwestern cities in the second half of the twentieth century.

While economic forces determine overall levels of economic growth and inequality, social stratification across social groups determines *who* becomes poor. The main status groups in today's society are generally defined by the intersection of ethnic, gender, and class affiliations. Social stratification across status groups occurs when social groups seek to maximize their rewards by restricting others' access to resources and opportunities. The process of stratification is usually a cumulative one. A person may begin life at a disadvantage, and disadvantages may accrue through the stages of people's lives, such as during schooling, then in the labor market, and so on.

Policy may reduce (or increase) the harmful effects of inequality. The rise of the welfare state in the 1930s was a response to the hardship of the Great Depression, which exposed some of the weakness of the unregulated market. Even earlier, Theodore Roosevelt sought to curb the power of the corporations and monopolies that threatened to undermine the competitive marketplace. Policy, however, has limits within the context of the market system. It is not always used as an instrument for promoting equality, because any push for broad-based economic equality of outcomes (as opposed to equality of opportunity) tends to reduce, if even by a modest amount, incentives to work. Supplying a guaranteed income runs contrary to the central ethos of the market system.

To answer the second question, What does it mean to be poor? I would note that views of poverty are rooted in a particular time and place. As described in chapter 2, the poverty line in the United States is considerably higher than the poverty line in developing countries, as defined by the World Bank. In poor countries, particularly in South Asia and Africa, a high proportion of the population fails to earn even $1 or $2 a day. Moreover, even within the United States, the level of income that people believe is needed to avoid poverty is higher today than it was at the beginning of the twentieth century. This is not to say that efforts to define and use an absolute, subsistence poverty measure are devoid of value. It is informative to gauge changes in the number of people with incomes below a very low, fixed poverty threshold. But we need to be aware that any fixed line is somewhat arbitrary and would eventually need to be updated if it were to continue to be socially meaningful.

While poverty in general refers to material deprivation, it is a multifaceted experience with many different effects on those who are struggling to get by. It certainly involves economic hardship, such as having difficulty paying food bills or living in housing in severe disrepair. For some, poverty means lacking some of the basic consumer items that their neighbors have, such as telephones and cars. A majority of people manage to escape poverty after a short spell of being poor, though a significant minority are not so fortunate. A substantial number also face recurrent bouts of poverty between periods of adequate earnings. Also rising over the last few decades has been the number of people living in high-poverty neighborhoods, where problems such as crime, substandard education, and low levels of civic engagement are common. It should be noted that a vast majority of the poor (as defined by the official measure) do not live in high-poverty neighborhoods.

The third question posed at the beginning of this chapter is, Are people from particular racial and ethnic backgrounds, age groups, or family types inevitably more likely to continue to be poor? The answer is no. Today, minorities, women, children, and female-headed families are more likely to be poor, and in the short run we may see only small shifts in the composition of the poverty population. But in recent years we have also witnessed some very significant declines in poverty among these groups. The poverty rate among African Americans plummeted from 55 percent in 1959 to 22 percent in 2000. Similarly, the poverty rate of people in female-headed families has also declined substantially, from about 50 percent in 1959 to 28 percent in 2000. Poverty rates among these groups are still higher than the overall 11 percent poverty rate in 2000. Yet these dramatic drops suggest that there is nothing inherent about very high poverty rates among certain groups.

For the nonwhite population, the removal of legal barriers to employment and reduction in other forms of discrimination have played a large role in the narrowing of the poverty gap. Nevertheless, disparities remain, particularly for African Americans, and they are fueled by economic dislocation, continuing racism and racial animosity, wealth differentials, segregated housing and employment networks, family insta-bility, and substandard schooling in lower-income areas. These prob-lems are also evident, if less pronounced, among the Latino population. Continued high levels of immigration from Latin American countries make it hard to discern what accounts for high Latino poverty rates (which match African American poverty rates). Newly arrived immi-grants often fare worse than the native population because of language barriers, unfamiliarity with local labor markets, and lower levels of education. Latinos in particular display high employment rates but low wages. Asian Americans have poverty rates only modestly higher than those of the white population. Higher poverty rates among Asian immi-grants explain most of the disparity. Asian American educational levels equal or surpass those of whites and other groups, as does their median household income, particularly among the native-born. Discrimination against Asian Americans does not appear to be so extreme as to increase significantly their likelihood of poverty.

Single-parent families tend to be considerably more vulnerable to economic hardship than married-couple families. Single parents are more likely to face the multiple challenge of working and raising children by themselves. Women, who are far more likely to head such families, face the additional obstacle of having lower earnings than men. While gender disparities in earnings have narrowed considerably, particularly among younger cohorts of women, there is still a gap that is difficult to account for; research suggests that gender discrimination continues to play a role in producing unequal outcomes in the labor market. Despite the greater economic vulnerability of single-parent families, they are not inherently disposed to high poverty rates. One reason is that increasing levels of employment and rising wages among all women, including female heads, have driven down the poverty rates among such families. Another is that policy can reduce poverty among single-parent families, whether in the form of income support, child care, or back-to-work programs. Countries that provide generous support, such as Sweden, have greatly reduced poverty among these types of families.

Contrary to conventional wisdom, then, shifts in family structure have not been the most important factor explaining trends in American poverty rates, though they did have a very significant effect on child poverty in the 1970s and 1980s. Economic growth played the largest role in explaining absolute poverty rates over the last half of the twen-tieth century, while changes in income inequality played a prominent role in explaining relative poverty levels. The effect of changes in family structure peaked in the 1969 to 1990 period and then had no discernible association with trends in poverty in the 1990s.

What do these answers to the questions posed earlier say about future trends in poverty? They suggest that poverty rates depend mostly on trends in income growth and inequality. If the economy remains strong, we should expect to see a long-run downward trend in absolute poverty levels. Two facts bode well for long-term declines in absolute poverty: the effect of changes in family structure stabilized in the 1990s, and the trend of increasing income inequality also plateaued in that decade by some measures (though the very rich did especially well in the economic boom).

Setbacks will occur in periods of recession, however, in the form of short-term, sometimes considerable, increases in poverty. Economic shocks, such as the oil crisis in the mid-1970s, severe political instability, or war could also have significant effects on trends in poverty. Technological and organizational economic changes, such as industrialization and then deindustrialization, cause short- and medium-term increases in poverty as some skills become devalued, employment in certain industries shrinks, and new types of employment opportunities and skills gain currency. In spite of all these variables, the long-term trend of economic growth since colonial times provides a compelling argument for believing that absolute poverty rates will continue to fall.

Predicting future trends in relative poverty levels is more difficult. The key factor driving relative poverty is income inequality, the long-term trend of which is less discernible than the economic growth trend. Inequality is sensitive to the measures used to estimate it. It certainly has risen and fallen over different time periods in the United States, declining or remaining stable from the 1940s through the 1960s, before increasing in the 1970s and 1980s by all measures. Given the lack of a predictable long-term trend, such as what we see for economic growth, we should continue to see moderate levels of relative poverty for the indefinite future.

The final question is, What are the limits of policy? The American public accepts a certain amount of income inequality as an inherent part of the market system, more so as compared with Northern and Western European countries, nearly all which have lower GNPs per capita but also lower poverty rates than in the United States (even when measured by U.S. standards). At the same time, the American public favors at least some of the income support structures of the modern welfare state. There is wide acceptance of the policies, such as Social

Security and Medicare, that reduce poverty and hardship and provide some degree of income security, particularly for middle-class families.

Changes in public investment depend on the amount of public support they muster. Racial and ethnic friction often serve to drive down support for public investment because they reduce people's sense of a broader community—of common goals, aims, and civic responsibilities. Lingering racial animosities translate into greater acceptance of economic inequality among those who control economic institutions. Fostering the goals of pluralism, democracy, and true equality of opportunity, building shared institutions that benefit all groups, such as schools, and supporting broadly targeted social insurance programs that do not markedly inhibit economic growth—these are all critical tasks in efforts to reduce poverty in the United States.

This is also a time to look outward—to promote efforts to reduce poverty that are beneficial to people around the world. The poverty and inequality underlying much of the international turmoil at the beginning of the twenty-first century threaten to rock the foundations of our own democratic and pluralistic ideals. The wealth and high standards of living enjoyed by the majority of Americans (and Europeans) are simultaneously alluring and repellent to those with little hope of sharing in it. The resulting resentment fuels conflict. Poverty is not just the problem of those who are poor. Understanding the sources and nature of poverty is in fact the basis for addressing some of the larger social problems of our day.

Data and Methods for the Analysis in Chapter 6

Data are drawn from the 1950 and 1970 Integrated Public-Use Micro-data (IPUMS) files and from the Annual (March) Demographic Supplement to the 1991 and 2000 Current Population Survey (CPS), all of which contain information on income and poverty for the preceding calendar year. The IPUMS consists of multiple years of the Public-Use Microdata Series (PUMS) files originally issued by the Census Bureau but compiled and made comparable over time by researchers at the University of Minnesota. Using data from different sources potentially affect estimates of trends. To address this possibility, I examined data from the 1990 IPUMS sample (for calendar year 1989) and found they were consistent with CPS data from the same year; using CPS data instead of IPUMS data does not affect conclusions.

The absolute measure of poverty used here uses the current official-U.S.-measure methodology. The measure consists of a set of poverty thresholds that vary by family size and composition and that are compared to a family's gross cash income. If the family's income falls below the threshold, then that family, and everyone in it, is considered poor. It should be noted that, while the official poverty rate time series published by the Census Bureau begins in 1959, I employ the official poverty measure methodology described above to compute analogous rates for the 1949 to 1959 period. Thresholds used in this measure were adjusted over time using the Consumer Price Index for Urban Consumers (CPI-U) from 1949 to 1969 and the CPI-U-X1, an alternative index meant to improve inflation adjustments, for adjustments thereafter (1990 and 1999). I also conducted the analysis using the CPI-U-X1 for the whole time period. The CPI-U-X1 produces only modestly higher declines in poverty over the 1949 to 1999 period (29.7 percentage points versus 27.7 percentage points), and it does not affect conclusions about the relative impact of the various processes on poverty.

The relative poverty measure implemented here uses a reference family poverty threshold equal to one-half the median income of a two-adult, two-child family. To adjust the poverty threshold for families of different sizes, a single parameter equivalence scale—with a square-root-of-household-size factor—is used. This equivalence scale, a common one used by researchers implementing relative poverty measures, takes into account greater economies of scale in larger households.[1] The income measure used is total family income, the same as is used in the official poverty measure. Note that this is one variation of a number of possible relative poverty measures. Some researchers have used after-tax median household income as the threshold.[2] This is not used here because the IPUMS data does not contain tax information. I did, however, test the relative poverty measure using this threshold for the 1990–1999 period (using the CPS data), and this did not affect the conclusions. Note that the NAS poverty measure used here uses pre-tax thresholds and income. Because this study focuses on trends over time, it is less important to focus on any one particular figure as representing a "true" poverty rate than it is to track trends using consistent measures.

The quasi-relative measure here is based on the NAS panel's recommendations and on the corresponding implementation procedures developed by the Census Bureau.[3] Thresholds under the NAS measure (as it is called in the Census Bureau reports) are represented by a dollar amount for food, clothing, shelter, and utilities, and a small amount for other needs (such as household supplies and personal care) for a family of four. This is then adjusted, using an equivalence scale, to reflect the needs of different family sizes and types. The NAS panel recommended a two-parameter scale; one parameter takes into account that children consume less than adults, and the other that there are greater economies of scale in larger families. Thresholds are further adjusted for geographic variations in housing costs in different regions and city sizes.

Family resources in the NAS measure are defined as the value of cash income from all sources (e.g., earnings, welfare income), plus the value of near-money benefits that are available to buy goods and services covered by the new thresholds, minus "nondiscretionary" expenses. Near-money benefits include food stamps, housing subsidies, school lunch subsidies, home energy assistance, and the Earned Income Tax Credit (EITC). Nondiscretionary expenses subtracted include taxes, child care and other work-related expenses, and medical out-of-pocket costs. This measure is available only for the 1990–1999 period in this analysis. The U.S. Census Bureau report by Kathleen Short and her colleagues in 1999 contains detail on the implementation of the NAS poverty measure.[4]

To gauge the effect of income growth, economic inequality, and changes in family structure on poverty, I use Sheldon Danziger and Peter Gottschalk's method of employing direct standardization and simulations to calculate adjusted rates under different assumptions.[5]

A three-step procedure is used. First, to estimate the effect of income growth on poverty, I gauge the increase in per-capita income over the period.[6] For the analysis using the NAS poverty measure for the years 1990 to 1999, per-capita income growth is measured using the definition of disposable family income consistent with the income measure used in the NAS poverty calculation, as described above.[7] Using initial time t microdata, I then simulate what poverty would have been in current year $t + 1$ if everyone's income had grown at the same rate. I then compare each family's simulated income with the actual poverty line for that family size in year $t + 1$. This simulated income distribution has the same shape, or inequality, as in time t, but the mean income of $t + 1$. These adjusted poverty rates are also computed for different family types and racial/ethnic groups.

Second, I weight the group-specific poverty rates by the observed $t + 1$ demographic composition of the population (which takes family structure and changes in the racial/ethnic composition of the population into account). Four family-type categories were used: married-couple family, female-headed family, male-headed family, and unrelated individual. While unrelated individuals are not families per se, they are separate units that are included in poverty statistics. Four racial/ethnic categories were used: non-Hispanic white, non-Hispanic black, Hispanic, and non-Hispanic other. This second simulation incorporates the inequality of time t but has the mean income and demographic composition of time $t + 1$. The difference between the poverty rates from the first two simulations equals the percentage-point change in poverty that is accounted for by demographic change.

Third, the difference between the poverty rate for all persons from this second simulation and the observed $t + 1$ poverty rate equals the change in poverty that is accounted for by changes in income inequality. By construction, the sum of these three components will equal the observed percentage-point change in the poverty rate over the period.

As one would expect, controlling for changes in racial and ethnic composition modestly reduces the estimated effect of changes in inequality. To calculate the impact of inequality without controlling for racial/ethnic composition changes, one need simply subtract the effect of changes in racial/ethnic composition and the family structure–race/ethnicity interaction from the inequality effect.

Despite the limitations of this analysis—which are described at length in chapter 6—it is informative because it shows the relative association between poverty and broad trends in economic and family structure and illustrates how these associations vary by how we think about poverty.

Notes

1. INTRODUCTION

1. Robert Lampman, *Ends and Means of Reducing Income Poverty* (Chicago: Markham, 1971).

2. James Tobin, "It Can Be Done! Conquering Poverty in the U.S by 1976," *New Republic,* 3 June 1967, 14.

3. For a review of these studies, see Daniel T. Lichter and Martha L. Crowley, "Poverty in America: Beyond Welfare Reform," *Population Bulletin* 57, 2 (June 2002): 1–36.

4. Barry Bluestone and Bennett Harrison, *Growing Prosperity: The Battle for Growth with Equity in the Twenty-First Century* (Boston: Houghton Mifflin, 2000).

5. Joseph Dalaker, "Poverty in the United States: 2000," U.S. Census Bureau, Current Population Reports, series P60-214 (Washington, DC: U.S. Government Printing Office, 2001).

6. William P. O'Hare, "A New Look at Poverty in America," *Population Bulletin* 51, 2 (1996): 41–48.

7. National Research Council, *Measuring Poverty: A New Approach,* ed. Constance F. Citro and Robert T. Michael (Washington, DC: National Academy Press, 1995).

2. EARLY VIEWS OF POVERTY IN AMERICA

1. National Research Council, *Measuring Poverty,* p. 24.

2. Martin Ravallion, *Poverty Comparisons,* Fundamentals of Pure and Applied Economics, no. 56 (Chur, Switzerland: Harwood Academic Press,

1994); Martin Ravallion, "Issues in Measuring and Modeling Poverty," Policy Research Working Paper no. 1615 (Washington, DC: World Bank, 1996).

3. Adam Smith, *An Inquiry into the Nature and Causes of the Wealth of Nations* (1776; reprint, Oxford, UK: Clarendon Press, 1976), pp. 351–52.

4. Peter Townsend, *The International Analysis of Poverty* (Hemel Hempstead, UK: Harvester-Wheatsheaf, 1993), p. 10.

5. Michael B. Katz, "The Urban 'Underclass' as a Metaphor of Social Transformation," in *The "Underclass" Debate: Views from History*, ed. Michael B. Katz (Princeton, NJ: Princeton University Press, 1993), pp. 3–23.

6. Walter I. Trattner, *From Poor Law to Welfare State: A History of Social Welfare in America* (New York: The Free Press, 1994), p. 22.

7. Trattner, *From Poor Law to Welfare State*, p. 26.

8. Michael B. Katz, *In the Shadow of the Poorhouse: A Social History of Welfare in America* (New York: Basic Books, 1996).

9. Thomas J. Sugrue, "The Structure of Urban Poverty: The Reorganization of Space and Work in Three Periods of American History," in *The "Underclass" Debate*, pp. 87, 91.

10. Charles Burroughs, *A Discourse Delivered in the Chapel of the New Alms-House, in Portsmouth, N.H.* (Portsmouth, NH: J. W. Foster, 1835), p. 9, quoted in Katz, "The Urban 'Underclass,'" p. 6.

11. Herbert J. Gans, *The War against the Poor* (New York: Basic Books, 1995), p. 15.

12. See Kyle D. Kauffman and L. Lynne Kiesling, "Was There a Nineteenth Century Welfare Magnet in the United States? Preliminary Results from New York City and Brooklyn," *Quarterly Review of Economics and Finance* 37, 2 (summer 1997): 439–48; Katz, *In the Shadow of the Poorhouse*; L. Lynne Kiesling and Robert A. Margo, "Explaining the Rise in Antebellum Pauperism, 1850–1860: New Evidence," *Quarterly Review of Economics and Finance* 37, 2 (summer 1997): 405–17; Eric H. Monkkonen, "Nineteenth-Century Institutions: Dealing with the Urban 'Underclass,'" in *The "Underclass" Debate*, pp. 334–65.

13. Katz, *In the Shadow of the Poorhouse*, p. 7; Monkkonen, "Dealing with the Urban 'Underclass,'" p. 343.

14. Katz, *In the Shadow of the Poorhouse*, pp. 8, 10.

15. Sugrue, "Structure of Urban Poverty," pp. 93–94.

16. *Second Annual Report of the Children's Aid Society of New York* (New York, 1855), p. 3, quoted in Katz, "The Urban 'Underclass,'" p. 9.

17. S. Humphreys Gurteen, *Handbook of Charity Organization* (Buffalo: published by the author, 1882), p. 38, quoted in Katz, *In the Shadow of the Poorhouse*, p. 76.

18. Sugrue, "Structure of Urban Poverty," p. 95.

19. Michael B. Katz, "Reframing the 'Underclass' Debate," in *The "Underclass" Debate*, p. 446.

20. Katz, *In the Shadow of the Poorhouse*, p. 10.

21. Sugrue, "Structure of Urban Poverty," pp. 91–92.

22. Kiesling and Margo, "Explaining the Rise in Antebellum Pauperism," p. 409.

23. Robert Hunter, *Poverty* (New York: Macmillan, 1904; reprint, New York: Harper Torchbooks, 1964), pp. 11–17, quoted in Alice O'Connor, *Poverty Knowledge: Social Science, Social Policy, and the Poor in Twentieth-Century U.S. History* (Princeton, NJ: Princeton University Press, 2001), p. 33.

24. Jacqueline Jones, "Southern Diaspora: Origins of the Northern "Underclass," in *The "Underclass" Debate*, p. 31.

25. Joe William Trotter Jr., "Blacks in the Urban North: The 'Underclass Question' in Historical Perspective," in *The "Underclass" Debate*, p. 60.

26. Trotter, "Blacks in the Urban North," p. 61.

27. W. E. B. DuBois, *The Philadelphia Negro: A Social Study* (1899; reprint, Philadelphia: University of Pennsylvania Press, 1996), p. 171.

28. DuBois, *The Philadelphia Negro*, p. 273.

29. O'Connor, *Poverty Knowledge*, p. 36.

30. Trotter, "Blacks in the Urban North," pp. 58–69.

31. Sugrue, "Structure of Urban Poverty," p. 97.

32. Jonathan H. Turner, Leonard Beeghley, and Charles H. Powers, *The Emergence of Sociological Theory* (Belmont, CA: Wadsworth, 1989).

33. Gordon M. Fisher, "From Hunter to Orshansky: An Overview of (Unofficial) Poverty Lines in the United States from 1904 to 1965," U.S. Census Bureau, Poverty Measurement Working Paper, 1997 (http://www.census.gov /hhes/poverty/povmeas/papers/hstorsp4.html).

34. Charles Booth, *Life and Labour of the People of London. First Series: Poverty* (London: Macmillan and Co., 1892–1897; reprint, New York: AMS Press, 1970); Fisher, "From Hunter to Orshansky," p. 3.

35. Charles Booth, *Labour and Life of the People. Volume I: East London* (London: Williams and Norgate, 1889), p. 33, quoted in Fisher, "From Hunter to Orshansky," p. 3.

36. Fisher, "From Hunter to Orshansky," p. 5.

37. Fisher, "From Hunter to Orshansky," p. 7.

38. Gordon M. Fisher, "Is There Such a Thing as an Absolute Poverty Line over Time? Evidence from the United States, Britain, Canada, and Australia on the Income Elasticity of the Poverty Line." U.S. Census Bureau, Poverty Measurement Working Paper, 1995 (http://www.census.gov/hhes/poverty/povmeas /papers/elastap4.html), p. 7.

39. Fisher, "From Hunter to Orshansky," p. 22.

40. Fisher, "From Hunter to Orshansky," p. 48.

41. Fisher, "From Hunter to Orshansky," p. 30.

42. Fisher, "From Hunter to Orshansky," pp. 32–41.

43. John Kenneth Galbraith, *The Affluent Society* (1958; reprint, New York: New American Library, 1964), p. 251.

44. Michael Harrington, *The Other America: Poverty in the United States* (New York: Macmillan, 1962).

45. O'Connor, "Poverty Knowledge," p. 152.

46. O'Connor, "Poverty Knowledge," p. 154.

47. Mollie Orshansky, "Children of the Poor," *Social Security Bulletin* 26, 7 (1963): 3–13; Mollie Orshansky, "Counting the Poor: Another Look at the Poverty Profile," *Social Security Bulletin* 28, 1 (1965): 3–29.

3. METHODS OF MEASURING POVERTY

1. Kate Shatzkin, "Old Poverty Line Inadequate to Reflect Today's Family Needs: Experts Struggle to Find an Alternative," *Baltimore Sun,* 13 September 2000 (available through www.baltimoresun.com).

2. Emil Munsterberg, "The Problem of Poverty," *American Journal of Sociology* 10, 3 (November 1904): 335.

3. National Research Council, *Measuring Poverty,* p. 31. An interesting discussion of these issues is also contained in James E. Foster, "Absolute versus Relative Poverty," *American Economic Review* 88, 2, Papers and Proceedings of the 110th Annual Meeting of the American Economic Association (May 1998): 335–41.

4. National Research Council, *Measuring Poverty,* pp. 1, 24.

5. National Research Council, *Measuring Poverty,* p. 31. See also Amartya Sen, "Poor, Relatively Speaking," *Oxford Economic Papers* 35, 2 (1983): 153–69.

6. National Research Council, *Measuring Poverty,* p. 24. For details on the development of the U.S. official measure, see also Gordon M. Fisher, "The Development of the Orshansky Poverty Thresholds and Their Subsequent History as the Official U.S. Poverty Measure," U.S. Census Bureau, Poverty Measurement Working Paper, 1997 (http://www.census.gov/hhes/poverty/povmeas /papers/orshansky.html).

7. The food plan also reflected the differing food needs of adults under and over sixty-five, and for units with only one or two people. Orshansky followed different procedures to calculate thresholds for one- and two-person units to allow for the relatively larger fixed costs that small family units face.

8. Since its adoption, the official poverty measure has undergone minor changes. In 1969 the Consumer Price Index (CPI) began to be used to update thresholds to reflect price changes, instead of the per-capita cost of foods in the Economy Food Plan. Farm thresholds were also raised from 70 to 85 percent of the nonfarm thresholds. In 1981 nonfarm thresholds were applied to all families, and thresholds for families headed by women and men were averaged, and the largest family size category for the thresholds was raised from families of seven or more to families of nine or more people.

9. Sen, "Poor, Relatively Speaking," p. 159.

10. Fisher, "From Hunter to Orshansky," pp. 26–38.

11. Fisher, "From Hunter to Orshansky," pp. 5–11.

12. For a detailed discussion, see Peter Townsend, *International Analysis of Poverty.*

13. Many of the problems are also discussed in Patricia Ruggles, *Drawing the Line: Alternative Poverty Measures and Their Implications for Public Policy* (Washington, DC: Urban Institute Press, 1990); and National Research Council, *Measuring Poverty.*

14. For a complete list of items included in the official Census Bureau income definition, see Joseph Dalaker and Mary Naifeh, "Poverty in the United States: 1997," U.S. Census Bureau, Current Population Reports, series P60-201 (Washington, DC: U.S. Government Printing Office, 1998).

15. Evidence for the growing effect of the EITC comes from Center on Budget and Policy Priorities, "Strengths of the Safety Net: How the EITC, Social Security, and Other Government Programs Affect Poverty," Center on Budget and Policy Priorities Research Report 98-020, March 1998; John Iceland and Josh Kim, "Poverty among Working Families: Insights from an Improved Measure," *Social Science Quarterly* 82, 2 (June 2001): 253–67; John Iceland, Kathleen Short, Thesia I. Garner, and David Johnson, "Are Children Worse Off? Evaluating Child Well-Being Using a New (and Improved) Measure of Poverty," *Journal of Human Resources* 36, 2 (2001): 398–412.

16. National Research Council, *Measuring Poverty,* pp. 1–13.

17. National Research Council, *Measuring Poverty,* pp. 1–13.

18. Note that a "family" unit under the official measure can also consist of a single unrelated individual. That is, even though these individuals are not a "family" per se they are counted as separate units in the family unit of analysis.

19. Trends in cohabitation are found in Lynne M. Casper and Philip N. Cohen, "How Does POSSLQ Measure Up? Historical Estimates of Cohabitation," *Demography* 37, 2 (May 2000): 237–45. Discussion of how using different units affects poverty measurement is in John Iceland, "The 'Family/Couple/Household' Unit of Analysis in Poverty Measurement," *Journal of Economic and Social Measurement* 26 (2000): 253–65.

20. See National Research Council, *Measuring Poverty.*

21. These themes are discussed in detail in, among other works, Amartya Sen, *Inequality Reexamined* (Cambridge, MA: Harvard University Press, 1992); Townsend, *International Analysis of Poverty.*

22. Smith, *The Wealth of Nations,* quoted in National Research Council, *Measuring Poverty,* p. 21.

23. Examples of relative poverty lines defined in this way can be found in, among other papers, Gary Burtless and Timothy M. Smeeding, "The Level, Trend, and Composition of Poverty," in *Understanding Poverty,* ed. Sheldon Danziger and Robert Haveman (Cambridge, MA: Harvard University Press, 2001), pp. 27–68; Michael O'Higgins and Stephen Jenkins, "Poverty in the EC: Estimates for 1975, 1980, and 1985," in *Analysing Poverty in the European Community: Policy Issues, Research Options, and Data Sources,* ed. Rudolph Teekens and Bernard M.S. van Praag (Luxembourg: Office of Official Publications of the European Communities, 1990), pp. 187–211; Paul Johnson and Steven Webb, "Official Statistics on Poverty in the United Kingdom," in *Poverty Measurement for Economies in Transition in Eastern European Countries* (Warsaw: Polish Statistical Association and Polish Central Statistical Office, 1992), pp. 135–54.

24. Barbara Ehrenreich, *Nickel and Dimed: On (Not) Getting By in America* (New York: Metropolitan Books, 2001), 199–200.

25. Organization for Economic Cooperation and Development, *OECD Employment Outlook* (Paris: OECD, June 2001).

26. John Micklewright, "Social Exclusion and Children: A European View for a US Debate," Center for Analysis and Social Exclusion paper no. 51 (London School of Economics, February 2002), p. 1.

27. John F. Cogan, "Dissent," in National Research Council, *Measuring Poverty,* pp. 385–90.

28. National Research Council, *Measuring Poverty,* p. 126; Sen, "Poor, Relatively Speaking," p. 156.

29. See James D. Davidson, "Theories and Measures of Poverty: Toward a Holistic Approach," *Sociological Focus* 18, 3 (August 1985): 187–88.

30. United Nations Children's Fund (UNICEF) Innocenti Research Centre, "Child Poverty in Rich Nations," *Innocenti Report Card,* no. 1 (June 2000): 6.

31. UNICEF Innocenti Research Centre, "Child Poverty in Rich Nations," p. 6.

32. These criticisms are discussed in National Research Council, *Measuring Poverty,* p. 125; Sen, "Poor, Relatively Speaking," p. 156.

33. UNICEF Innocenti Research Centre, "Child Poverty in Rich Nations," p. 22.

34. A discussion of these studies is in Gordon Fisher, "'Enough for a Family to Live On?'—Questions from Members of the American Public and New Perspectives from British Social Scientists" (paper presented at the Association for Public Policy Analysis and Management annual research conference, Washington, DC, 2 November 2001); Martin Ravallion, "Poverty Lines in Theory and Practice," Living Standards Measurement Study (LSMS) working paper no. 133 (Washington, DC: World Bank, 1998).

35. Denton R. Vaughan, "Exploring the Use of the Public's Views to Set Income Poverty Thresholds and Adjust Them over Time," *Social Security Bulletin* 56, 2 (1993): 22.

36. National Research Council, *Measuring Poverty,* p. 136. The variations in question wording among these three studies were minor, though there were also some differences in the estimation methodologies used. The $32,530 figure comes from Klaas De Vos and Thesia I. Garner, "An Evaluation of Subjective Poverty Definitions: Comparing Results from the U.S and the Netherlands," *Review of Income and Wealth* 37, 3 (September 1991): 267–85. The lower figure, $12,160, comes from Diane Colasanto, Arie Kapteyn, and Jacques van der Gaag, "Two Subjective Definitions of Poverty: Results from the Wisconsin Basic Needs Study," *Journal of Human Resources* 28, 1 (1984): 127–38. This study asked a sample of Wisconsin residents about after-tax income needed. The third study is Sheldon H. Danziger, Jacques van der Gaag, Michael K. Taussig, and Eugene Smolensky, "The Direct Measurement of Welfare Levels: How Much Does It Cost to Make Ends Meet?" *Review of Economics and Statistics* 66, 3 (1984): 500–05. This study estimated a threshold figure of $24,680. The questions did not specify whether respondents were to answer in before-tax or in after-tax terms.

37. See also Sen, *Inequality Reexamined*; Robert Haveman and Andrew Bershadker, "Self-Reliance as a Poverty Criterion: Trends in Earnings-Capacity Poverty, 1975–1992," *AEA Papers and Proceedings* 88, 2 (May 1998): 342–47.

38. Discussion of hardship measures can be found in Susan E. Mayer and Christopher Jencks, "Poverty and the Distribution of Material Hardship," *Journal of Human Resources* 24, 1 (winter 1989): 88–114; Kurt J. Bauman, "Extended Measures of Well-Being: Meeting Basic Needs," U.S. Census Bureau, Current Population Reports, series P70-67 (Washington, DC: U.S. Government

Printing Office, 1999); Sondra G. Beverly, "Using Measures of Material Hardship," *Focus* 21, 2 (fall 2000): 65–69.

39. Beverly, "Using Measures of Material Hardship," p. 65.

40. Robert E. Rector, Kirk A. Johnson, and Sarah E. Youssef, "The Extent of Material Hardship and Poverty in the United States," *Review of Social Economy* 57, 3 (September 1999): 351–87.

41. Sondra G. Beverly, "Measures of Material Hardship: Rationale and Recommendations," *Journal of Poverty* 5, 1 (2001): 23–41.

42. Micklewright, "Social Exclusion and Children," p. 3.

43. A. B. Atkinson and John Hills, "Social Exclusion, Poverty and Unemployment," Centre for Analysis of Social Exclusion paper no. 4 (1998); see also Micklewright, "Social Exclusion and Children," 9.

44. Kurt J. Bauman, "Direct Measures of Poverty as Indicators of Economic Need: Evidence from the Survey of Income and Program Participation," U.S. Census Bureau, Population Division Technical Working Paper no. 30 (1998).

45. Amartya Sen, "Poverty: An Ordinal Approach to Measurement," *Econometrica* 44 (1976): 219–31; James E. Foster and Anthony F. Shorrocks, "Poverty Orderings," *Econometrica* 56, 1 (January 1998): 173–77.

46. See, for example, Dalaker, "Poverty in the United States: 2000."

47. National Research Council, *Measuring Poverty.*

48. See Kathleen Short, "Experimental Poverty Measures: 1999," U.S. Census Bureau, Current Population Report, Consumer Income, series P60-216 (Washington, DC: U.S. Government Printing Office, 2001); Kathleen Short, Thesia I. Garner, David Johnson, and Patricia Doyle, "Experimental Poverty Measures: 1990 to 1997," U.S. Census Bureau, Current Population Report, Consumer Income, series P60-205 (Washington, DC: U.S. Government Printing Office, 1999).

49. Short et al., "Experimental Poverty Measures: 1990 to 1997," pp. 4–5.

50. The NAS panel recommended a two-parameter scale. One parameter takes into account that children consume less than adults and the other that there are economies of scale in larger families. The Short et al. report, "Experimental Poverty Measures: 1990 to 1997," also discusses a three-parameter scale developed by David Betson in "Is Everything Relative? The Role of Equivalence Scales in Poverty Measurement" (unpublished manuscript, University of Notre Dame, 1996), in which the third parameter provides more economies of scale between singles and childless couples and more similarity between the scales for families of one parent with two children and those of two parents with one child.

51. Interested readers should refer to National Research Council, *Measuring Poverty,* for a more detailed discussion of these various elements. Short et al., "Experimental Poverty Measures: 1990 to 1997," also contains detail on the actual operationalization and implementation of the NAS poverty measure.

52. Details are contained in Short et al., "Experimental Poverty Measures: 1990 to 1997," and Short, Experimental Poverty Measures: 1999."

53. After-tax income is used in order to make this threshold consistent with how the other three thresholds were originally devised and constructed.

54. This question has not been asked by Gallup or the General Social Survey (the sources of the earlier data) since 1993.

55. National Research Council, *Measuring Poverty,* pp. 55–56, 106, and 153–54.

56. See Short, "Experimental Poverty Measures: 1999"; Short et al., "Experimental Poverty Measures: 1990 to 1997."

57. To adjust the poverty threshold for families of different sizes, a single-parameter equivalence scale—with a square-root-of-household-size factor—is used in the relative measure. Details about the calculation of the NAS measure are in Short et al., "Experimental Poverty Measures: 1990 to 1997," pp. C1–C27.

58. National Research Council, *Measuring Poverty.*

4. CHARACTERISTICS OF THE POVERTY POPULATION

1. These results are reported by Martin Gilens, "Race and Poverty in America: Public Misperceptions and the American News Media," *Public Opinion Quarterly* 60, 4 (1996): 516–17. The first set of responses come from an analysis of data collected in the 1991 National Race and Politics Study, administered by the Survey Research Center at the University of California–Berkeley, and the second from a CBS–*New York Times* national telephone survey, conducted December 6–9, 1994. Gilens notes that people's perceptions of what constitutes poverty may differ from the official measure. Using a lower poverty threshold would tend to produce higher estimates of the proportion of the poor who are black. However, since the public's view tends to support a *higher* poverty threshold, as reported in chapter 2, blacks would comprise an even smaller proportion of the poverty population.

2. Dalaker, "Poverty in the United States: 2000," pp. 18–20.

3. Gilens, "Race and Poverty in America," pp. 521, 524.

4. Gilens, "Race and Poverty in America," p. 517.

5. Dalaker, "Poverty in the United States: 2000," p. 18.

6. For more discussion of the effect of Social Security on poverty, see Center on Budget and Policy Priorities, "Strengths of the Safety Net"; Bradly R. Schiller, *The Economics of Poverty and Discrimination,* 8th ed. (Upper Saddle River, NJ: Prentice Hall, 2001).

7. National Research Council, *Measuring Poverty.*

8. Due to the small sample size of American Indians and Alaska Natives in the Current Population Survey, three years of data are pooled to produce a reliable poverty rate estimate.

9. Iceland and Kim, "Poverty among Working Families"; John Iceland, Kathleen Short, Thesia I. Garner, and David Johnson, "Are Children Worse Off?"; Short et al., "Experimental Poverty Measures: 1990 to 1997."

10. Amartya Sen, "Poverty: An Ordinal Approach to Measurement."

11. Dalaker, "Poverty in the United States: 2000."

12. Mark S. Littman, "Poverty in the 1980's: Are the Poor Getting Poorer?" *Monthly Labor Review* (June 1989): 13–18; O'Hare, "A New Look at Poverty in America."

13. Heather Boushey, Chauna Brocht, Bethney Gundersen, and Jared Bernstein, *Hardships in America: The Real Story of Working Families* (Washington, DC: Economic Policy Institute, 2001).

14. The Survey of Income and Program Participation (SIPP) is a nationally representative longitudinal survey. The data on hardships from the 1993 panel were collected in 1995, the last year of that panel. The data from the 1997 National Survey of American Families (NSAF) reflected responses about hardships in 1996. The NSAF is a survey of economic, health, and social characteristics of children, adults under age sixty-five, and their families.

15. Rector, Johnson, and Youssef, "The Extent of Material Hardship and Poverty in the United States."

16. Lichter and Crowley, "Poverty in America: Beyond Welfare Reform"; Chanjin Chung and Samuel L. Myers Jr., "Do the Poor Pay More for Food? An Analysis of Grocery Store Availability and Food Price Disparities," *Journal of Consumer Affairs* 33, 2 (1999): 276–91; Phil R. Kaufman, "Rural Poor Have Less Access to Supermarkets, Large Grocery Stores," *Rural Development* 13, 3 (1999): 19–25.

17. Townsend, *International Analysis of Poverty,* p. 10.

18. Two authors who held this view, though they had otherwise differed on many points, include Michael Harrington (*The Other America*) and Oscar Lewis ("The Culture of Poverty," *Scientific American* 215 [1966]: 19–25).

19. For more on longitudinal studies on poverty, see Mary Jo Bane and David Ellwood, "Slipping into and out of Poverty: The Dynamics of Spells," *Journal of Human Resources* 21 (1986): 1–23; Peter Gottschalk, Sara McLanahan, and Gary Sandefur, "The Dynamics and Intergenerational Transmission of Poverty and Welfare Participation," in *Confronting Poverty,* ed. Sheldon Danziger, Gary Sandefur, and Daniel Weinberg (Cambridge, MA: Harvard University Press, 1994), pp. 85–108; Patricia Ruggles and Roberton Williams, "Longitudinal Measures of Poverty: Accounting for Income and Assets over Time," *Review of Income and Wealth* 35, 3 (1989): 225–43; Ann Huff Stevens, "The Dynamics of Poverty Spells: Updating Bane and Ellwood," *AEA Papers and Proceedings* 84, 2 (May 1994): 34–37: Ann Huff Stevens, "Climbing out of Poverty, Falling Back In: Measuring the Persistence of Poverty over Multiple Spells," *Journal of Human Resources* 34, 3 (summer 1999): 557–88.

20. Rebecca Blank, *It Takes a Nation: A New Agenda for Fighting Poverty* (Princeton, NJ: Princeton University Press, 1997).

21. These statistics likely underestimate the actual length of all poverty spells, given that poverty spells whose beginnings are not observed in a given longitudinal survey tend to be longer in duration (John Iceland, *The Dynamics of Poverty Spells and Issues of Left-Censoring,* Population Studies Center research report 97-378, University of Michigan–Ann Arbor, 1997).

22. Bane and Ellwood, "Dynamics of Spells," p. 12.

23. Mary Naifeh, "Dynamics of Economic Well-Being, Poverty, 1993–94: Trap Door? Revolving Door? Or Both?" U.S. Census Bureau, Current Population Reports, series P70-63 (Washington, DC: U.S. Government Printing Office, 1998), p. 1.

24. Stevens, "Climbing out of Poverty, Falling Back In."

25. Bane and Ellwood, "Dynamics of Spells," p. 12.

26. Stevens, "Updating Bane and Ellwood," pp. 34–37.

27. Stevens, "Climbing out of Poverty, Falling Back In."

28. Joel A. Devine, Mark Plunkett, and James D. Wright, "The Chronicity of Poverty: Evidence from the PSID, 1968–1987," *Social Forces* 70, 3 (March 1992): 787–812.

29. Blank, *It Takes a Nation,* pp. 23–24.

30. See Greg Duncan, "The Economic Environment of Childhood," in *Children in Poverty: Child Development and Public Policy,* ed. A. Huston (New York: Cambridge University Press, 1991).

31. Gottschalk, McLanahan, and Sandefur, "Dynamics and Intergenerational Transmission of Poverty and Welfare Participation," p. 85.

32. Gary Solon, "Intergenerational Income Mobility in the United States," *American Economic Review* 82 (1992): 393–408.

33. Mary Corcoran, "Mobility, Persistence, and the Intergenerational Determinants of Children's Success," *Focus* 21, 2 (fall 2000): 16–20.

34. See Mary Corcoran and Terry Adams, "Race, Sex, and the Intergenerational Transmission of Poverty," in *Consequences of Growing Up Poor,* ed. Greg J. Duncan and Jeanne Brooks-Gunn (New York: Russell Sage Foundation, 1997), pp. 461–517.

35. Lawrence Mead, *Beyond Entitlement: The Social Obligations of Citizenship* (New York: Free Press, 1986).

36. William Julius Wilson, *The Truly Disadvantaged: The Inner City, the Underclass, and Public Policy* (Chicago: University of Chicago Press, 1987).

37. Corcoran and Adams, "Race, Sex, and the Intergenerational Transmission of Poverty," pp. 511–15.

38. For more on rural poverty, see Daniel H. Weinberg, "Rural Pockets of Poverty," *Rural Sociology* 52 (1987): 398–408; Daniel T. Lichter and Leif Jensen, "Rural America in Transition: Poverty and Welfare at the Turn of the 21st Century" (paper presented at Rural Dimensions of Welfare Reform: A Research Conference on Poverty, Welfare, and Food Assistance, sponsored by the Joint Center for Poverty Research, Northwestern University/University of Chicago, May 4, 2000); Lichter and Crowley, "Poverty in America: Beyond Welfare Reform"; Thomas A. Lyson and William W. Falk, *Forgotten Places* (Lawrence: University Press of Kansas, 1992).

39. Robert Gibbs, "Nonmetro Labor Markets in the Era of Welfare Reform," *Rural America* 16, 3 (fall 2001): 11–21.

40. Lichter and Crowley, "Poverty in America: Beyond Welfare Reform," pp. 23–24.

41. Lichter and Crowley, "Poverty in America: Beyond Welfare Reform," p. 24.

42. See Paul A. Jargowsky, *Poverty and Place: Ghettos, Barrios, and the American City* (New York: Russell Sage Foundation, 1997); also see Wilson, *The Truly Disadvantaged.*

43. Sugrue, "The Structure of Urban Poverty," pp. 92–93.

44. Jargowsky, *Poverty and Place,* p. 11.

45. Jargowsky, *Poverty and Place,* pp. 38–43.

46. O'Hare, "A New Look at Poverty in America," p. 26.

47. Jargowsky, *Poverty and Place*, p. 38.

48. Jargowsky, *Poverty and Place*, pp. 89–115.

49. Paul A. Jargowsky, "Beyond the Street Corner: The Hidden Diversity of High-Poverty Neighborhoods," *Urban Geography* 17, 7 (1996): 598.

50. Michael G. H. McGeary, "Ghetto Poverty and Federal Policies and Programs," in *Inner-City Poverty in the United States*, ed. Laurence Lynn Jr. and Michael McGeary (Washington, DC: National Academy Press, 1990).

51. Douglas S. Massey and Nancy Denton, *American Apartheid* (Cambridge, MA: Harvard University Press, 1993).

52. Massey and Denton, *American Apartheid*, p. 2.

53. John F. Kain, "Housing Segregation, Negro Employment, and Metropolitan Decentralization," *Quarterly Journal of Economics* 82 (1968): 175–97.

54. For more on skills mismatches, see Harry J. Holzer, "The Spatial Mismatch Hypothesis: What Has the Evidence Shown?" *Urban Studies* 28, 1 (1991): 105–22; John Kasarda, "Structural Factors Affecting the Location and Timing of Underclass Growth," *Urban Geography* 11 (1990): 234–64; Wilson, *The Truly Disadvantaged*.

55. Two influential proponents of this view are Charles Murray, *Losing Ground: American Social Policy, 1950–1980* (New York: Basic Books, 1984); Lawrence Mead, *The New Politics of Poverty: The Nonworking Poor in America* (New York: Basic Books, 1992).

56. See Murray, *Losing Ground*.

57. See Mead, *New Politics of Poverty*.

58. Wilson, *The Truly Disadvantaged*, p. 14.

59. See Wilson, *The Truly Disadvantaged*, for a detailed discussion.

60. Jargowsky, *Poverty and Place*, p. 183.

61. Swiss Agency for Development and Cooperation (SDC), "The SDC Policy for Social Development," in *The Challenge of Eliminating World Poverty*, ed. SDC Publications on Development (Berne: SDC, 2000), pp. 14–61.

62. Christian Comeliau, "Poverty—A Hopeless Battle?" in *The Challenge of Eliminating World Poverty*, pp. 74–95.

63. World Bank, *World Development Report, 2000/2001: Attacking Poverty* (Oxford: Oxford University Press, 2001), p. 45.

64. World Bank, "Income Poverty: The Latest Global Numbers," *Data on Poverty* website: www.worldbank.org/poverty/data/trends/income.htm (2001).

65. The $1 a day figure was measured in purchasing power parity (PPP) terms. The numbers in the table are estimated from the countries in each region for which at least one survey was available during the 1985–1998 period. The proportion of the population covered by each survey varied across regions, ranging from 52.5 percent in the Middle East and North Africa to 97.9 percent in South Asia. The World Bank (*World Development Report, 2000/2001*, p. 17) notes that survey dates often do not coincide with dates given in the table. To line them up with the dates given, the survey estimates were adjusted using the closest available survey for each country and applying the consumption growth rate from national accounts. Assuming that the sample of countries covered by surveys is representative of the region as a whole, the numbers of

poor are then estimated by region. Further details of the methodology can be found in Shaohua Chen and Martin Ravallion, "How Did the World's Poorest Fare in the 1990s?" World Bank, Policy Research Working Paper, 2000.

66. World Bank, "Income Poverty: The Latest Global Numbers."

67. World Bank, *World Development Report, 2000/2001*, p. 13.

68. World Bank, "Social Indicators—Health: Life Expectancy, Infant and Child Mortality, Malnutrition," *Data on Poverty* (www.worldbank.org/poverty /data/trends/mort.htm), 2001.

69. Centers for Disease Control and Prevention, "Infant Mortality Rates, Fetal Mortality Rates, and Perinatal Mortality Rates, According to Race: United States, Selected Years, 1950–99," National Center for Health Statistics, Health Data, table 23 (www.cdc.gov/nchs/about/major/dvs/mortdata.htm), 2001.

70. World Bank, "Social Indicators—Health."

71. Timothy Smeeding, Lee Rainwater, and Gary Burtless, "United States Poverty in a Cross-National Context," Luxembourg Income Study Working Paper no. 244, September 2000.

72. Construction of an absolute poverty threshold that is consistent across countries is challenging because national poverty rates are sensitive to the PPP rate chosen. PPP exchange rates were developed to compare gross domestic product (GDP) across countries, not poverty in particular. Smeeding, Rainwater, and Burtless, "United States Poverty in a Cross-National Context," p. 6, chose 1999 OECD PPPs. Several limitations of using PPPs are noted by Bruce Bradbury and Markus Jantti, "Child Poverty across Twenty-Five Countries," in *The Dynamics of Child Poverty in Industrialised Countries*, ed. Bruce Bradbury, Stephen P. Jenkins, and John Micklewright (Cambridge, UK: Cambridge University Press, 2001). First, because different population groups have different consumption patterns, they may face different average prices; second, the goods priced may not be of comparable quality in different countries; third, PPPs were developed for comparison of GDP, which includes capital goods prices that do not directly affect consumer living standards; fourth, there is the challenge of generating comparable price indexes for components of personal consumption where there is substantial government contribution toward these services. An example is health care, where in many industrialized countries the bulk of such costs are met by the state. The United States, in contrast, tends to have lower government contributions to such services and higher family out-of-pocket costs. The net effect is that absolute poverty may be a little overestimated in countries with high levels of government subsidies vis-à-vis the United States.

73. For both the absolute and relative poverty measures Smeeding, Rainwater, and Burtless ("United States Poverty in a Cross-National Context," pp. 6–7) use the broadest income definition that still preserves comparability across nations. They define income as disposable cash and noncash income: money income minus direct income and payroll taxes and including all cash and near-cash government transfers, such as food stamps and cash housing allowances, and refundable tax credits, such as the Earned Income Tax Credit.

74. Smeeding, Rainwater, and Burtless, "United States Poverty in a Cross-National Context," pp. 1–2.

75. See Susan E. Mayer, "A Comparison of Poverty and Living Conditions in the United States, Canada, Sweden, and Germany," in *Poverty, Inequality, and the Future of Social Policy*, ed. Katherine McFate, Roger Lawson, and William Julius Wilson (New York: Russell Sage Foundation, 1996).

76. Mayer, "Comparison of Poverty and Living Conditions," pp. 127–40.

77. For more on sources of differences, see Lee Rainwater and Timothy M. Smeeding, "Doing Poorly: The Real Income of American Children in a Comparative Perspective," in *Crisis in American Institutions,* ed. J. H. Skolnick and E. Currie (Boston: Allyn & Bacon, 1995); Smeeding, Rainwater, and Burtless, "United States Poverty in a Cross-National Context"; Bradbury and Jantti, "Child Poverty across Twenty-Five Countries."

78. Mayer, "Comparison of Poverty and Living Conditions," p. 109.

79. All figures from Bradbury and Jantti, "Child Poverty across Twenty-Five Countries."

80. Rainwater and Smeeding, "Doing Poorly," p. 19.

81. See Amartya Sen, *Development as Freedom* (New York: Knopf, 1999).

5. CAUSES OF POVERTY

1. Oscar Lewis, *La Vida* (New York: Random House, 1966), quoted in Schiller, *Economics of Poverty and Discrimination,* p. 127.

2. Lichter and Crowley, "Poverty in America: Beyond Welfare Reform," p. 19.

3. O'Connor, *Poverty Knowledge,* p. 143.

4. David B. Grusky, "The Contours of Social Stratification," in *Social Stratification in Sociological Perspective*, ed. David B. Grusky (Boulder, CO: Westview Press, 1994), p. 11.

5. Karl Marx, "Classes in Capitalism and Pre-capitalism," reprinted in *Social Stratification in Sociological Perspective*, pp. 69–78.

6. Karl Marx, "Value and Surplus Value," reprinted in *Social Stratification in Sociological Perspective*, pp. 80–82.

7. Max Weber, "Class, Status, Party," reprinted in *Social Stratification in Sociological Perspective*, p. 121.

8. U.S. Census Bureau, "Population and Housing Counts: 1790–1990," Selected Historical Census Data, Population and Housing Counts Internet report, CPH-2-1, table 16 (www.census.gov/population/www/censusdata/pop-hc.html), 1993; U.S. Census Bureau, "DP-1. Profile of General Demographic Characteristics: 2000," Census 2000 summary file 1 (SF 1), 100-Percent Data Quick Table, American FactFinder tabulation (factfinder.census.gov), 2000.

9. U.S. Census Bureau, "Percent of People 25 Years Old and Over Who Have Completed High School or College, by Race, Hispanic Origin and Sex: Selected Years 1940 to 1999," Educational Attainment Historical Tables, table A-2, Internet release data (www.census.gov/population/socdemo/education/tableA-2.txt), 15 September 2000.

10. See Bluestone and Harrison, *Growing Prosperity.*

11. While the official time series of poverty statistics begins in 1959, researchers have extended the time series backward, using the constant official

threshold (adjusted only for inflation), as defined by Mollie Orshansky in the mid-1960s.

12. World Bank, *World Development Report 2000/2001*.

13. See, for example, Robert Haveman and Jonathan Schwabish, "Economic Growth and Poverty: A Return to Normalcy?" *Focus* 20, 2 (1999): 1–7; Rebecca Blank, "Why Has Economic Growth Been Such an Ineffective Tool against Poverty in Recent Years?" in *Poverty and Inequality: The Political Economy of Redistribution*, ed. Jon Neil (Kalamazoo, MI: W. E. Upjohn Institute for Employment Research, 1997); Blank, *It Takes a Nation*.

14. Bluestone and Harrison, *Growing Prosperity*, pp. 28–30.

15. Richard Freeman, "The Rising Tide Lifts . . ." *Focus* 21, 2 (2000): 27–31.

16. Danziger and Gottschalk, *America Unequal*.

17. Sugrue, "Structure of Urban Poverty," p. 87.

18. Sugrue, "Structure of Urban Poverty," pp. 88–91.

19. Sugrue, "Structure of Urban Poverty," pp. 95–97.

20. Bluestone and Harrison, *Growing Prosperity*, p. 183.

21. Bluestone and Harrison, *Growing Prosperity*, pp. 183, 185.

22. Freeman, "Rising Tide," pp. 27–31.

23. Changes in family structure and the demographic composition of the population have likely played a role (see Sara McLanahan and Lynne Casper, "Growing Diversity and Inequality in the American Family," in *State of the Union: America in the 1990s*, vol. 2, ed. Reynolds Farley [New York: Russell Sage Foundation, 1995]); the effect of family structure on poverty is discussed later in this chapter and in chapter 6.

24. For a more detailed description of the skills mismatch hypothesis, see Harry J. Holzer and Wayne Vroman, "Mismatches and the Urban Labor Market," in *Urban Labor Markets and Job Opportunity*, ed. George Peterson and Wayne Vroman (Washington, DC: Urban Institute Press, 1992), pp. 81–112; George E. Peterson and Wayne Vroman, "Urban Labor Markets and Economic Opportunity," in *Urban Labor Markets and Job Opportunity*, pp. 1–29; Harry J. Holzer, *What Employers Want: Job Prospects for Less-Educated Workers* (New York: Russell Sage Foundation, 1996).

25. See, for example, Richard Murnane, "Education and the Well-Being of the Next Generation," in *Confronting Poverty*, pp. 289–307; Barry Bluestone, "The Inequality Express," *The American Prospect* 20 (winter 1994): 81–93; Sheldon Danziger and Daniel H. Weinberg, "The Historical Record: Trends in Family Income, Inequality, and Poverty," in *Confronting Poverty*, pp. 18–50.

26. Blank, *It Takes a Nation*, p. 61.

27. See John Kasarda, "Caught in the Web of Change," *Society* (November–December 1983): 41–47; John Kasarda, "Urban Industrial Transition and the Underclass," *Annals of the American Academy* 501 (January 1989): 26–47.

28. John Iceland, "Urban Labor Markets and Individual Transitions out of Poverty," *Demography* 34, 3 (1997): 429–41; Bennet Harrison and Barry Bluestone, *The Great U-Turn: Corporate Restructuring and the Polarizing of America* (New York: Basic Books, 1990).

29. Danziger and Gottschalk, *America Unequal,* p. 137.

30. Danziger and Gottschalk, *America Unequal,* pp. 140–43; Bluestone and Harrison, *Growing Prosperity,* pp. 190–97.

31. Bluestone and Harrison, *Growing Prosperity,* pp. 190–97.

32. Danziger and Gottschalk, *America Unequal,* pp. 130–31.

33. Jared Bernstein, Elizabeth C. McNichol, Lawrence Mishel, and Robert Zahradnik, "Pulling Apart: A State-by-State Analysis of Income Trends," Center on Budget and Policy Priorities and Economic Policy Institute Report, January 2000.

34. See Paul Osterman, *Securing Prosperity* (Princeton, NJ: Princeton University Press, 1999).

35. Iceland and Kim, "Poverty among Working Families." A "full-time working family" is defined as one in which family members work at least 1,750 hours in total over the previous year. The 1,750 figure is equivalent to a work effort of 35 hours a week for fifty weeks. A "part-time working family" is defined here as one in which the total number of hours worked by family members ranges from 50 to 1,749 hours in the previous year.

36. See chapter 3 for more details about the two measures.

37. See Linda Barrington, "Does a Rising Tide Lift All Boats?" The Conference Board, research report 1271-00-RR, 2000.

38. Interested readers should refer to Grusky's edited volume, *Social Stratification in Sociological Perspective,* for an in-depth discussion of these perspectives.

39. Max Weber, "Open and Closed Relationships," in *Social Stratification in Sociological Perspective,* p. 128.

40. Frank Parkin, "Marxism and Class Theory: A Bourgeois Critique," in *Social Stratification in Sociological Perspective,* pp. 141–54.

41. Peter M. Blau, Otis Dudley Duncan, and Andrea Tyree, "The Process of Stratification," in *Social Stratification in Sociological Perspective,* pp. 317–29.

42. O'Hare, "A New Look at Poverty in America."

43. C. Price, "The Study of Assimilation," in *Sociological Studies: Migration,* ed. J. A. Jackson (Cambridge, UK: Cambridge University Press, 1969).

44. Schiller, *Economics of Poverty and Discrimination,* pp. 159–66.

45. See E. Bonacich, "A Theory of Ethnic Antagonism: The Split Labor Market," *American Sociological Review* 37 (October 1972): 547–59; Gary S. Becker, *The Economics of Discrimination* (Chicago: University of Chicago Press, 1971).

46. Dennis P. Hogan and M. Pazul, "The Occupational and Earnings Returns to Education among Black Men in the North," *American Journal of Sociology* 90 (1982): 584–607; Michael J. Piore, "The Dual Labor Market: Theory and Implications," in *Social Stratification in Sociological Perspective,* pp. 359–61.

47. Shelly J. Lundberg and Richard Startz, "Inequality and Race: Models and Policy," in *Meritocracy and Economic Inequality,* ed. Kenneth Arrow, Samuel Bowles, and Steven Durlauf (Princeton, NJ: Princeton University Press, 2000), p. 273.

48. Jones, "Southern Diaspora" p. 31; Trotter, "Blacks in the Urban North," p. 60.

49. William Julius Wilson, *The Declining Significance of Race: Blacks and Changing American Institutions* (Chicago: University of Chicago Press, 1978).

50. Wilson, *The Truly Disadvantaged*.

51. Glenn C. Loury, "What's Next? Some Reflections on the Poverty Conference," *Focus* 21, 2 (fall 2000): 60.

52. Michael Hout, "Occupational Mobility of Black Men, 1962 to 1973," in *Social Stratification in Sociological Perspective*, pp. 531–42; Reynolds Farley, *Blacks and Whites: Narrowing the Gap?* (Cambridge, MA: Harvard University Press, 1984); Arthur Sakamoto, Huei-Hsia Wu, and Jessie M. Tzeng, "The Declining Significance of Race among American Men during the Latter Half of the Twentieth Century," *Demography* 37, 1 (2000): 41–51; G. Farkas and K. Vicknair, "Appropriate Tests of Racial Wage Discrimination Require Controls for Cognitive Skill: Comment on Cancio, Evans, and Maume," *American Sociological Review* 1 (1996): 557–60.

53. Sakamoto, Wu, and Tzeng, "Declining Significance of Race," pp. 8–9.

54. See Harry Cross, Genevieve Kenney, Jane Mell, and Wendy Zimmermann, *Employer Hiring Practices* (Washington, DC: Urban Institute Press, 1990); Margery Turner, Michael Fix, and Raymond Struyk, *Opportunities Denied, Opportunities Diminished: Discrimination in Hiring* (Washington, DC: Urban Institute Press, 1991).

55. Reynolds Farley and William H. Frey, "Changes in the Segregation of Whites from Blacks during the 1980s: Small Steps toward a More Integrated Society," *American Sociological Review* 59, 1 (February 1994): 23–45; Michael J. White, *American Neighborhoods and Residential Differentiation* (New York: Russell Sage Foundation, 1987).

56. Massey and Denton, *American Apartheid*, pp. 2–3.

57. Keith R. Ihlanfeldt and David L. Sjoquist, "The Impact of Job Decentralization on the Economic Welfare of Central City Blacks," *Journal of Urban Economics* 26 (1989): 110–30.

58. See, for example, James H. Johnson and Melvin L. Oliver, "Structural Changes in the U.S. Economy and Black Male Joblessness: A Reassessment," in *Urban Labor Markets and Job Opportunity*, pp. 113–47; Massey and Denton, *American Apartheid*, pp. 2–3; Ted Mouw, "Job Relocation and the Racial Gap in Unemployment in Detroit and Chicago, 1980 to 1990," *American Sociological Review* 65, 5 (2000): 730–53.

59. John Yinger, "Housing Discrimination and Residential Segregation as Causes of Poverty," *Focus* 21, 2 (fall 2000): 51–55.

60. George C. Galster, "A Cumulative Causation Model of the Underclass: Implications for Urban Economic Development Policy," in *The Metropolis in Black and White: Place, Power, and Polarization*, ed. George Galster and Edward W. Hill (New Brunswick, NJ: Center for Urban Policy Research, Rutgers University, 1992).

61. John Bound and Richard Freeman, "What Went Wrong? The Erosion of Relative Earnings and Employment among Young Black Men in the 1980s,"

Quarterly Journal of Economics 107 (1992): 201–32; John Bound and Harry J. Holzer, "Industrial Shifts, Skills Levels, and the Labor Market for White and Black Males," *Review of Economics and Statistics* 75, 3 (1993): 387–96; Leslie McCall, "Sources of Racial Inequality in Metropolitan Labor Markets: Racial, Ethnic, and Gender Differences," *American Sociological Review* 66, 4 (2001): 520–41; Iceland, "Urban Labor Markets and Individual Transitions out of Poverty."

62. John Bound and Laura Dresser, "Losing Ground: The Erosion of the Relative Earnings of African American Women during the 1980s," in *Latinas and African American Women at Work*, ed. Irene Browne (New York: Russell Sage Foundation, 1999), pp. 61–104.

63. John Kasarda, "Industrial Restructuring and the Changing Location of Jobs," in *State of the Union: America in the 1990s*, vol. 1, ed. Reynolds Farley (New York: Russell Sage Foundation, 1995), pp. 215–67.

64. June O'Neill, "The Role of Human Capital in Earnings Differentials between Black and White Men," *Journal of Economic Perspectives* 4, 4 (1990): 25–46; Farkas and Vicknair, "Appropriate Tests of Racial Wage Discrimination," pp. 557–60.

65. Arthur Sakamoto and Satomi Furuichi, "Wages among White and Japanese-American Male Workers," *Research in Stratification and Mobility* 15 (1997): 177–206.

66. Roderick J. Harrison and Claudette Bennett, "Racial and Ethnic Diversity," in *State of the Union*, vol. 2, pp. 141–210.

67. Barry R. Chiswick and Teresa A. Sullivan, "The New Immigrants," in *State of the Union*, vol. 2, pp. 211–70.

68. Dalaker, "Poverty in the United States: 2000," p. 2.

69. See George J. Borjas, "Assimilation, Changes in Cohort Quality, and the Earnings of Immigrants," *Journal of Labor Economics* 3 (1987), 463–89; George J. Borjas, *Friends or Strangers: The Impact of Immigrants on the U.S. Economy* (New York: Basic Books, 1990); Nancy S. Landale and Avery M. Guest, "Generation, Ethnicity, and Occupational Opportunity in Late 19th Century America," *American Sociological Review* 55 (April 1990): 280–96; Victor Nee and Jimy Sanders, "The Road to Parity: Determinants of the Socioeconomic Achievements of Asian Americans," *Ethnic and Racial Studies* 8, 1 (January 1985): 75–93; Barry R. Chiswick, "The Effect of Americanization on the Earnings of Foreign-Born Men," *Journal of Political Economy* 86, 5 (1978): 897–921; Sharon M. Lee and Barry Edmonston, "The Socioeconomic Status and Integration of Asian Immigrants," in *Immigration and Ethnicity: The Integration of America's Newest Arrivals*, ed. Barry Edmonston and Jeffrey S. Passel (Washington, DC: Urban Institute Press, 1994); Chiswick and Sullivan, "The New Immigrants."

70. See Borjas, "Assimilation, Changes in Cohort Quality, and the Earnings of Immigrants"; Borjas, *Friends or Strangers;* Chiswick and Sullivan, "The New Immigrants."

71. McCall, "Sources of Racial Inequality in Metropolitan Labor Markets," pp. 520–41.

72. Chiswick and Sullivan, "The New Immigrants," p. 265.

73. H. R. Barringer, R. W. Gardner, and M. J. Levin, *Asian and Pacific Islanders in the United States* (New York: Russell Sage Foundation, 1993).

74. See Chiswick and Sullivan, "The New Immigrants."

75. Gillian Stevens and Joo Hyun Cho, "Socioeconomic Indexes and the New 1980 Census Occupational Classification Scheme," *Social Science Research* 14, 2 (1985): 142–68.

76. John Iceland, "Earnings Returns to Occupational Status: Are Asian Americans Disadvantaged?" *Social Science Research* 28 (1999): 45–65; Sharon M. Lee, "Poverty and the U.S. Asian Population," *Social Science Quarterly* 75 (September 1994): 541–59; Sakamoto, Wu, and Tzeng, "Declining Significance of Race."

77. C. W. Reimers, "A Comparative Analysis of the Wages of Hispanics, Blacks, and Non-Hispanic Whites," in *Hispanics in the U.S. Economy*, ed. George Borjas and Marta Tienda (New York: Academic Press, 1985); Sakamoto, Wu, and Tzeng, "Declining Significance of Race."

78. Gary Sandefur and W. J. Scott, "Minority Group Status and the Wages of Indian and Black Males," *Social Science Research* 12 (1983): 44–68; Sakamoto, Wu, and Tzeng, "Declining Significance of Race."

79. Diana Pearce, "The Feminization of Poverty: Women, Work, and Welfare," *Urban Sociological Change* 11 (1978): 128–36.

80. Larry Bumpass and R. Raley, "Redefining Single-Parent Families: Cohabitation and Changing Family Reality," *Demography* 32 (1995): 97–109.

81. McLanahan and Casper, "Growing Diversity and Inequality in the American Family."

82. Suzanne Bianchi, "Feminization and Juvenilization of Poverty: Trends, Relative Risks, Causes, and Consequences," *Annual Review of Sociology* 25 (1999): 307–33.

83. U.S. Census Bureau, "Poverty of People, by Sex: 1966 to 2000," Historical Poverty Tables, Table 7, Internet release data (www.census.gov/hhes /poverty/histpov/hstpov7.html), 13 February 2002.

84. Lichter and Crowley, "Poverty in America: Beyond Welfare Reform," 7.

85. Devine, Plunkett, and Wright, "The Chronicity of Poverty"; Majorie Starrels, Sally Bould, and Leon J. Nicholas, "The Feminization of Poverty in the United States," *Journal of Family Issues* 15, 4 (December 1994): 590–607; Stevens, "Dynamics of Poverty Spells"; Stevens, "Climbing Out of Poverty."

86. Starrels, Bould, and Nicholas, "Feminization of Poverty in the United States."

87. Bianchi, "Feminization and Juvenilization of Poverty," pp. 307–33.

88. Paula England, "Wage Appreciation and Depreciation: A Test of Neoclassical Economic Explanations of Occupational Sex Segregation," in *Social Stratification in Sociological Perspective*, pp. 590–603; Heidi Hartmann, "The Unhappy Marriage of Marxism and Feminism: Towards a More Progressive Union," in *Social Stratification in Sociological Perspective*, pp. 570–76.

89. Hartmann, "Unhappy Marriage of Marxism and Feminism," p. 570.

90. England, "Wage Appreciation and Depreciation," p. 599.

91. Solomon W. Polachek and W. Stanley Siebert, "Gender in the Labour Market," in *Social Stratification in Sociological Perspective,* pp. 583–89.

92. T. Daymont and P. Andrisani, "Job Preferences, College Major, and the Gender Gap in Earnings," *Journal of Human Resources* 19 (1984): 408–28.

93. Suzanne Bianchi, "Changing Economic Roles of Women and Men," in *State of the Union,* vol. 1, pp. 107–54.

94. U.S. Census Bureau, "Women's Earnings as a Percentage of Men's Earnings by Race and Hispanic Origin: 1960 to 2000," Historical Income Tables, table P-40, Internet release data (www.census.gov/hhes/income/histinc/p40x1.html), 21 March 2002.

95. Francine D. Blau, Marianne A. Ferber, and Anne E. Winkler, *The Economics of Women, Men, and Work* (Upper Saddle River, NJ: Prentice Hall, 1998), p. 137.

96. See Bianchi, "Changing Economic Roles of Women and Men."

97. Francine D. Blau and Lawrence M. Kahn, "Swimming Upstream: Trends in the Gender Wage Differential in the 1980s," *Journal of Labor Economics* 15, 1, part 1 (1997): 1–42.

98. Jane Waldfogel and Susan Mayer, "Differences between Men and Women in the Low-Wage Labor Market," *Focus* 20, 1 (winter 1998–1999): 11–16.

99. E. Franklin Frazier, *The Negro Family in the United States* (Chicago: University of Chicago Press, 1939); E. Franklin Frazier, *The Negro Family in Chicago* (Chicago: University of Chicago Press, 1932); Gunnar Myrdal, *An American Dilemma* (New York: Harper and Row, 1944); Daniel Patrick Moynihan, *The Negro Family: The Case for National Action* (Washington, DC: U.S. Department of Labor, 1965); Suzanne Bianchi, "America's Children: Mixed Prospects," *Population Bulletin* 45 (1990): 1–43; Dennis Hogan and Daniel Lichter, "Children and Youth: Living Arrangements and Welfare," in *State of the Union,* pp. 93–139; Daniel T. Lichter, "Poverty and Inequality among Children," *Annual Review of Sociology* 23 (1997): 121–45.

100. Poverty rates from 1959 and 1970 are from Dalaker, "Poverty in the United States: 2000," p. 18; the 2000 poverty rates are based on my tabulations of the Annual Demographic Supplement to the 2001 Current Population Survey.

101. O'Hare, "A New Look at Poverty in America," pp. 18, 21.

102. Blau, Ferber, and Winkler, *Economics of Women, Men, and Work,* p. 169.

103. Bianchi, "Feminization and Juvenilization of Poverty."

104. Elaine Sorenson, "Noncustodial Fathers: Can They Afford to Pay More Child Support?" Urban Institute working paper, December 1994; O'Hare, "A New Look at Poverty in America," pp. 21–23.

105. Daniel T. Lichter and Nancy S. Landale, "Parental Work, Family Structure, and Poverty among Latino Children," *Journal of Marriage and the Family* 57 (1995): 346–54; Starrels, Bould, and Nicholas, "Feminization of Poverty in the United States."

106. See Maria Cancian and Deborah Reed, "Changes in Family Structure: Implications for Poverty and Related Policy," *Focus* 21, 2 (2000): 21–26; David J. Eggebeen and Daniel T. Lichter, "Race, Family Structure, and Changing Poverty among American Children," *American Sociological Review* 56 (1991): 801–17; Robert I. Lerman, "The Impact of the Changing U.S. Family Structure on Poverty and Income Inequality," *Economica* 63 (1996): S119–S139; Donald J. Hernandez, *America's Children: Resources from Family, Government, and the Economy* (New York: Russell Sage Foundation, 1993); Bianchi, "America's Children: Mixed Prospects"; Lichter, "Poverty and Inequality among Children."

107. Cancian and Reed, "Changes in Family Structure."

108. Lichter and Landale, "Parental Work, Family Structure, and Poverty among Latino Children."

109. Danziger and Gottschalk, *America Unequal*, pp. 67–92; Lichter, "Poverty and Inequality among Children."

110. Cancian and Reed, "Changes in Family Structure."

111. Ron Haskins, "Giving Is Not Enough," *Brookings Review* 19, 3 (summer 2001): 13–15.

112. UNICEF Innocenti Research Centre, "Child Poverty in Rich Nations," p. 8.

113. UNICEF Innocenti Research Centre, "Child Poverty in Rich Nations," pp. 11–13.

114. For an extended discussion, see O'Connor, *Poverty Knowledge*, pp. 74–123.

115. Booker T. Washington, *The Future of the American Negro* (New York, 1902); Myrdal, *An American Dilemma*; Frazier, *The Negro Family in the United States*; Frazier, *The Negro Family in Chicago*.

116. O'Connor, *Poverty Knowledge*, p. 81.

117. Robert Cherry, "The Culture-of-Poverty Thesis and African Americans: The Work of Gunnar Myrdal and Other Institutionalists," *Journal of Economic Issues* 29, 4 (December 1995): 1119–32.

118. Schiller, *Economics of Poverty and Discrimination*, p. 127.

119. Edward C. Banfield, *The Unheavenly City* (Boston: Little, Brown, 1958), quoted in Michael B. Katz, *The Undeserving Poor: From the War on Poverty to the War on Welfare* (New York: Pantheon, 1989), pp. 31–32.

120. See Murray, *Losing Ground*; Robert Rector, "Welfare Reform, Dependency Reduction, and Labor Market Entry," *Journal of Labor Research* 14, 3 (summer 1993): 283–97.

121. Ronald Mincy, "The Underclass: Concept, Controversy, Evidence," in *Confronting Poverty*, pp. 108–46.

122. Michael B. Teitz and Karen Chapple, "The Causes of Inner-City Poverty: Eight Hypotheses in Search of Reality," *Cityscape* 3, 3 (1998): 33–70; Lee Rainwater, *Behind Ghetto Walls: Black Families in a Federal Slum* (Chicago: Aldine, 1970).

123. Rachel K. Jones and Ye Luo, "The Culture of Poverty and African-American Culture: An Empirical Assessment," *Sociological Perspectives* 42, 3

(1999): 439–58; Carole Marks, "The Urban Underclass," *American Review of Sociology* 17 (1991): 445–66.

124. Harrison and Bennett, "Racial and Ethnic Diversity."

6. WHY POVERTY REMAINS HIGH, REVISITED

1. Robert Rector, Kirk A. Johnson, and Patrick F. Fagan, "Understanding Differences in Black and White Child Poverty Rates," The Heritage Foundation, Center for Data Analysis report no. 01-04, May 23, 2001.

2. Robert Rector, Kirk A. Johnson, and Patrick F. Fagan, "The Effect of Marriage on Child Poverty," The Heritage Foundation, Center for Data Analysis report no. 02-04, April 15, 2002, p. 1.

3. World Bank, *World Development Report, 2000/2001*, p. 32.

4. David Ellwood and Lawrence Summers, "Poverty in America: Is Welfare the Answer or the Problem?" in *Fighting Poverty: What Works and What Doesn't*, ed. Sheldon H. Danziger and Daniel H. Weinberg (Cambridge, MA: Harvard University Press, 1986), p. 81, quoted in Sheldon H. Danziger and Peter Gottschalk, *America Unequal* (Cambridge, MA: Harvard University Press, 1995), p. 10.

5. Blank, *It Takes a Nation*, p. 52.

6. Danziger and Gottschalk, *America Unequal*, pp. 12–13.

7. Robert Lampman, *Ends and Means of Reducing Income Poverty* (Chicago: Markham, 1971); Tobin, "It Can Be Done!" p. 14.

8. Dalaker, "Poverty in the United States: 2000."

9. Danziger and Gottschalk, *America Unequal*, pp. 93–110; Robert Haveman and Jonathan Schwabish, "Economic Growth and Poverty: A Return to Normalcy?" *Focus* 20, 2 (spring 1999): 1–7.

10. Arthur Jones Jr. and Daniel H. Weinberg, "The Changing Shape of the Nation's Income Distribution," U.S. Census Bureau, Current Population Reports, series P60-204 (Washington, DC: U.S. Government Printing Office, 2000); Maria Cancian and Deborah Reed, "Changes in Family Structure: Implications for Poverty and Related Policy," *Focus* 21, 2 (fall 2000): 21–26; Dalaker, Poverty in the United States: 2000," p. 18.

11. Danziger and Gottschalk, *America Unequal*, pp. 93–110.

12. See, for example, Fisher, "Is There Such a Thing as an Absolute Poverty Line over Time?"; National Research Council, *Measuring Poverty;* Townsend, *International Analysis of Poverty.*

13. Fisher, "From Hunter to Orshansky."

14. Vaughan, "Exploring the Use of the Public's Views to Set Income Poverty Thresholds and Adjust Them over Time."

15. Danziger and Gottschalk, *America Unequal*, pp. 93–110.

16. Danziger and Gottschalk, p. 101 n. 4.

17. Note that this 1999 relative poverty figure differs from the 2000 one in Table 4.1 (21.1 percent). The principal reason for the difference is that the poverty threshold used in this chapter is equal to half the median income of a two-adult, two-child family in 1999 (the median for this type of family equals

$59,488), while the one in chapter 4 refers to half the overall household median income in 2000 ($50,565). The analysis in this chapter uses the median for a specific family size and composition over time to more effectively separate the effect of family structure (which affects the median household income figure) from that of economic growth.

18. As we would expect, the effect of income growth is generally smaller when using the relative poverty measure than when using the absolute one. Conceptually, income growth should actually have little effect (other things being equal) on relative poverty. However, because relative poverty measures are nearly always *operationalized* in terms of median income instead of mean income (as researchers tend to favor using poverty thresholds that are unaffected by a skewed income distribution) and the measure of general "income growth" used here is based on changes in the mean (as it nearly always is by researchers), we do see some effect. In my view, these findings illustrate not errors of measurement but rather the fact that how we commonly measure income-related phenomena affects their trends and our understanding of the factors that affect them.

19. See, for example, Danziger and Gottschalk, *America Unequal,* pp. 39–66, and their results on the effect of income growth, pp. 93–110. There are small differences in results because the time periods used in their study and this study do not exactly correspond. One additional source of differences is that, while Danziger and Gottschalk measure income growth using income-to-poverty ratios generated from the data set itself, I use published per-capita income figures. Finally, this analysis uses four categories of family types (married couple, female headed, male headed, and unrelated individual), while Danziger and Gottschalk collapse the unrelated-individual category into a male- or female-headed family category.

20. Danziger and Gottschalk, *America Unequal,* pp. 108–10.

21. It should be noted that, while the results in Figure 6.1, 6.2, or 6.3 do not show the magnitude of the effect of racial and ethnic composition changes on poverty, the analyses do take these factors into account, as discussed in appendix A. The effect of changes in racial/ethnic composition were +1.2, +0.7, and +0.7 percentage points when using the absolute measure over the 1949–1969, 1969–1990, and 1990–1999 time periods, respectively. Using the relative measure, these effects were +1.4, +1.1, and +1.0 percentage points over the three time periods. Using the NAS measure, the effect was +0.7 in the 1990–1999 period. Finally, there were small interaction effects between family structure and race/ethnicity changes, all ranging from −0.3 to −0.1 for all measures in all time periods.

22. See Eggebeen and Lichter, "Race, Family Structure, and Changing Poverty among American Children"; Lerman, "The Impact of the Changing U.S. Family Structure on Poverty and Income Inequality."

23. Cancian and Reed, "Changes in Family Structure," pp. 21–26; Jason Fields, "Living Arrangements of Children: Fall 1996," U.S. Census Bureau, Current Population Reports, series P70-74 (Washington, DC: U.S. Government Printing Office, 2001); Allen Dupree and Wendell Primus, "Declining Share of Children Lived with Single Mothers in the Late 1990s," Center on Budget and Policy Priorities research report, June 15, 2001.

24. Bernstein et al., "Pulling Apart: A State-by-State Analysis of Income Trends."

7. POVERTY AND POLICY

1. Sar A. Levitan, Garth L. Mangum, and Stephen L. Mangum, *Programs in Aid of the Poor* (Baltimore: Johns Hopkins University Press, 1998), p. 225.

2. Munsterberg, "The Problem of Poverty," p. 343.

3. Katz, *In the Shadow of the Poorhouse.*

4. Trattner, *From Poor Law to Welfare State,* pp. 10–12.

5. Trattner, *From Poor Law to Welfare State,* pp. 10–11; Katz, *In the Shadow of the Poorhouse,* pp. 13–15.

6. Katz, *In the Shadow of the Poorhouse,* p. 14.

7. Trattner, *From Poor Law to Welfare State,* pp. 23–24.

8. W. E. B. DuBois, *The Philadelphia Negro,* p. 269.

9. Trattner, *From Poor Law to Welfare State,* pp. 24–26.

10. Trattner, *From Poor Law to Welfare State,* pp. 47–56.

11. Katz, *In the Shadow of the Poorhouse,* pp. 22–36.

12. Trattner, *From Poor Law to Welfare State,* pp. 60–61.

13. Eric H. Monkkonen, "Nineteenth-Century Institutions: Dealing with the Urban 'Underclass,'" in *The "Underclass" Debate,* pp. 331–33.

14. Katz, *In the Shadow of the Poorhouse,* pp. 26–36.

15. Katz, *In the Shadow of the Poorhouse,* p. 38.

16. Trotter, "Blacks in the Urban North," pp. 64–65.

17. Trattner, *From Poor Law to Welfare State,* pp. 83–84.

18. Jones, "Southern Diaspora," pp. 33–34; Katz, "Reframing the 'Underclass' Debate," p. 458.

19. Trattner, *From Poor Law to Welfare State,* pp. 84–85.

20. Theda Skocpol, *The Missing Middle: Working Families and the Future of American Social Policy* (New York: W. W. Norton, 2000), pp. 25–26.

21. See Trattner, *From Poor Law to Welfare State,* pp. 77–103; Katz, *In the Shadow of the Poorhouse,* pp. 60–87.

22. Trattner, *From Poor Law to Welfare State,* p. 95.

23. Trattner, *From Poor Law to Welfare State,* pp. 99–102.

24. Katz, *In the Shadow of the Poorhouse,* p. 197.

25. See, for example, Theda Skocpol, Majorie Abend-Wein, Christopher Howard, and Susan Goodrich Lehmann, "Women's Associations and the Enactment of Mothers' Pensions in the United States," *American Political Science Review* 87, 3 (September 1993): 686–701.

26. Katz, *In the Shadow of the Poorhouse,* p. 148.

27. Trattner, *From Poor Law to Welfare State,* pp. 225, 250.

28. Trattner, *From Poor Law to Welfare State,* pp. 273–74.

29. Katz, *In the Shadow of the Poorhouse,* pp. 224–54.

30. Thomas F. Jackson, "The State, the Movement, and the Urban Poor: The War on Poverty and Political Mobilization in the 1960s," in *The "Underclass" Debate,* p. 437; Skocpol, *The Missing Middle,* pp. 22–58; Katz, *In the Shadow of the Poorhouse,* pp. 242–55.

31. Trattner, *From Poor Law to Welfare State*, p. 294.

32. Katz, *In the Shadow of the Poorhouse*, p. 254.

33. Skocpol, *The Missing Middle*, p. 26.

34. Trattner, *From Poor Law to Welfare State*, pp. 313–19.

35. See Jackson, "The State, the Movement, and the Urban Poor," pp. 403–39; Trattner, *From Poor Law to Welfare State*, pp. 322–31; O'Connor, *Poverty Knowledge*, pp. 166–95.

36. Trattner, *From Poor Law to Welfare State*, pp. 304–31.

37. Katz, "Reframing the 'Underclass' Debate," p. 476.

38. Trattner, *From Poor Law to Welfare State*, pp. 337–51.

39. Katz, *In the Shadow of the Poorhouse*, pp. 283–99; Trattner, *From Poor Law to Welfare State*, pp. 352–65.

40. Trattner, *From Poor Law to Welfare State*, pp. 393–97.

41. U.S. House of Representatives, Committee on Ways and Means, *Green Book: Background Material and Data on Programs within the Jurisdiction of the Committee on Ways and Means* (Washington, DC: U.S. Government Printing Office, 2000).

42. House Committee on Ways and Means, *Green Book*, table K-5.

43. O'Hare, "A New Look at Poverty in America," p. 42.

44. Skocpol, *The Missing Middle*, pp. 22–58.

45. Marc Roemer, "Assessing the Quality of the March Current Population Survey and the Survey of Income and Program Participation Income Estimates, 1990–1996," U.S. Census Bureau Staff Paper on Income, Internet release data (www.census.gov/hhes/income/papers.html), 16 June 2000, table 2b, p. 45, reports that the problem may be most serious for estimates of family assistance, which includes TANF, where CPS aggregate income (income totaled over all respondents) in 1996 was 67.7 percent of a benchmark total estimated from administrative records. The undercount of recipients (rather than income) is likely less severe, as aggregates tend to be underestimated due to both fewer people reporting income and lower amounts reported among those who do report receipt. SSI and Social Security aggregate income from the March CPS in 1996 was 84.2 and 91.7 percent of the estimated benchmark for those two items, respectively.

46. U.S. Census Bureau, "Income of Households from Specified Sources, by Poverty Status: 2000," Experimental Measures of Income and Poverty, Detailed Income Tabulations from the CPS, table 7, Internet release data (ferret.bls .census.gov/macro/032000/rdcall/toc.htm), 6 September 2001.

47. Harrell R. Rodgers Jr., *American Poverty in a New Era of Reform* (Armonk, NY: M. E. Sharpe, 2000), p. 126.

48. U.S. Census Bureau, "Income of Households from Specified Sources, by Poverty Status: 1995," Experimental Measures of Income and Poverty, Detailed Income Tabulations from the CPS, table 7 (ferret.bls.census.gov/macro/031996 /rdcall/7_000.htm), issued 1996, last revised on the internet on 10 March 1997; U.S. Census Bureau, "Income of Households from Specified Sources, by Poverty Status: 2000," table 7.

49. O'Hare, "A New Look at Poverty in America," p. 33. He defined major welfare programs as consisting of AFDC or other cash welfare programs, food stamps, Medicaid, or housing assistance.

50. U.S. Census Bureau, "Income of Households from Specified Sources, by Poverty Status: 2000," table 7.

51. Center on Budget and Policy Priorities, "Strengths of the Safety Net."

52. John Karl Sholz and Kara Levine, "The Evolution of Income Support Policy in Recent Decades," *Focus* 21, 2 (fall 2000): 9–15.

53. Center on Budget and Policy Priorities, "Strengths of the Safety Net," p. 4.

54. Iceland and Kim, "Poverty among Working Families."

55. Haskins, "Giving Is Not Enough"; Tommy G. Thompson, "Welfare Reform's Next Step," *Brookings Review* 19, 3 (summer 2001): 2–3.

56. Thompson, "Welfare Reform's Next Step," p. 3.

57. Mark Greenberg, "Welfare Reform and Devolution," *Brookings Review* 19, 3 (summer 2001): 20–24.

58. Robert Moffitt, "From Welfare to Work: What the Evidence Shows," Brookings Institution Policy Brief no. 13, January 2002.

59. See Moffitt, "From Welfare to Work"; Sarah Brauner and Pamela Loprest, "Where Are They Now? What States' Studies of People Who Left Welfare Tell Us," Urban Institute Research Report no. A-32, New Federalism: Issues and Options for States Series (1999).

60. Greenberg, "Welfare Reform and Devolution," p. 22.

61. Moffitt, "From Welfare to Work," pp. 1, 5.

62. Brauner and Loprest, "Where Are They Now?" pp. 8–9.

63. Rodgers, *American Poverty in a New Era of Reform,* pp. 144–54; O'Hare, "A New Look at Poverty in America," pp. 40–42; Rebecca Blank, "Why Has Economic Growth Been Such an Ineffective Tool against Poverty in Recent Years?" in *Poverty and Inequality: The Political Economy of Redistribution,* pp. 188–210.

64. For more discussion of these issues, see Ron Haskins, Isabel Sawhill, and Kent Weaver, "Welfare Reform Reauthorization: An Overview of Problems and Issues," Brookings Institution Welfare Reform and Beyond Policy Brief No. 2, January 2001; Katherine S. Newman, *No Shame in My Game: The Working Poor in the Inner City* (New York: Knopf and Russell Sage Foundation, 1999); Wendell Primus, "What Next for Welfare Reform? A Vision for Assisting Families," *Brookings Review* 19, 3 (summer 2001): 17–24; Thompson, "Welfare Reform's Next Step."

65. Danziger and Gottschalk, *America Unequal,* pp. 158–65.

66. Joseph V. Hotz, Charles H. Mullin, and John Karl Sholz, "The Earned Income Tax Credit and Labor Market Participation of Families on Welfare" (paper presented at the Institute for Research on Poverty Summer Research Workshop on Problems of the Low-Income Population, Madison, WI, 25–28 June 2001).

67. Hugh Heclo, "Poverty Politics," in *Confronting Poverty*, pp. 396–437.

68. Christopher Jencks, *Rethinking Social Policy: Race, Poverty, and the Underclass* (New York: Harper Perennial, 1992), pp. 87–91.

69. Samuel Bowles and Herbert Gintis, *Recasting Egalitarianism: New Rules for Communities, States and Markets*, The Real Utopias Project, vol. 3, ed. Erik Olin Wright (London: Verso, 1998).

70. Isabel Sawhill, "From Welfare to Work," *Brookings Review* 19, 3 (summer 2001): 4–7.

71. Michael B. Katz, *The Price of Citizenship: Redefining the American Welfare State* (New York: Metropolitan Books, Henry Holt, 2001), p. 31.

72. O'Hare, "A New Look at Poverty in America," p. 33.

73. Michael Harrington, *The Other America: Poverty in the United States* (New York: Macmillan, 1962; reprint with a new introduction, New York: Penguin Books, 1981), pp. xxviii–xxix.

74. Murray, *Losing Ground;* Rector, "Welfare Reform, Dependency Reduction, and Labor Market Entry."

75. See, for example, A. Lindbeck et al., *Turning Sweden Around* (Cambridge: MIT Press, 1994).

76. Robert Moffitt, "Incentive Effects of the U.S. Welfare System: A Review," *Journal of Economic Literature* 30 (March 1992): 56.

77. Daniel T. Lichter, Diane K. McLaughlin, and David Ribar, "Welfare and the Rise in Female-Headed Families," *American Journal of Sociology* 103, 1 (July 1997): 112–43.

78. Bradbury and Jantti, "Child Poverty across Twenty-Five Countries"; Markus Jantti and Sheldon Danziger, "Income Poverty in Advanced Countries," Luxembourg Income Study Working Paper no. 193, March 1999.

79. Smeeding, Rainwater, and Burtless, "United States Poverty in a Cross-National Context."

80. Timothy Smeeding, "The International Evidence on Income Distribution in Modern Economics," in *Poverty and Inequality*, pp. 79–103.

81. See Gary Burtless, "Public Spending on the Poor: Historical Trends and Economic Limits," in *Confronting Poverty*, pp. 51–84; Smeeding, Rainwater, and Burtless, "United States Poverty in a Cross-National Context."

82. Sara McLanahan and Irwin Garfinkel, "Single-Mother Families and Social Policy: Lessons for the United States from Canada, France, and Sweden," in *Poverty, Inequality, and the Future of Social Policy*, pp. 367–83; UNICEF Innocenti Research Centre, "Child Poverty in Rich Nations."

83. UNICEF Innocenti Research Centre, "Child Poverty in Rich Nations," 8.

84. Katz, *The Price of Citizenship*, pp. 15–16.

85. Roger Lawson and William Julius Wilson, "Poverty, Social Rights, and the Quality of Citizenship," in *Poverty, Inequality, and the Future of Social Policy*, p. 707.

86. A. B. Atkinson, *The Economic Consequences of Rolling Back the Welfare State* (Cambridge, MA: MIT Press, 1999).

87. Katz, *The Price of Citizenship*, p. 341.

88. Katz, *The Price of Citizenship*, p. 62.

89. Katz, *The Price of Citizenship*, pp. 26–31.

90. See Tom Smith, "Social Inequality in Cross-National Perspective," in *Attitudes to Inequality and the Role of Government,* ed. Duane Alwin et al. (Rijswijk, The Netherlands: Sociaal en Cultural Planbureau, 1990).

91. Lawson and Wilson, "Poverty, Social Rights, and the Quality of Citizenship," p. 712.

92. Munsterberg, "The Problem of Poverty," p. 336.

93. Amartya Sen, "Merit and Justice," in *Meritocracy and Economic Inequality,* pp. 5–16.

94. Roland Benabou, "Meritocracy, Distribution, and the Size of the Pie," in *Meritocracy and Economic Inequality,* p. 318.

95. John E. Roemer, "Equality of Opportunity," in *Meritocracy and Economic Inequality,* pp. 17–32.

96. Bowles and Gintis, *Recasting Egalitarianism,* p. 363.

97. U.S. Census Bureau, "Homeownership Rates for the U.S.: 1965–2002," Housing Vacancies and Homeownership Detailed Tables—First Quarter 2002, table 5, Internet re-release data (www.census.gov/hhes/www/housing/hvs /q102tab5.html), 25 April 2002.

98. Bowles and Gintis, *Recasting Egalitarianism,* pp. 3–59.

APPENDIX: DATA AND METHODS
FOR THE ANALYSIS IN CHAPTER 6

1. Burtless and Smeeding, "The Level, Trend, and Composition of Poverty."

2. Timothy Smeeding, B. B. Torrey, and M. Rein, "Patterns of Income and Poverty: The Economic Status of Children and the Elderly in Eight Countries," in *The Vulnerable,* ed. J. L. Palmer, Timothy Smeeding, and B. B. Torrey (Washington, DC: Urban Institute Press, 1988), pp. 89–119.

3. See Short et al., "Experimental Poverty Measures: 1990 to 1997"; U.S. Census Bureau, "Standardized and Unstandardized Experimental Poverty Rates: 1990 to 1999," Poverty 1999 table release package, Internet release data (www.census.gov/hhes/poverty/povmeas/exppov/suexppov.html), 23 October 2000; Iceland et al., "Are Children Worse Off?"

4. See Short et al., "Experimental Poverty Measures: 1990 to 1997."

5. Danziger and Gottschalk, *America Unequal,* pp. 93–110. This method is also described by Henry S. Shyrock and Jacob S. Siegel, *The Methods and Materials of Demography* (New York: Academic Press, 1976).

6. Per-capita income figures used in the official and relative poverty measure analyses were obtained from calculations based on data in U.S. Census Bureau, "Money Income in the United States: 1999," Current Population Reports, Consumer Income, series P60-209 (Washington, DC: U.S. Government Printing Office, 2000); and U.S. Census Bureau, "Historical National Population Estimates: July 1, 1900 to July 1, 1999," Population Estimates Program, Population Division, Internet release data (www.census.gov/population/estimates /nation/popclockest.txt), 11 April 2000, revised 28 June 2000. I also tried other measures of income growth, such as changes in the income-to-poverty ratio

from the data output. I did not adopt this method because income values are top coded in the public-use IPUMS data, and the methods of top coding also vary over the years.

7. Per-capita income figures for the NAS measure were obtained from the CPS data output. Top coding was not an issue because the data come from internal Census Bureau versions of the 1991–2000 CPS data files. There would be virtually no difference in results whether using changes in income-to-poverty ratios or per-capita income changes as measures of income growth.

References

Atkinson, A. B., and John Hills. 1998. "Social Exclusion, Poverty and Unemployment," Centre for Analysis of Social Exclusion paper no. 4.

————. 1999. *The Economic Consequences of Rolling Back the Welfare State.* Cambridge, MA: MIT Press.

Bane, Mary Jo, and David Ellwood. 1986. "Slipping into and out of Poverty: The Dynamics of Spells." *Journal of Human Resources* 21 (winter): 1–23.

Banfield, Edward C. 1958. *The Unheavenly City.* Boston: Little, Brown.

Barringer, H. R., R. W. Gardner, and M. J. Levin. 1993. *Asian and Pacific Islanders in the United States.* New York: Russell Sage Foundation.

Barrington, Linda. 2000. "Does a Rising Tide Lift All Boats?" The Conference Board. Research Report no. 1271-00-RR.

Bauman, Kurt J. 1998. "Direct Measures of Poverty as Indicators of Economic Need: Evidence from the Survey of Income and Program Participation." U.S. Census Bureau. Population Division Technical Working Paper no. 30.

————. 1999. "Extended Measures of Well-Being: Meeting Basic Needs." Current Population Reports, series P70-67. Washington, DC: U.S. Government Printing Office.

Becker, Gary S. 1971. *The Economics of Discrimination.* Chicago: University of Chicago Press.

Benabou, Roland. 2000. "Meritocracy, Distribution, and the Size of the Pie." In *Meritocracy and Economic Inequality,* edited by Kenneth Arrow, Samuel Bowles, and Steven Durlauf. Princeton, NJ: Princeton University Press.

Bernstein, Jared, Elizabeth C. McNichol, Lawrence Mishel, and Robert Zahradnik. 2000, January. "Pulling Apart: A State-by-State Analysis of Income Trends." Center on Budget and Policy Priorities and Economic Policy Institute Report.

Betson, David. 1996. "Is Everything Relative? The Role of Equivalence Scales in Poverty Measurement." Unpublished manuscript, University of Notre Dame.

Beverly, Sondra G. 2000. "Using Measures of Material Hardship." *Focus* 21, 2 (fall): 65–69.

———. 2001. "Measures of Material Hardship: Rationale and Recommendations." *Journal of Poverty* 5, 1: 23–41.

Bianchi, Suzanne. 1990. "America's Children: Mixed Prospects." *Population Bulletin* 45: 1–43.

———. 1995. "Changing Economic Roles of Women and Men." In *State of the Union: America in the 1990s*, vol. 1, edited by Reynolds Farley. New York: Russell Sage Foundation.

———. 1999. "Feminization and Juvenilization of Poverty: Trends, Relative Risks, Causes, and Consequences." *Annual Review of Sociology* 25: 307–33.

Blank, Rebecca. 1997. "Why Has Economic Growth Been Such an Ineffective Tool Against Poverty in Recent Years?" In *Poverty and Inequality: The Political Economy of Redistribution*, edited by Jon Neil. Kalamazoo, MI: W. E. Upjohn Institute for Employment Research.

———. 1997. *It Takes a Nation: A New Agenda for Fighting Poverty*. Princeton, NJ: Princeton University Press.

Blau, Francine D., and Lawrence M. Kahn. 1997. "Swimming Upstream: Trends in the Gender Wage Differential in the 1980s." *Journal of Labor Economics* 15, 1, part 1 (January): 1–42.

Blau, Francine D., Marianne A. Ferber, and Anne E. Winkler. 1998. *The Economics of Women, Men, and Work*. Upper Saddle River, NJ: Prentice Hall.

Blau, Peter M., Otis Dudley Duncan, and Andrea Tyree. 1994. "The Process of Stratification." In *Social Stratification in Sociological Perspective*, edited by David B. Grusky. Boulder, CO: Westview Press.

Bluestone, Barry. 1994. "The Inequality Express." *The American Prospect* 20 (winter): 81–93.

Bluestone, Barry, and Bennett Harrison. 2000. *Growing Prosperity: The Battle for Growth with Equity in the Twenty-First Century*. Boston: Houghton Mifflin.

Bonacich, E. 1972. "A Theory of Ethnic Antagonism: The Split Labor Market." *American Sociological Review* 37 (October): 547–59.

Booth, Charles. 1889. *Labour and Life of the People*, vol. 1: *East London*. London: Williams and Norgate.

———. 1892–1897. *Life and Labour of the People of London*, First Series: *Poverty*. London: Macmillan; reprint, New York: AMS Press, 1970.

Borjas, George J. 1987. "Assimilation, Changes in Cohort Quality, and the Earnings of Immigrants." *Journal of Labor Economics* 3: 463–89.

———. 1990. *Friends or Strangers: The Impact of Immigrants on the U.S. Economy*. New York: Basic Books.

Bound, John, and Harry J. Holzer. 1993. "Industrial Shifts, Skills Levels, and the Labor Market for White and Black Males." *The Review of Economics and Statistics* 75, 3 (August): 387–96.

Bound, John, and Laura Dresser. 1999. "Losing Ground: The Erosion of the Relative Earnings of African American Women during the 1980s." In *Latinas and African American Women at Work*, edited by Irene Browne. New York: Russell Sage Foundation.

Bound, John, and Richard Freeman. 1992. "What Went Wrong? The Erosion of Relative Earnings and Employment among Young Black Men in the 1980s." *Quarterly Journal of Economics* 107: 201–32.

Boushey, Heather, Chauna Brocht, Bethney Gundersen, and Jared Bernstein. 2001. *Hardships in America: The Real Story of Working Families*. Washington, DC: Economic Policy Institute.

Bowles, Samuel, and Herbert Gintis. 1998. *Recasting Egalitarianism: New Rules for Communities, States and Markets*. The Real Utopias Project, vol. III. edited by Erik Olin Wright. London: Verso.

Bradbury, Bruce, and Markus Jantti. 2001. "Child Poverty across Twenty-Five Countries." In *The Dynamics of Child Poverty in Industrialised Countries*, edited by Bruce Bradbury, Stephen P. Jenkins, and John Micklewright. Cambridge, UK: Cambridge University Press.

Brauner, Sarah, and Pamela Loprest. 1999. "Where Are They Now? What States' Studies of People Who Left Welfare Tell Us." Urban Institute Research Report no. A-32, New Federalism: Issues and Options for States Series.

Bumpass, Larry, and R. Raley. 1995. "Redefining Single-Parent Families: Cohabitation and Changing Family Reality." *Demography* 32: 97–109.

Bureau of Economic Analysis. 2002. "Gross Domestic Product, in Current Dollars and in Chained (1996) Dollars." *National Accounts Data*, Times Series Estimates of Gross Domestic Product (http://www.bea.doc.gov/bea/dn1.htm).

Burroughs, Charles. 1835. *A Discourse Delivered in the Chapel of the New Alms-House, in Portsmouth, N.H.* Portsmouth, NH: J. W. Foster.

Burtless, Gary. 1994. "Public Spending on the Poor: Historical Trends and Economic Limits." In *Confronting Poverty*, edited by Sheldon Danziger, Gary Sandefur, and Daniel Weinberg. Cambridge, MA: Harvard University Press.

Burtless, Gary, and Timothy M. Smeeding. 2001. "The Level, Trend, and Composition of Poverty." In *Understanding Poverty*, edited by Sheldon Danziger and Robert Haveman. Cambridge, MA: Harvard University Press.

Cancian, Maria, and Deborah Reed. 2000. "Changes in Family Structure: Implications for Poverty and Related Policy." *Focus* 21, 2 (fall): 21–26.

Casper, Lynne M., and Philip N. Cohen. 2000. "How Does POSSLQ Measure Up? Historical Estimates of Cohabitation." *Demography* 37, 2 (May): 237–45.

Center on Budget and Policy Priorities. 1998, March. "Strengths of the Safety Net: How the EITC, Social Security, and Other Government Programs Affect Poverty." Center on Budget and Policy Priorities research report 98-020.

Centers for Disease Control and Prevention. 2001. "Infant Mortality Rates, Fetal Mortality Rates, and Perinatal Mortality Rates, According to Race: United States, Selected Years, 1950–99." National Center for Health Statistics, Health Data, table 23 (http://www.cdc.gov/nchs/about/major/dvs/mortdata.htm).

Chen, Shaohua, and Martin Ravallion. 2000. "How Did the World's Poorest Fare in the 1990s?" Policy Research Working Paper. Washington, DC: World Bank.

Cherry, Robert. 1995. "The Culture-of-Poverty Thesis and African Americans: The Work of Gunnar Myrdal and Other Institutionalists." *Journal of Economic Issues* 29, 4 (December): 1119–32.

Chiswick, Barry R. 1978. "The Effect of Americanization on the Earnings of Foreign-Born Men." *Journal of Political Economy* 86, 5: 897–921.

Chiswick, Barry R., and Teresa A. Sullivan. 1995. "The New Immigrants." In *State of the Union America in the 1990s*, vol. 2, edited by Reynolds Farley. New York: Russell Sage Foundation.

Chung, Chanjin, and Samuel L. Myers, Jr. 1999. "Do the Poor Pay More for Food? An Analysis of Grocery Store Availability and Food Price Disparities." *The Journal of Consumer Affairs* 33, 2: 276–91.

Cogan, John F. 1995. "Dissent." In *Measuring Poverty: A New Approach*, edited by Constance F. Citro and Robert T. Michael. Washington, DC: National Academy Press.

Colasanto, Diane, Arie Kapteyn, and Jacques van der Gaag. 1984. "Two Subjective Definitions of Poverty: Results from the Wisconsin Basic Needs Study." *Journal of Human Resources* 28, 1: 127–38.

Comeliau, Christian. 2000. "Poverty—A Hopeless Battle?" In *The Challenge of Eliminating World Poverty*, edited by Swiss Agency Development and Cooperation (SDC) Publications on Development. Berne: SDC.

Corcoran, Mary. 2000. "Mobility, Persistence, and the Intergenerational Determinants of Children's Success." *Focus* 21, 2 (fall): 16–20.

Corcoran, Mary, and Terry Adams. 1997. "Race, Sex, and the Intergenerational Transmission of Poverty." In *Consequences of Growing Up Poor* edited by Greg J. Duncan and Jeanne Brooks-Gunn. New York: Russell Sage Foundation.

Cross, Harry, Genevieve Kenney, Jane Mell, and Wendy Zimmermann. 1990. *Employer Hiring Practices*. Washington, DC: Urban Institute Press.

Dalaker, Joseph. 2001. "Poverty in the United States: 2000." U.S. Census Bureau, Current Population Reports, series P60-214. Washington, DC: U.S. Government Printing Office.

Dalaker, Joseph, and Mary Naifeh. 1998. "Poverty in the United States: 1997." U.S. Census Bureau, Current Population Reports, series P60-201. Washington, DC: U.S. Government Printing Office.

Danziger, Sheldon, and Daniel H. Weinberg. 1994. "The Historical Record: Trends in Family Income, Inequality, and Poverty." In *Confronting Poverty*, edited by Sheldon Danziger, Gary Sandefur, and Daniel Weinberg. Cambridge, MA: Harvard University Press.

Danziger, Sheldon H., Jacques van der Gaag, Michael K. Taussig, and Eugene Smolensky. 1984. "The Direct Measurement of Welfare Levels: How Much Does It Cost to Make Ends Meet?" *Review of Economics and Statistics* 66, 3: 500–05.

Danziger, Sheldon H., and Peter Gottschalk. 1995. *America Unequal*. Cambridge, MA: Harvard University Press.

Davidson, James D. 1985. "Theories and Measures of Poverty: Toward a Holistic Approach." *Sociological Focus* 18, 3 (August): 187–88.

Daymont, T., and P. Andrisani. 1984. "Job Preferences, College Major, and the Gender Gap in Earnings." *Journal of Human Resources* 19: 408–28.

Devine, Joel A., Mark Plunkett, and James D. Wright. 1992. "The Chronicity of Poverty: Evidence from the PSID, 1968–1987." *Social Forces* 70, 3 (March): 787–812.

De Vos, Klaas, and Thesia I. Garner. 1991. "An Evaluation of Subjective Poverty Definitions: Comparing Results from the U.S and the Netherlands." *The Review of Income and Wealth* 37, 3 (September): 267–85.

DuBois, W. E. B. 1899. *The Philadelphia Negro: A Social Study.* Reprint, Philadelphia: University of Pennsylvania Press, 1996.

Duncan, Greg. 1991. "The Economic Environment of Childhood." In *Children in Poverty: Child Development and Public Policy,* edited by A. Huston. New York: Cambridge University Press.

Dupree, Allen, and Wendell Primus. 2001, June 15. "Declining Share of Children Lived with Single Mothers in the Late 1990s." Center on Budget and Policy Priorities Research Report.

Eggebeen, David J., and Daniel T. Lichter. 1991. "Race, Family Structure, and Changing Poverty among American Children." *American Sociological Review* 56: 801–17.

Ehrenreich, Barbara. 2001. *Nickel and Dimed: On (Not) Getting By in America.* New York: Metropolitan Books.

England, Paula. 1994. "Wage Appreciation and Depreciation: A Test of Neoclassical Economic Explanations of Occupational Sex Segregation." In *Social Stratification in Sociological Perspective,* edited by David B. Grusky. Boulder, CO: Westview Press.

Farkas, G., and K. Vicknair. 1996. "Appropriate Tests of Racial Wage Discrimination Require Controls for Cognitive Skill: Comment on Cancio, Evans, and Maume." *American Sociological Review* 1: 557–60.

Farley, Reynolds. 1984. *Blacks and Whites: Narrowing the Gap?* Cambridge, MA: Harvard University Press.

Farley, Reynolds, and William H. Frey. 1994. "Changes in the Segregation of Whites from Blacks during the 1980s: Small Steps toward a More Integrated Society." *American Sociological Review* 59, 1 (February): 23–45.

Fields, Jason. 2001. "Living Arrangements of Children: Fall 1996." U.S. Census Bureau, Current Population Reports, series P70-74. Washington, DC: U.S. Government Printing Office.

Fisher, Gordon M. 2001, November 2. "'Enough for a Family to Live On?'— Questions from Members of the American Public and New Perspectives from British Social Scientists." Paper presented at the Association for Public Policy Analysis and Management annual research conference, Washington, DC.

———. 1986. "Estimates of the Poverty Population under the Current Official Definition for Years before 1959." Mimeo, Office of the Assistant Secretary for Planning and Evaluation: U.S. Department of Health and Human Services.

———. 1995. "Is There Such a Thing as an Absolute Poverty Line over Time? Evidence from the United States, Britain, Canada, and Australia on the Income Elasticity of the Poverty Line." U.S. Census Bureau, Poverty Measurement Working Paper (www.census.gov/hhes/poverty/povmeas/papers /elastap4.html).

———. 1997. "From Hunter to Orshansky: An Overview of (Unofficial) Poverty Lines in the United States from 1904 to 1965." U.S. Census Bureau, Poverty Measurement Working Paper (www.census.gov/hhes/poverty /povmeas/papers/hstorsp4.html).

———. 1997. "The Development of the Orshansky Poverty Thresholds and Their Subsequent History as the Official U.S. Poverty Measure." U.S. Census Bureau, Poverty Measurement Working Paper (www.census.gov/hhes /poverty/povmeas/papers/orshansky.html).

Foster, James E. 1998. "Absolute versus Relative Poverty." *American Economic Review* 88, 2, Papers and Proceedings of the 110th Annual Meeting of the American Economic Association (May): 335–41.

Foster, James E., and Anthony F. Shorrocks. 1988. "Poverty Orderings." *Econometrica* 56, 1 (January): 173–77.

Frazier, E. Franklin. 1939. *The Negro Family in the United States.* Chicago: University of Chicago Press.

———. 1932. *The Negro Family in Chicago.* Chicago: University of Chicago Press.

Freeman, Richard. 2000. "The Rising Tide Lifts . . . " *Focus* 21, 2 (fall): 27–31.

Galbraith, John Kenneth. 1958. *The Affluent Society.* New York: New American Library, 1964.

Galster, George C. 1992. "A Cumulative Causation Model of the Underclass: Implications for Urban Economic Development Policy." In *The Metropolis in Black and White: Place, Power, and Polarization,* edited by George Galster and Edward W. Hill. New Brunswick, NJ: Center for Urban Policy Research, Rutgers University.

Gans, Herbert J. 1995. *The War against the Poor.* New York: Basic Books.

Gibbs, Robert. 2001. "Nonmetro Labor Markets in the Era of Welfare Reform." *Rural America* 16, 3 (fall): 11–21.

Gilens, Martin. 1996. "Race and Poverty in America: Public Misperceptions and the American News Media." *Public Opinion Quarterly* 60, 4: 515–41.

Gottschalk, Peter, Sara McLanahan, and Gary Sandefur. 1994. "The Dynamics and Intergenerational Transmission of Poverty and Welfare Participation." In *Confronting Poverty,* edited by Sheldon Danziger, Gary Sandefur, and Daniel Weinberg. Cambridge, MA: Harvard University Press.

Greenberg, Mark. 2001. "Welfare Reform and Devolution." *Brookings Review* 19, 3 (summer): 20–24.

Grusky, David. 1994. "The Contours of Social Stratification." In *Social Stratification in Sociological Perspective,* edited by David B. Grusky. Boulder, CO: Westview Press.

Gurteen, S. Humphreys. 1882. *Handbook of Charity Organization.* Buffalo, NY: published by the author.

Harrington, Michael. 1962. *The Other America: Poverty in the United States.* New York: Macmillan.

———. 1981. *The Other America: Poverty in the United States.* Reprint with a new introduction, New York: Penguin Books.

Harrison, Bennett, and Barry Bluestone. 1990. *The Great U-Turn: Corporate Restructuring and the Polarizing of America.* New York: Basic Books.

Harrison, Roderick J., and Claudette Bennett. 1995. "Racial and Ethnic Diversity." In *State of the Union America in the 1990s,* vol. 2, edited by Reynolds Farley. New York: Russell Sage Foundation.

Hartmann, Heidi. 1994. "The Unhappy Marriage of Marxism and Feminism: Towards a More Progressive Union." In *Social Stratification in Sociological Perspective,* edited by David B. Grusky. Boulder, CO: Westview Press.

Haskins, Ron. 2001. "Giving Is Not Enough." *Brookings Review* 19, 3 (summer): 13–15.

Haskins, Ron, Isabel Sawhill, and Kent Weaver. 2001, January. "Welfare Reform Reauthorization: An Overview of Problems and Issues." Brookings Institution Welfare Reform and Beyond Policy Brief no. 2.

Haveman, Robert, and Andrew Bershadker. 1998. "Self-Reliance as a Poverty Criterion: Trends in Earnings-Capacity Poverty, 1975–1992." *AEA Papers and Proceedings* 88, 2 (May): 342–47.

Haveman, Robert, and Jonathan Schwabish. 1999. "Economic Growth and Poverty: A Return to Normalcy?" *Focus* 20, 2 (spring): 1–7.

Heclo, Hugh. 1994. "Poverty Politics." In *Confronting Poverty,* edited by Sheldon Danziger, Gary Sandefur, and Daniel Weinberg. Cambridge, MA: Harvard University Press.

Hernandez, Donald J. 1993. *America's Children: Resources from Family, Government, and the Economy.* New York: Russell Sage Foundation.

Hogan, Dennis, and Daniel Lichter. 1995. "Children and Youth: Living Arrangements and Welfare." In *State of the Union: America in the 1990s,* vol. 2, edited by Reynolds Farley. New York: Russell Sage Foundation.

Hogan, Dennis P., and M. Pazul. 1982. "The Occupational and Earnings Returns to Education among Black Men in the North." *American Journal of Sociology* 90: 584–607.

Holzer, Harry J. 1996. *What Employers Want: Job Prospects for Less-Educated Workers.* New York: Russell Sage Foundation.

———. 1991. "The Spatial Mismatch Hypothesis: What Has the Evidence Shown?" *Urban Studies* 28, 1: 105–22.

Holzer, Harry J., and Wayne Vroman. 1992. "Mismatches and the Urban Labor Market." In *Urban Labor Markets and Job Opportunity,* edited by George Peterson and Wayne Vroman. Washington, DC: Urban Institute Press.

Hotz, V. Joseph, Charles H. Mullin, and John Karl Scholz. 2001, June 25–28. "The Earned Income Tax Credit and Labor Market Participation of Families on Welfare." Paper presented at the Institute for Research on Poverty Summer Research Workshop on Problems of the Low-Income Population, Madison, WI.

Hout, Michael. 1994. "Occupational Mobility of Black Men: 1962 to 1973." In *Social Stratification in Sociological Perspective*, edited by David B. Grusky. Boulder, CO: Westview Press.

Hunter, Robert. 1904. *Poverty*. New York: Macmillan; reprint, New York: Harper Torchbooks, 1964.

Iceland, John. 2001, August. "Why Poverty Remains High: Reassessing the Effect of Economic Growth, Income Inequality, and Changes in Family Structure on Poverty, 1949–1999." American Sociological Association meetings, Anaheim, CA.

———. 2000. "The 'Family/Couple/Household' Unit of Analysis in Poverty Measurement." *Journal of Economic and Social Measurement* 26: 253–65.

———. 1999. "Earnings Returns to Occupational Status: Are Asian Americans Disadvantaged?" *Social Science Research* 28: 45–65.

———. 1997. "The Dynamics of Poverty Spells and Issues of Left-Censoring." Research report no. 97-378. Population Studies Center, University of Michigan–Ann Arbor.

———. 1997. "Urban Labor Markets and Individual Transitions out of Poverty." *Demography* 34, 3 (August): 429–41.

Iceland, John, and Josh Kim. 2001. "Poverty among Working Families: Insights from an Improved Measure." *Social Science Quarterly* 82, 2 (June): 253–67.

Iceland, John, Kathleen Short, Thesia I. Garner, and David Johnson. 2001. "Are Children Worse Off? Evaluating Child Well-Being Using a New (and Improved) Measure of Poverty." *Journal of Human Resources* 36, 2: 398–412.

Ihlanfeldt, Keith R., and David L. Sjoquist. 1989. "The Impact of Job Decentralization on the Economic welfare of Central City Blacks." *Journal of Urban Economics* 26: 110–30.

Jackson, Thomas F. 1993. "The State, the Movement, and the Urban Poor: The War on Poverty and Political Mobilization in the 1960s." In *The "Underclass" Debate: Views from History*, edited by Michael B. Katz. Princeton, NJ: Princeton University Press.

Jantti, Markus, and Sheldon Danziger. 1999, March. "Income Poverty in Advanced Countries." Luxembourg Income Study Working Paper no. 193.

Jargowsky, Paul A. 1997. *Poverty and Place: Ghettos, Barrios, and the American City*. New York: Russell Sage Foundation.

———. 1996. "Beyond the Street Corner: The Hidden Diversity of High-Poverty Neighborhoods." *Urban Geography*, 17, 7: 579–603.

Jencks, Christopher. 1992. *Rethinking Social Policy: Race, Poverty, and the Underclass*. New York: Harper Perennial.

Jencks, Christopher, and Paul E. Peterson, eds. 1991. *The Urban Underclass*. Washington, DC: Brookings Institution.

Johnson, James H., and Melvin L. Oliver. 1992. "Structural Changes in the U.S. Economy and Black Male Joblessness: A Reassessment." In *Urban Labor Markets and Job Opportunity*, edited by George Peterson and Wayne Vroman. Washington, DC: Urban Institute Press.

Johnson, Paul, and Steven Webb. 1992. "Official Statistics on Poverty in the United Kingdom." In *Poverty Measurement for Economies in Transition in*

Eastern European Countries. Warsaw: Polish Statistical Association and Polish Central Statistical Office.

Jones, Arthur F., Jr., and Daniel H. Weinberg. 2000. "The Changing Shape of the Nation's Income Distribution." U.S. Census Bureau, Current Population Reports, series P60-204. Washington, DC: U.S. Government Printing Office.

Jones, Jacqueline. 1993. "Southern Diaspora: Origins of the Northern 'Underclass.'" In *The "Underclass" Debate: Views from History,* edited by Michael B. Katz. Princeton, NJ: Princeton University Press.

Jones, Rachel K., and Ye Luo. 1999. "The Culture of Poverty and African-American Culture: An Empirical Assessment." *Sociological Perspectives* 42, 3 (fall): 439–58.

Kain, John F. 1968. "Housing Segregation, Negro Employment, and Metropolitan Decentralization." *Quarterly Journal of Economics* 82: 175–97.

Kasarda, John. 1995. "Industrial Restructuring and the Changing Location of Jobs." In *State of the Union: America in the 1990s,* vol. 1, edited by Reynolds Farley. New York: Russell Sage Foundation.

———. 1990. "Structural Factors Affecting the Location and Timing of Underclass Growth." *Urban Geography* 11: 234–64.

———. 1989. "Urban Industrial Transition and the Underclass." *The Annals of the American Academy* 501 (January): 26–47.

———. 1983. "Caught in the Web of Change." *Society* (November–December): 41–47.

Katz, Michael B. 2001. *The Price of Citizenship: Redefining the American Welfare State.* New York: Metropolitan Books, Henry Holt.

———. 1996. *In the Shadow of the Poorhouse: A Social History of Welfare in America.* New York: Basic Books.

———. 1993. "The Urban 'Underclass' as a Metaphor of Social Transformation." In *The "Underclass" Debate: Views from History,* edited by Michael B. Katz. Princeton, NJ: Princeton University Press.

———. 1993. "Reframing the 'Underclass' Debate." In *The "Underclass" Debate: Views from History,* edited by Michael B. Katz. Princeton, NJ: Princeton University Press.

———. 1989. *The Undeserving Poor: From the War on Poverty to the War on Welfare.* New York: Pantheon.

Kauffman, Kyle D., and L. Lynne Kiesling. 1997. "Was There a Nineteenth Century Welfare Magnet in the United States? Preliminary Results from New York City and Brooklyn." *Quarterly Review of Economics and Finance* 37, 2 (summer): 439–48.

Kaufman, Phil R. 1999. "Rural Poor Have Less Access to Supermarkets, Large Grocery Stores." *Rural Development* 13, 3: 19–25.

Kiesling, L. Lynne, and Robert A. Margo. 1997. "Explaining the Rise in Antebellum Pauperism, 1850–1860: New Evidence." *Quarterly Review of Economics and Finance* 37, 2 (summer): 405–17.

Lampman, Robert. 1971. *Ends and Means of Reducing Income Poverty.* Chicago: Markham.

Landale, Nancy S., and Avery M. Guest. 1990. "Generation, Ethnicity, and Occupational Opportunity in Late 19th Century America." *American Sociological Review* 55 (April): 280–96.

Lawson, Roger, and William Julius Wilson. 1996. "Poverty, Social Rights, and the Quality of Citizenship." In *Poverty, Inequality, and the Future of Social Policy,* edited by Katherine McFate, Roger Lawson, and William Julius Wilson. New York: Russell Sage Foundation.

Lee, Sharon M. 1994. "Poverty and the U.S. Asian Population." *Social Science Quarterly* 75 (September): 541–59.

Lee, Sharon M., and Barry Edmonston. 1994. "The Socioeconomic Status and Integration of Asian Immigrants." In *Immigration and Ethnicity: The Integration of America's Newest Arrivals,* edited by Barry Edmonston and Jeffrey S. Passel. Washington, DC: Urban Institute Press.

Lerman, Robert I. 1996. "The Impact of the Changing U.S. Family Structure on Poverty and Income Inequality." *Economica* 63: S119–S139.

Levitan, Sar A., Garth L. Mangum, and Stephen L. Mangum. 1998. *Programs in Aid of the Poor.* Baltimore: Johns Hopkins University Press.

Lewis, Oscar. 1966. "The Culture of Poverty." *Scientific American* 215: 19–25.

———. 1966. *La Vida.* New York: Random House.

Lichter, Daniel T., Diane K. McLaughlin, and David Ribar. 1997. "Welfare and the Rise in Female-Headed Families." *American Journal of Sociology* 103, 1 (July): 112–43.

Lichter, Daniel T., and Leif Jensen. 2000, May 4. "Rural America in Transition: Poverty and Welfare at the Turn of the 21st Century." Paper presented at "Rural Dimensions of Welfare Reform: A Research Conference on Poverty, Welfare, and Food Assistance," sponsored by the Joint Center for Poverty Research, Northwestern University/University of Chicago.

Lichter, Daniel T., and Martha L. Crowley. 2002. "Poverty in America: Beyond Welfare Reform." *Population Bulletin* 57, 2 (June): 1–36.

Lichter, Daniel T., and Nancy S. Landale. 1995. "Parental Work, Family Structure, and Poverty among Latino Children." *Journal of Marriage and the Family* 57 (May): 346–54.

Lichter, Daniel T. 1997. "Poverty and Inequality among Children." *Annual Review of Sociology* 23: 121–45.

Lindbeck, A., P. Molander, T. Persson, O. Petersson, A. Sandmo, B. Swedenborg, and N. Thygesen. 1994. *Turning Sweden Around.* Cambridge, MA: MIT Press.

Littman, Mark S. 1989. "Poverty in the 1980's: Are the Poor Getting Poorer?" *Monthly Labor Review* (June): 13–18.

Loury, Glenn C. 2000. "What's Next? Some Reflections on the Poverty Conference." *Focus* 21, 2 (fall): 58–60.

Lundberg, Shelly J., and Richard Startz. 2000. "Inequality and Race: Models and Policy." In *Meritocracy and Economic Inequality,* edited by Kenneth Arrow, Samuel Bowles, and Steven Durlauf. Princeton, NJ: Princeton University Press.

Lyson, Thomas A., and William W. Falk. 1992. *Forgotten Places*. Lawrence: University Press of Kansas.

Marks, Carole. 1991. "The Urban Underclass." *American Review of Sociology*, 17: 445–66.

Marx, Karl. 1994. "Classes in Capitalism and Pre-Capitalism." Reprinted from *The Communist Manifesto* in *Social Stratification in Sociological Perspective*, edited by David B. Grusky. Boulder, CO: Westview Press.

Marx, Karl. 1994. "Value and Surplus Value." Reprinted in *Social Stratification in Sociological Perspective*, edited by David B. Grusky. Boulder, CO: Westview Press.

Massey, Douglas S., and Nancy Denton. 1993. *American Apartheid*. Cambridge, MA: Harvard University Press.

Mayer, Susan E. 1996. "A Comparison of Poverty and Living Conditions in the United States, Canada, Sweden, and Germany." In *Poverty, Inequality, and the Future of Social Policy*, edited by Katherine McFate, Roger Lawson, and William Julius Wilson. New York: Russell Sage Foundation.

Mayer, Susan E., and Christopher Jencks. 1989. "Poverty and the Distribution of Material Hardship." *The Journal of Human Resources* 24, 1 (winter): 88–114.

McCall, Leslie. 2001 "Sources of Racial Inequality in Metropolitan Labor Markets: Racial, Ethnic, and Gender Differences." *American Sociological Review* 66, 4 (August): 520–41.

McGeary, Michael G. H. 1990. "Ghetto Poverty and Federal Policies and Programs." In *Inner-City Poverty in the United States*, edited by Laurence Lynn Jr. and Michael G. H. McGeary. Washington, DC: National Academy Press.

McLanahan, Sara, and Irwin Garfinkel. 1996. "Single-Mother Families and Social Policy: Lessons for the United States from Canada, France, and Sweden." In *Poverty, Inequality, and the Future of Social Policy*, edited by Katherine McFate, Roger Lawson, and William Julius Wilson. New York: Russell Sage Foundation.

McLanahan, Sara, and Lynne Casper. 1995. "Growing Diversity and Inequality in the American Family." In *State of the Union America in the 1990s*, vol. 2, edited by Reynolds Farley. New York: Russell Sage Foundation.

Mead, Lawrence. 1992. *The New Politics of Poverty: The Nonworking Poor in America*. New York: Basic Books.

———. 1986. *Beyond Entitlement: The Social Obligations of Citizenship*. New York: Free Press.

Micklewright, John. 2002, February. "Social Exclusion and Children: A European View for a US Debate." Center for Analysis and Social Exclusion paper no. 51. London School of Economics.

Mincy, Ronald. 1994. "The Underclass: Concept, Controversy, Evidence." In *Confronting Poverty*, edited by Sheldon Danziger, Gary Sandefur, and Daniel Weinberg. Cambridge, MA: Harvard University Press.

Moffitt, Robert. 2002, January. "From Welfare to Work: What the Evidence Shows." Brookings Institution Policy Brief no. 13.

————. 1992. "Incentive Effects of the U.S. Welfare System: A Review." *Journal of Economic Literature* 30 (March): 1–61.

Monkkonen, Eric H. 1993. "Nineteenth-Century Institutions: Dealing with the Urban 'Underclass.'" In *The "Underclass" Debate: Views from History,* edited by Michael B. Katz. Princeton, NJ: Princeton University Press.

Mouw, Ted. 2000. "Job Relocation and the Racial Gap in Unemployment in Detroit and Chicago, 1980 to 1990." *American Sociological Review* 65, 5 (October): 730–53.

Moynihan, Daniel Patrick. 1965. *The Negro Family: The Case for National Action.* Washington, DC: U.S. Department of Labor.

Murnane, Richard. 1994. "Education and the Well-Being of the Next Generation." In *Confronting Poverty,* edited by Sheldon Danziger, Gary Sandefur, and Daniel Weinberg. Cambridge, MA: Harvard University Press.

Murray, Charles. 1984. *Losing Ground: American Social Policy, 1950–1980.* New York: Basic Books.

Munsterberg, Emil. 1904. "The Problem of Poverty." *American Journal of Sociology* 10, 3 (November): 335–53.

Myrdal, Gunnar. 1944. *An American Dilemma.* 2 vols. New York: Harper and Row.

Naifeh, Mary. 1998. "Dynamics of Economic Well-Being, Poverty, 1993–94: Trap Door? Revolving Door? Or Both?" U.S. Census Bureau, Current Population Reports, series P70-63, Washington, DC: U.S. Government Printing Office.

National Research Council. 1995. *Measuring Poverty: A New Approach,* edited by Constance F. Citro and Robert T. Michael. Washington, DC: National Academy Press.

Nee, Victor, and Jimy Sanders. 1985. "The Road to Parity: Determinants of the Socioeconomic Achievements of Asian Americans." *Ethnic and Racial Studies* 8, 1 (January): 75–93.

Newman, Katherine S. 1999. *No Shame in My Game: The Working Poor in the Inner City.* New York: Knopf and Russell Sage Foundation.

O'Connor, Alice. 2001. *Poverty Knowledge: Social Science, Social Policy, and the Poor in Twentieth-Century U.S. History.* Princeton, NJ: Princeton University Press.

O'Hare, William P. 1996. "A New Look at Poverty in America." *Population Bulletin* 51, 2: 1–48.

O'Higgins, Michael, and Stephen Jenkins. 1990. "Poverty in the EC: Estimates for 1975, 1980, and 1985." In *Analysing Poverty in the European Community: Policy Issues, Research Options, and Data Sources,* edited by Rudolph Teekens and Bernard M. S. van Praag. Luxembourg: Office of Official Publications of the European Communities.

O'Neill, June. 1990. "The Role of Human Capital in Earnings Differentials between Black and White Men." *Journal of Economic Perspectives* 4, 4: 25–46.

Organization for Economic Cooperation and Development. 2001, June. *OECD Employment Outlook.* Paris: OECD.

Orshansky, Mollie. 1963. "Children of the Poor." *Social Security Bulletin* 26, 7 (July): 3–13.

Orshansky, Mollie. 1965. "Counting the Poor: Another Look at the Poverty Profile." *Social Security Bulletin* 28, 1 (January): 3–29.

Osterman, Paul. 1999. *Securing Prosperity*. Princeton, NJ: Princeton University Press.

Parkin, Frank. 1994. "Marxism and Class Theory: A Bourgeois Critique." In *Social Stratification in Sociological Perspective,* edited by David B. Grusky. Boulder, CO: Westview Press.

Pearce, Diana. 1978. "The Feminization of Poverty: Women, Work, and Welfare." *Urban Sociological Change* 11: 128–36.

Peterson, George E., and Wayne Vroman. 1992. "Urban Labor Markets and Economic Opportunity." In *Urban Labor Markets and Job Opportunity,* edited by George E. Peterson and Wayne Vroman. Washington, DC: Urban Institute Press.

Piore, Michael J. 1994. "The Dual Labor Market: Theory and Implications." In *Social Stratification in Sociological Perspective,* edited by David B. Grusky. Boulder, CO: Westview Press.

Plotnick, Robert D., Eugene Smolensky, Eirik Evenhouse, and Siobhan Reilly. 1998, August 23–29. "The Twentieth Century Record of Inequality and Poverty in the United States." Paper presented at the General Conference of the International Association for Research on Income and Wealth. Cambridge, UK.

Polachek, Solomon W., and W. Stanley Siebert. 1994. "Gender in the Labour Market." In *Social Stratification in Sociological Perspective,* edited by David B. Grusky. Boulder, CO: Westview Press.

Price, C. 1969. "The Study of Assimilation." In *Sociological Studies: Migration,* edited by J. A. Jackson. Cambridge, UK: Cambridge University Press.

Primus, Wendell. 2001. "What Next for Welfare Reform? A Vision for Assisting Families." *Brookings Review* 19, 3 (summer): 17–24.

Rainwater, Lee. 1970. *Behind Ghetto Walls: Black Families in a Federal Slum.* Chicago: Aldine.

Rainwater, Lee, and Timothy M. Smeeding. 1995. "Doing Poorly: The Real Income of American Children in a Comparative Perspective." In *Crisis in American Institutions,* edited by J. H. Skolnick and E. Currie. Boston: Allyn and Bacon.

Ravallion, M. 1994. *Poverty Comparisons.* Fundamentals of Pure and Applied Economics no. 56. Chur, Switzerland: Harwood Academic Press.

Ravallion, M. 1996. "Issues in Measuring and Modeling Poverty." Policy Research Working Paper no. 1615. Washington, DC: World Bank.

Ravallion, Martin. 1998. "Poverty Lines in Theory and Practice." Living Standards Measurement Study (LSMS) Working Paper no. 133. Washington, DC: World Bank.

Rector, Robert. 1993. "Welfare Reform, Dependency Reduction, and Labor Market Entry." *Journal of Labor Research* 14, 3 (summer): 283–97.

Rector, Robert, Kirk A. Johnson, and Patrick F. Fagan. 2002, April 15. "The Effect of Marriage on Child Poverty." Heritage Foundation, Center for Data Analysis report no. 02-04.

———. 2001, May 23. "Understanding Differences in Black and White Child Poverty Rates." The Heritage Foundation, Center for Data Analysis report no. 01-04.

Rector, Robert, Kirk A. Johnson, and Sarah E. Youssef. 1999. "The Extent of Material Hardship and Poverty in the United States." *Review of Social Economy* 57, 3 (September): 351–87.

Reimers, C. W. 1985. "A Comparative Analysis of the Wages of Hispanics, Blacks, and Non-Hispanic Whites." In *Hispanics in the U.S. Economy,* edited by George Borjas and Marta Tienda. New York: Academic Press.

Rodgers, Harrell R., Jr. 2000. *American Poverty in a New Era of Reform.* Armonk, NY: M. E. Sharpe.

Roemer, John E. 2000. "Equality of Opportunity." In *Meritocracy and Economic Inequality,* edited by Kenneth Arrow, Samuel Bowles, and Steven Durlauf. Princeton, NJ: Princeton University Press.

Roemer, Marc I. 2000. "Assessing the Quality of the March Current Population Survey and the Survey of Income and Program Participation Income Estimates, 1990–1996." U.S. Census Bureau Staff Paper on Income, Internet release data (http://www.census.gov/hhes/income/papers.html), June 16, 2000.

Ruggles, Patricia. 1990. *Drawing the Line: Alternative Poverty Measures and Their Implications for Public Policy.* Washington, DC: The Urban Institute Press.

Ruggles, Patricia, and Roberton Williams. 1989. "Longitudinal Measures of Poverty: Accounting for Income and Assets over Time." *Review of Income and Wealth* 35, 3 (September): 225–43.

Sakamoto, Arthur, and Satomi Furuichi. 1997. "Wages among White and Japanese-American Male Workers." *Research in Stratification and Mobility* 15: 177–206.

Sakamoto, Arthur, Huei-Hsia Wu, and Jessie M. Tzeng. 2000. "The Declining Significance of Race among American Men during the Latter Half of the Twentieth Century." *Demography* 37, 1: 41–51.

Sandefur, Gary, and W. J. Scott. 1983. "Minority Group Status and the Wages of Indian and Black Males." *Social Science Research* 12: 44–68.

Sawhill, Isabel. 2001. "From Welfare to Work." *Brookings Review* 19, 3 (summer): 4–7.

Schiller, Bradly R. 2001. *The Economics of Poverty and Discrimination,* 8th ed. Upper Saddle River, NJ: Prentice Hall.

Second Annual Report of the Children's Aid Society of New York. 1855. New York.

Sen, Amartya. 2000. "Merit and Justice." In *Meritocracy and Economic Inequality,* edited by Kenneth Arrow, Samuel Bowles, and Steven Durlauf. Princeton, NJ: Princeton University Press.

———. 1999. *Development as Freedom.* New York: Knopf.

————. 1992. *Inequality Reexamined.* Cambridge, MA: Harvard University Press.

————. 1983. "Poor, Relatively Speaking." *Oxford Economic Papers* 35, 2: 153–69.

————. 1976. "Poverty: An Ordinal Approach to Measurement." *Econometrica* 44: 219–31.

Shatzkin, Kate. 2000, September 13. "Old Poverty Line Inadequate to Reflect Today's Family Needs; Experts Struggle to Find an Alternative." *Baltimore Sun.*

Sholz, John Karl, and Kara Levine. 2000. "The Evolution of Income Support Policy in Recent Decades." *Focus* 21, 2 (fall): 9–15.

Short, Kathleen. 2001. "Experimental Poverty Measures: 1999." U.S. Census Bureau, Current Population Reports, Consumer Income, series P60-216. Washington, DC: U.S. Government Printing Office.

Short, Kathleen, Thesia I. Garner, David Johnson, and Patricia Doyle. 1999. *Experimental Poverty Measures: 1990 to 1997.* U.S. Census Bureau, Current Population Reports, Consumer Income, series P60-205. Washington, DC: U.S. Government Printing Office.

Shyrock, Henry S., and Jacob S. Siegel. 1976. *The Methods and Materials of Demography.* New York: Academic Press.

Skocpol, Theda. 2000. *The Missing Middle: Working Families and the Future of American Social Policy.* New York: W. W. Norton.

Skocpol, Theda, Majorie Abend-Wein, Christopher Howard, and Susan Goodrich Lehmann. 1993. "Women's Associations and the Enactment of Mothers' Pensions in the United States." *American Political Science Review* 87, 3 (September): 686–701.

Smeeding, Timothy, Lee Rainwater, and Gary Burtless. 2000, September. "United States Poverty in a Cross-National Context." Luxembourg Income Study Working Paper no. 244.

Smeeding, Timothy, B. B. Torrey, and M. Rein. 1988. "Patterns of Income and Poverty: The Economic Status of Children and the Elderly in Eight Countries." In *The Vulnerable*, edited by J. L. Palmer, Timothy Smeeding, and B. B. Torrey. Washington, DC: Urban Institute Press.

Smeeding Timothy. 1997. "The International Evidence on Income Distribution in Modern Economics." In *Poverty and Inequality: The Political Economy of Redistribution,* edited by Jon Neil. Kalamazoo, MI: W. E. Upjohn Institute for Employment Research.

Smith, Adam. 1776. *An Inquiry into the Nature and Causes of the Wealth of Nations.* 1776; reprint, Oxford, UK: Clarendon Press, 1976.

Smith, Tom W. 1990. "Social Inequality in Cross-National Perspective." In *Attitudes to Inequality and the Role of Government,* edited by Duane Alwin et al. Rijswijk, The Netherlands: Sociaal en Cultural Planbureau.

Solon, Gary. 1992. "Intergenerational Income Mobility in the United States." *American Economic Review* 82: 393–408.

Sorenson, Elaine. 1994, December. "Noncustodial Fathers: Can They Afford to Pay More Child Support?" Urban Institute working paper.

Starrels, Marjorie E., Sally Bould, and Leon J. Nicholas. 1994. "The Feminization of Poverty in the United States." *Journal of Family Issues* 15, 4 (December): 590–607.

Stevens, Ann Huff. 1999. "Climbing out of Poverty, Falling Back In: Measuring
the Persistence of Poverty over Multiple Spells." *Journal of Human Resources*
34, 3 (summer): 557–88.

———. 1994. "The Dynamics of Poverty Spells: Updating Bane and Ellwood."
AEA Papers and Proceedings 84, 2 (May): 34–37.

Stevens, Gillian, and Joo Hyun Cho. 1985. "Socioeconomic Indexes and the
New 1980 Census Occupational Classification Scheme." *Social Science
Research* 14, 2: 142–68.

Sugrue, Thomas J. 1993. "The Structure of Urban Poverty: The Reorganization
of Space and Work in Three Periods of American History." In *The "Underclass" Debate: Views from History,* edited by Michael B. Katz. Princeton:
Princeton University Press.

Swiss Agency for Development and Cooperation (SDC). 2000. "The SDC Policy for Social Development." In *The Challenge of Eliminating World Poverty,* edited by SDC Publications on Development. Berne: SDC.

Teitz, Michael B., and Karen Chapple. 1998. "The Causes of Inner-City
Poverty: Eight Hypotheses in Search of Reality." *Cityscape* 3, 3: 33–70.

Thompson, Tommy G. 2001. "Welfare Reform's Next Step." *Brookings Review*
19, 3 (summer): 2–3.

Tobin, James. 1967, June 3. "It Can Be Done! Conquering Poverty in the U.S
by 1976. *New Republic,* pp. 14–18.

Townsend, Peter. 1993. *The International Analysis of Poverty.* Hemel Hempstead, UK: Harvester-Wheatsheaf.

Trattner, Walter I. 1994. *From Poor Law to Welfare State: A History of Social
Welfare in America.* New York: Free Press.

Trotter, Joe William, Jr. 1993. "Blacks in the Urban North: The 'Underclass
Question' in Historical Perspective." In *The "Underclass" Debate: Views
from History,* edited by Michael B. Katz. Princeton: Princeton University
Press.

Turner, Jonathan H., Leonard Beeghley, and Charles H. Powers. 1989. *The
Emergence of Sociological Theory.* Belmont, CA: Wadsworth.

Turner, Margery, Michael Fix, and Raymond Struyk. 1991. *Opportunities
Denied, Opportunities Diminished: Discrimination in Hiring.* Washington,
DC: Urban Institute Press.

UNICEF Innocenti Research Centre. 2000. "Child Poverty in Rich Nations."
Innocenti Report Card, no. 1 (June): 1–28.

U.S. Census Bureau. 1993. "Population and Housing Counts: 1790–1990."
Selected Historical Census Data, Population and Housing Counts Internet
report, CPH-2-1, table 16 (www.census.gov/population/www/censusdata
/pop-hc.html).

———. 1993. "Summary of Occupation, Income, and Poverty Characteristics:
1990." 1990 Census of Population: Social and Economic Characteristics,
series CP 2-1, table 3. United States Summary.

———. 1996. "Income of Households from Specified Sources, by Poverty Status: 1995." Experimental Measures of Income and Poverty, Detailed Income Tabulations from the CPS, table 7 (Last revised on the Internet on March 10, 1997: ferret.bls.census.gov/macro/031996/rdcall/7_000.htm).

———. 2000. "DP-1. Profile of General Demographic Characteristics: 2000." Census 2000 summary file 1 (SF 1), 100-Percent Data Quick Table (American FactFinder tabulation available at: factfinder.census.gov).

———. 2000. "Money Income in the United States: 1999." Current Population Reports, Consumer Income, series P60-209. Washington, DC: U.S. Government Printing Office.

———. 2000, April 11. "Historical National Population Estimates: July 1, 1900, to July 1, 1999." Population Estimates Program, Population Division. Internet release data (revised June 28, 2000: www.census.gov/population /estimates/nation/popclockest.txt).

———. 2000, September 15. "Percent of People 25 Years Old and Over Who Have Completed High School or College, by Race, Hispanic Origin and Sex: Selected Years 1940 to 1999." Educational Attainment Historical Tables, table A-2. Internet release data (www.census.gov/population/socdemo/education/tableA-2.txt).

———. 2000, October 23. "Standardized and Unstandardized Experimental Poverty Rates: 1990 to 1999." Poverty 1999 table release package. Internet release data (www.census.gov/hhes/poverty/povmeas/exppov/suexppov .html).

———. 2000, December 13. "Persons by Poverty Status in 1969, 1979, and 1989, by State." Census Historical Poverty Tables, table CPHL-162. Internet release data (www.census.gov/hhes/poverty/census/cphl162.html).

———. 2001, February 7. "Race and Hispanic Origin of People (Both Sexes Combined) by Median and Mean Income: 1947 to 1999." Historical Income Tables—People, table P-4. Internet data release (www.census.gov /hhes/income/histinc/p04.html).

———. 2001, June 29. "America's Families and Living Arrangements: March 2000." Current Population Reports, series P20-537. Detailed Tables Series, table F1. "Family Households, by Type, Age of Own Children, Age of Family Members, and Age, Race and Hispanic Origin of Householder: March 2000." Internet release data (www.census.gov/population/socdemo/hh-fem /p20-537/2000/tabF1.pdf).

———. 2001, September 6. "Income of Households from Specified Sources, by Poverty Status: 2000." Experimental Measures of Income and Poverty, Detailed Income Tabulations from the CPS, table 7. Internet release data (ferret.bls.census.gov/macro/032000/rdcall/toc.htm).

———. 2002. "Profile of Selected Economic Characteristics: 2000." Census Bureau Demographic Profiles, table DP-3.

———. 2002, February 13. "Poverty of People, by Sex: 1966 to 2000." Historical Poverty Tables, table 7. Internet release data (www.census.gov /hhes/poverty/histpov/hstpov7.html).

———. 2002, March 21. "Women's Earnings as a Percentage of Men's Earnings by Race and Hispanic Origin: 1960 to 2000." Historical Income Tables,

table P-40. Internet release data (www.census.gov/hhes/income/histinc
/p40x1.html).

———. 2002, April 25. "Homeownership Rates for the U.S.: 1965–2002."
Housing Vacancies and Homeownership Detailed Tables—First Quarter
2002, table 5. Internet re-release data (www.census.gov/hhes/www/housing
/hvs/q102tab5.html).

U.S. House of Representatives, Committee on Ways and Means. 2000. *Green
Book: Background Material and Data on Programs within the Jurisdiction
of the Committee on Ways and Means.* Washington, DC: U.S. Government
Printing Office.

Vaughan, Denton R. 1993. "Exploring the Use of the Public's Views to Set
Income Poverty Thresholds and Adjust Them over Time." *Social Security
Bulletin* 56, 2 (summer): 22–46.

Waldfogel, Jane, and Susan Mayer. 1998–1999. "Differences between Men and
Women in the Low-Wage Labor Market." *Focus* 20, 1 (winter): 11–16.

Washington, Booker T. 1902. *The Future of the American Negro.* New York:
Metro Books, 1969.

Weber, Max. 1994. "Class, Status, Party." In *Social Stratification in Sociological Perspective,* edited by David B. Grusky. Boulder, CO: Westview Press.

———. 1994. "Open and Closed Relationships." In *Social Stratification in
Sociological Perspective,* edited by David B. Grusky. Boulder, CO: Westview
Press.

Weinberg, Daniel H. 1987. "Rural Pockets of Poverty." *Rural Sociology* 52:
398–408.

White, Michael J. 1987. *American Neighborhoods and Residential Differentiation.* New York: Russell Sage Foundation.

Wilson, William Julius. 1978. *The Declining Significance of Race: Blacks and
Changing American Institutions.* Chicago: University of Chicago Press.

———. 1987. *The Truly Disadvantaged: The Inner City, the Underclass, and
Public Policy.* Chicago: University of Chicago Press.

World Bank. 2001. *World Development Report, 2000/2001: Attacking Poverty.*
Oxford, UK: Oxford University Press.

———. 2001. "Income Poverty: The Latest Global Numbers." Data on Poverty
Website (www.worldbank.org/poverty/data/trends/income.htm).

———. 2001. "Social Indicators—Health: Life Expectancy, Infant and Child
Mortality, Malnutrition." Data on Poverty Web site: (www.worldbank.org
/poverty/data/trends/mort.htm).

Yinger, John. 2000. "Housing Discrimination and Residential Segregation as
Causes of Poverty." *Focus* 21, 2 (fall): 51–55.

Index

Compositor:	Michael Bass Associates
Indexer:	Ron Strauss
Text:	10/13 Sabon
Display:	Sabon
Printer and binder:	Edwards Brothers, Inc.

- contract - limit to absolute
  (at least)
- CG — emph absolute + partic.
  (relative)